The READING Test

Mastery of the Georgia Regents' Reading Test

SECOND EDITION
Revised Printing

Linda L. Arthur
Louise Keys
Jeanne McDougald
Martha Nolen
Rose Marie Stallworth-Clark
Durelle Tuggle
Georgia Southern University

KENDALL/HUNT PUBLISHING COMPANY
4050 Westmark Drive   Dubuque, Iowa 52002

Credit lines: See pages 221–224, which are considered extensions of the copyright page.

Contents

Preface

This revised edition of The Reading Test: Mastery of the Georgia Regents' Reading Test has been expanded and enhanced to include new and modified exercises and practice test passages. It is written for the student preparing for the Georgia Regents' Reading Test. The text has been developed primarily for use in Regents' Reading review courses. In order to accommodate review course objectives, the text provides an introduction to the Regents' Reading Test, suggestions for basic test preparations, review of reading skills which are tested, and numerous (ten) practice tests.

Features of the Book

The text is divided into seven units. Units One and Two provide an introduction to the test and basic suggestions for test preparation. Units Three through Six furnish reviews of specific reading skills which are tested on the Regents' Reading Test. Unit Seven is comprised of ten practice tests, all of which are designed to be used as diagnostic tools to identify reading skill areas which may need to be strengthened. This pinpointing of weak skill areas is accomplished through the item analysis chart located at the bottom of each scantron. The Diagnostic Practice Test (Test One) includes explanations of correct answers. In addition, facsimiles of the scantron forms which students will use at the test site are provided for convenient use during practice test-taking sessions. Answer keys for both the chapters and practice tests are found in the back of the textbook, and all pages are perforated to facilitate removal.

Selected Readings

The passages and topics selected for inclusion in the text were drawn from subject areas in the social sciences, the humanities, the sciences, and business, and are, in the authors' judgments, representative of those which appear on the Regents' Reading Test.

Suggested Use of Text

Because of the comprehensiveness of the text, instructors will find it useful both for first-time review course students as well as for those students who have taken the review course more than once. Where courses are designed to remediate students more than once, the use of the practice tests may be distributed (and limited) throughout the course sessions. The book's content and organization make it a highly usable text in review courses as well as a text of self instruction for the individual student who seeks familiarization with the Regents' Reading Test.

Acknowledgments

Our motivation for writing the book was, first and foremost, our students. They have helped us determine those types of instructional materials which seem to be most helpful when preparing for the test, and it is our sincere hope that the book will provide the instruction and the encouragement which will lead them to success on the Regents' Reading Test.

We appreciate our colleagues and friends who have served as special sources of information; we thank Frank Fortune for the cover photograph and Peggy Smith who tirelessly typed the manuscript.

Finally, we thank our families, who were understanding as work progressed on the book, and we thank each other for the opportunity of working together to produce materials for our classes.

```
╔══════════════════════════════════╗
║          Unit One                 ║
║                                   ║
║       Introduction to the         ║
║   Georgia Regents' Reading Test   ║
╚══════════════════════════════════╝
```

The Georgia University System Board of Regents requires that all students enrolled in undergraduate degree programs in University System institutions in the state of Georgia must take and pass the Georgia Regents' Reading Test before graduation. The purpose of the reading test is to assess competency in college-level reading.

Georgia Board of Regents' Policy

The reading test policy of the Georgia Board of Regents states:

Each institution of the University System of Georgia will ensure the other institutions and the system as a whole that students obtaining a degree from the institution possess literacy competence. The Regents' Testing Program has been developed to attain this goal. The objectives of the Testing Program are: (1) to provide system wide information on the status of student competence in the areas of (reading and writing), and (2) to provide a uniform means of identifying those students who fail to reach the minimum levels of competence in these areas.

A student must pass all components of the test by scoring above the cut off score specified for each component. The test may be administered either in its entirety or as one or more components (reading or writing) depending on the student's needs. If one component of the test is passed, that component shouldn't be retaken; this provision is open to all students who have taken the test in any form since the beginning of the program.

Students should pass the Regents' Test before the end of their sophomore year. All students who fail the test must retake and pass it. Each institution will require deficient students to participate in Regents' remedial courses before retaking the exam.

Bulletin of Georgia Southern University, General Catalog, 1994-1995, p. 87.

General Description of the Regents' Reading Test

The University-System Committee on the Regents' Reading Test describes the Regents' Reading Test as follows:

The Reading Test is a 60-item, multiple-choice test comprised of ten reading passages and five to eight questions about each passage. It has an administration time of one hour. The content and skills covered by the test have been defined by a joint committee. This committee consists of the Testing Subcommittee of the Academic Committee on English and the Committee on the Regents' Reading Test. When a new form of the test is developed, the members of the joint committee approve the passages and the items that appear on the new test form.

1

The passages on the test usually range from 175 to 325 words in length, treat topics drawn from a variety of subject areas, e.g., social science, mathematics, natural science, and the humanities, and entail various modes of discourse, e.g., exposition, narration, and argumentation. Passages are selected from published materials which, in the committee members' judgment, students receiving a degree from a University-System institution should be able to comprehend.

Testing Committee Guidelines

The following is a summary of specifications which are adhered to by the test writers of the Regents' Reading Test. The reading terminology used in this book is equivalent to that found in the committee proceedings.

The items of each form of the Reading Test assess each of the following four major aspects of reading. The approximate numbers of items within each category are given in parentheses:

1. Vocabulary, (12-14)

2. Literal Comprehension, (12-14)

3. Inferential Comprehension, (20-24)

4. Analysis (12-14)

Four Major Types of Reading Questions

Literal Comprehension 22%
The author states that...
As underlined, <u>him</u> refers to...
According to the passage, all are
    reasons...EXCEPT...
The narrator lists

Vocabulary 22%
As used in the passage, _____ means...
As used in the passage, _____ nearly means...
The underlined phrase (word) _____ means...

Inference 34%
The author implies that...
The passage is primarily concerned
    with...
What is the main idea of this passage?
The author would probably agree that...

Analysis 22%
For what purpose did the author use the
    example _____ in line (30)?
The author's attitude toward _____
    could best be described as...
Which of the following does the author
    use to support his ideas?
Which of the following statements could
    be a fact and NOT an opinion?

1. *Vocabulary:* The student must identify the meanings of words as they are used in passages. Context clues, structural analysis and/or a general understanding of the meaning of the passage may be used to determine the meanings of words. Context clues are found in the form of: formal definition and definition by example, description, comparison, contrast, synonym, or antonym. Words in apposition, words in a series, transitional expressions such as conjunctive adverbs or other modifiers, and the general logic of the passage may provide definition clues to those specific words being tested. Structural analysis clues include common affixes and roots. (Foreign words or phrases are not tested.) Note: some words selected in the vocabulary category have more than one dictionary meaning. Questions about such words require the student to use clues within the passage to identify the meaning which fits the context.

2. *Literal Comprehension:* The student must recognize information and ideas presented directly in passages.

   1. details or facts--identification of a single fact, concept or event, or recognition of several facts, concepts, or events.

   2. a sequence of events--recognition of time order. Signals may be words such as *then, next, before, finally, in the first place, in the meantime, subsequently, thereafter, latter, former, respectively.*

   3. comparative relationships--identification of likenesses or differences among periods, events, characters, philosophies, actions, or ideas. Signals may be provided by words or phrases such as *in the same way, just as, likewise, similarly,* and *furthermore.*

   4. cause and effect relationships--identification of the reason(s) for events, actions, or decision, or the outcome of an event, action, or decision. Signals may be words or phrases such as *hence, therefore, consequently, for this purpose, accordingly, as a result,* or *because.*

   5. referential relationships--identification of the referent for which a word or group of words has been substituted in a passage. Referring words or phrases may include pronouns, nouns, or noun phrases.

   All details tested are important to understanding the passage. Students are tested on their ability to identify details which are supportive of major ideas presented in the passage even though the question items do not necessarily use the exact wordings provided in the passage.

3. *Inferential Comprehension:* The student must synthesize and interpret material that is presented in a passage. Inferential comprehension items involve the following skills:

   1. identification of the main idea of a passage or paragraph. (This idea or focus is not likely to be stated directly.)

   2. utilization of inductive reasoning skills--The student may be required to draw conclusions, make generalizations, summarize ideas presented in the passage, identify relationships and interpret an author's beliefs about his or her subject.

   3. utilization of deductive reasoning skills--The student may be asked to apply one or more of the ideas presented in a passage to a new situation not referred to in the passage.

   4. interpretation of figurative or other language--The student must draw inferences which indicate comprehension of the author's implied meaning.

3

4. Analysis: The student must identify author's purpose and organization of ideas. Drawing inferences about the author's style, purpose, or pattern of presentation may be required. Although these inferences are *based on* the content and structure of the passage, the analysis categories differ from the inferential categories in that analysis questions do not specifically test comprehension of the content of the passage. Analysis items require the student to identify the following:

1. *author's style--*

♦ tone . . . identification of the author's perspective or attitude toward the topic of the passage, attitude toward the reader, the author's attitude toward him/herself, and shifts in tone that occur within a passage.

♦ point of view . . . identification of the author's position, the *place* of the author in the passage, i.e., as an observer, as a participant.

♦ type of language . . . identification of language, i.e. humorous, argumentative, entertaining, serious, formal, informal, academic, etc.

♦ literary devices . . . identification of specific literary tools commonly utilized by writers such as analogy, fact and opinion statements, irony, factual narration, sensory appeal, and figurative expression.

2. *author's purpose--*

♦ identification of the author's purpose in writing a paragraph or a passage . . . such purposes might be: to explain an idea, to argue a point of view, to describe an item or event, to instruct, to contrast or compare, or to discuss causes and/or effects.

♦ recognition of functional relationships . . . the student may be required to identify the author's manner of functionally relating words, phrases, sentences, and paragraphs. Example: The student may be asked to select the word, phrase, or sentence which would be a logical transition between portions of the passage. To choose the correct answer, the student would have to understand the functional relationships between the items being connected. Possible transitional words or phrases may include: *in addition, for example, likewise, as a result, in fact, furthermore, indeed, but, on the contrary, certainly, however, yet, now, here, then, in other words, nevertheless.*

Institution Specific Regents' Test Policies

Each institution in the state of Georgia may vary its policies; therefore, it is advised that the student make inquiries at his/her college/university's registrar. The Registrar's Office at Georgia Southern University states that the following are Board of Regents' and Georgia Southern University policies which must be adhered to concerning the Regents' Test. The registrar suggests that each student read these policies carefully and become familiar with them. These policies are strictly enforced.

When to Take the Regents' Test

1. Students who have completed the two composition courses (ENG 151 and 152) are eligible to take the Regents' Test immediately following the second composition course (and stand a better chance of passing the test).

2. Students who have earned 60 cumulative quarter hours are required to take the Regents' Test each quarter they are enrolled until both sections (Reading and Essay) are passed, *regardless,* of whether English 151 and 152 are passed.

3. Students are required to take only the portion(s) of the Regents' Test they have not passed.

Transfer Students

1. Transfer students from non-University System institutions who receive 60 hours or more of transfer credit must take the Test within two quarters attendance. Thereafter, they are subject to all other provisions of the policies.

2. Transfer students from University System institutions must follow all requirements of the policy, including the requirements that they be enrolled in review classes if they have earned 75 credit hours.

Review Course Requirements

Students who have not passed or who have not taken both sections of the Regents' Test by the time they have earned 75 quarter hours *must* enroll in and attend review courses in the area(s) they have not passed. The courses are **English 090** and **Reading 090.** These review courses are specifically designed to help students pass the Regents' Test. A student who is required to enroll in these courses will be allowed to register for no more than eighteen (18) quarter hours *including* these courses. Each course carries three (3) hours of institutional credit and will be considered a part of the student's academic load. These courses will meet for approximately four weeks immediately preceding the Regents' Test for four days a week, two hours a day.

Attendance Policy

A student must attend at least 75% of the classes and complete at least 75% of the assigned work in order to be eligible to take the Regents' Test that same quarter. Failure to attend at least 50% of the class sessions will result in suspension for the subsequent quarter. Students who are required to enroll in review courses for the Regents' Test and do not register for them before the first day of class are in violation of Regents' and institutional policy. Such students will be administratively withdrawn from the university.

Exceptions to the Policy

Any exceptions to these policies must be approved by the Vice President of Academic Affairs. Only appeals for extreme hardships related to taking the review courses and/or the Regents' Test will be considered.

When taking a timed reading test like the Georgia Board of Regents' Reading Test, it is important to utilize techniques which will maximize the test score. Reading skills are obviously vital to success, but testwiseness provides for the application of techniques to enhance the reading skills. Many test strategies contribute to increased reading efficiency and ability to remain calm during the test. For example, in addition to understanding what is being read, it is crucial to maintain an adequate reading speed in order to complete the maximum number of passages and questions. Inability to finish the passages can be as devastating to the final score as not comprehending the passages. Testwiseness also includes many physical and psychological factors which may affect a student. Consider first of all, the foundation of *reading* testwiseness.

Reading Comprehension Efficiency

Some passages may be more difficult than others. The difficulty levels of the passages are directly related to the background knowledge and vocabulary of the reader. Using the systematic approach will enhance concentration, and thus improve comprehension.

1. Read the passages this way:

    A   Do a quick overview to get an idea of what the passage is about. Skim for key words in the passage. Underline these as the passage is skimmed as you are allowed to write in your test booklet. Hint: Key words are usually nouns.

    B   Read the selection carefully (try to ''see'' what is happening). Hint: Draw pictures or diagrams in your mind or on the test copy as you read.

    C   Read to *understand* the passage. As you read through the complete passage, try to identify the most important idea presented. Approaching the questions with a clear understanding of the passage is your most valuable test strategy.

2. Work through the questions this way:

    A   Read stems, recognizing the four question types: vocabulary in context, literal comprehension inferential comprehension, and analysis. (These question categories are explained in subsequent chapters.)

    B   Read all the options (the first one that looks correct may not be the best answer).

C   Eliminate obviously wrong answers first. Cross these out completely so that you do not re-read them. You greatly enhance your chances of selecting the best answer when you narrow your choices: one in two is much better odds than one in four.

D   Choose the *best answer*. Hint: Mark the answer immediately on the answer sheet. Darken the circle completely so that the scantron will not record any circles as "omits." Make sure your answer sheet is on a hard surface. Check often to ensure that you are placing the answer marks in the right places. REMINDER: all stray marks must be erased from the answer sheet because the "scantron reader" will not read an answer which has two marks recorded.

E   Spend no extra time on any one question. You can come back to those questions you are unsure of. (Place a light mark on your answer sheet through the number and option circles of the question so that you can find it again easily.) If you mark the question in the test booklet, it may be too difficult to locate quickly. An interesting possibility is that the brain will "covertly" rehearse that puzzling question for you as you continue to work through the remainder of the test. When you get back to the items you were uncertain of, the brain may present you with the answer directly. CAUTION: Be sure to allow time at the end of the test to go back and to select those answers you left blank.

F   Review all answer choices based on supporting details in the passage. Remember, this is not a memory test. It is a comprehension test.

G   YOUR SCORE IS BASED ON THE NUMBER OF CORRECT ANSWERS YOU MARK; therefore, do not choose options randomly as this lessens your chance of a correct answer. For all your empty circles, choose the same number.

3. Some of the strategies mentioned below will help you focus your concentration:

Write in your test booklet. This privilege of writing and marking helps you to be an active reader rather than a passive one. It will also help you attend to the printed page and keep your mind from wandering.

A   Mark the key words in the passages as you read them.

B   Draw simple pictures or diagrams that may help you to visualize the content and organization of the passage.

C   Use your pencil as a pacer to keep you moving mentally--and physically--through the passage and to help you not lose your place.

Reading Rate Efficiency

Do you read fast enough to complete the test? Check your speed for the test this way: Select a passage from one of this tests in this book. As you read and answer the questions, time yourself. Allow only six minutes for the entire exercise. Evaluate your reading rate. Do you need to speed up? Did you finish comfortably? Some passages may require more time than others, but a "mathematical test pace" would allow six minutes for reading each passage and answering its corresponding questions. If you believe that you need to speed up your reading rate, try these practical suggestions:

1. *Decide* to *read faster.* Simply deciding to read faster will help. Force your eyes to move faster across the lines. Re-read only when you know you have lost concentration. NOTE: Re-reading is a valid strategy for ensuring comprehension; however, don't rely on re-reading. It can be a time bandit.

2. *Practice reading faster.* Use newspaper or magazine columns for forced speed practice. Use your pencil as a pointer to keep your eyes moving forward.

3. *Use computer programs.* Work on Pacer Passages in NOVANET available through most Learning Resource Centers. This program times you while you read, asks questions, and gives percentages of correct answers.

4. *Practice, practice, practice. The* key to your increased reading speed will be regular workouts for several minutes at a time. Maintain your practice for several weeks prior to the test.

Physical Factors

To a great extent the physical preparations you make before the test will determine how prepared you are to cope with the stresses of test taking. A good idea is to establish these habits long before the test date:

Diet. Maintain a well-balanced diet. Make diet choices from the following food groups: fruits, vegetables, lean meats, lean dairy products, and whole grains. Adequate nutrition gives your body the flow of energy you need to prevent fatigue during the test. Also, curtail or eliminate foods a few days before the test which have dramatic effects on your blood sugar and blood-oxygen levels, i.e., sugary foods, caffeine, and alcoholic beverages.

Rest. Get enough rest. Don't wait until the night before the test to start "getting enough sleep." Fatigue caused by lack of sleep can be extremely detrimental to your ability to concentrate.

Exercise. Get adequate exercise. Exercise is an excellent way to reduce body tension which can, in turn, affect your academic performance. In addition, exercise can increase your energy level.

Psychological Factors

It is important to remember that life will continue after the test. Put the test into proper perspective. Failing scores are not recorded on your transcript, and if you take the test several times, only the *pass* will be recorded. It is important to realize, also, that it is normal to be nervous when you are about to take the Regents' Reading Test. Actually, some anxiety may help you to focus on the test and motivate you to do your best. Too much anxiety, however, will interfere with your concentration. Practice some of the following simple techniques during the days before the test to learn how to relax when you are tense. The more you practice relaxation techniques, the more effective they will be when you need them. Learn how to relax.

Breathe deeply. Taking deep breaths can help you relax, and it can also increase your brain power. The brain, like the rest of the body, requires oxygen to function efficiently. The healthy habit of deep breathing will be beneficial to you even before you realize you are tense.

Breathe deeply through your nose, expanding your diaphragm fully. Hold your breath for 3 to 5 seconds. Exhale slowly through the mouth. Repeat several times. Remember to breathe deeply before and sometime during the test.

Practice Body Awareness Scans. This is a concentration technique which focuses your attention *away from* anxiety. It is a good technique to use during your waiting time just prior to the test.

Begin by becoming aware of your feet; be sensitive to any tension there. Release and relax the muscles in your feet. Gradually, mentally moving up your body, following the same focusing process-- all the way to your eyebrows.

Tighten and Release Muscles. Use this technique as needed during the test. Be alert to the tension that builds in the neck and shoulder area.

Raise your shoulders as high as you can, tightening the muscles in your shoulders and neck. Hold briefly. Release.

Affirm Success. Your brain has a powerful control over your body. It believes what you tell it. Be sure you speak to it with positive affirmations. Affirm your success on the test.

Be Prepared. Have three specific strategies in mind that you will utilize for the test! Before you begin reading, write these strategies down somewhere on the test (preferably the instruction page). Some examples are: timing yourself, wearing earplugs, drawing or mapping, blacking out wrong choices, eating candy midpoint, underlining or circling, using your pencil as a pacer, and so forth. Thinking about your strategies and being mindful of them should keep you from being nervous.

A. Pre-test Checklist

Exercise 1. Please place a check (✓) in the space provided if you followed the strategy last time you took the Regents' Reading Test.

___ 1. Register for the test during the designated registration days.

___ 2. Do not associate with persons also taking the test. They may transfer their nervousness.

___ 3. Visit the testing site. Become acquainted with the testing environment.

___ 4. Get adequate rest the night before the test.

___ 5. Eat a light snack before the test. Do not arrive hungry or overfed at testing time.

___ 6. Wear comfortable clothing that can be layered to adjust to the temperature of the testing room.

B. Test-day Check List

___ 7. Bring a pictured ID.

___ 8. Bring (2) two sharpened no. 2 pencils. The answer sheet *must* be marked with no. 2 lead. It cannot be scored without no. 2 lead.

___ 9. Arrive early on the day of the test. Be prepared to wait for preliminary ''carding'' identifications, seating, and test distribution procedures.

____ 10. While you wait for the test to begin, do some brief relaxation exercises, such as deep breathing and/or body awareness scans.

____ 11. Do not talk about the test with others. Discussing tests just prior to taking them usually causes anxiety. Maintain a positive attitude.

____ 12. Unwrap candy.

____ 13. Write down strategies.

C. Taking-test Check List: Passages

____ 14. Survey each passage before you read it carefully.

____ 15. Read each passage carefully before you read the questions.

____ 16. Read for the main idea as you read.

____ 17. Draw, map, underline or circle.

D. Taking-test Check List: Questions

____ 18. Read each stem carefully. You will recognize the question types.

____ 19. Read all options.

____ 20. Eliminate obviously wrong answers first.

____ 21. Check answer choices by locating supporting details in passages.

____ 22. Choose best answer.

____ 23. Keep moving. Do not spend extra time on any one question.

____ 24. Eat candy midpoint.

____ 25. Mark all answers. Do not leave any question blank. Remember: Your score is based on the number of correct answers you mark.

____ 26. Mark clearly.

____ 27. Pace yourself through the test. Be aware of the clock. Six minutes per passage.

Unit Three

Vocabulary

Having the skill to discover the meanings of unfamiliar words is indispensable to successfully mastering the Regents' Test. Each passage on the Regents' Test is taken from college level materials and contains vocabulary appropriate to that level. The passages are drawn from the humanities, sciences and social sciences textbooks and from articles in current scholarly periodicals. The student will be required to understand and answer specific questions about one to two designated words per passage. A total of ten to twelve questions or about twenty percent of the test is devoted specifically to vocabulary items.

The vocabulary items on the Regents' Test are designed to test the student's ability to use context clues from the passages and to use structural analysis of words. Clues may appear in the same sentence as the unknown word, in preceding or following sentences, or in separate paragraphs. Having prior knowledge of words is an extremely valuable asset for the student, but the test items are designed so that structural and/or context clues are available in the passages.

Strategies for Determining Word Meanings

Strategy One: Check the question format.

A discussion of strategies must begin with recognition of the vocabulary question format. The vocabulary items on the Regents' Test are formulated using the following stems:

1. As used in the passage, _____ means
2. The underlined phrase (word) _____ most nearly means
3. As used in the passage, _____ most nearly means
4. The underlined word _____ means
5. _____, underlined in the passage, means

These stems qualify the degree to which the word's definition is affected by the context, i.e. stems 1, 2, and 3 indicate words with meanings directly affected by this particular paragraph and which could, in fact, have entirely different meanings in a different context. Stems 4 and 5 indicate words that may be answered by using prior knowledge of the word.

Strategy Two: Check the context.

Many context clues which enable the reader to understand unfamiliar words appear in the Regents' Test passages. A clue to the meaning of the word may appear in several forms: a direct or formal definition, an explanation by example, a contrasting word or phrase, a comparison, a synonym, an antonym, or a description. In addition, the clue may be derived from the general sense of the passage. Punctuation and transitional words and phrases may also indicate context clues.

Exercise 1 Utilizing context clues, work through the following illustrations to determine the meanings of the underlined words:

1. Synonym/Comparison

    Mary is a <u>perennial optimist:</u> no matter what <u>travail</u> she suffers, her spirits are always up.

<u>perennial optimist</u> means: _____

<u>travail</u> means: _____

2. Antonym/Contrast

    At first the changes in his appearance were so <u>subtle</u> he had been able to persuade himself it was his imagination, but now the changes were too obvious.

<u>Subtle</u> means: _____

3. Definition

    You need to give the Registrar's Office your <u>transcripts</u>, the official records of your grades.

<u>transcripts</u> means: _____

4. Example

    In the early 1900's America's policy toward Native Americans was really forced <u>assimilation;</u> Indian children were sent off to boarding schools, given English names, and weren't allowed to use their native languages and religious ceremonies.

<u>assimilation</u> means: _____

5. Description

    People who live in big cities have expressed feelings of <u>alienation</u> from their neighbors because there is no sense of community; neighbors do not know each other and feel no attachment to others.

<u>alienation</u> means: _____

6. General Sense of the Passage

    The man's <u>disheveled</u> clothing and <u>labored</u> breathing led us to conclude he had been engaged in vigorous exercise of some sort.

<u>disheveled</u> means _____

<u>labored</u> means: _____

Strategy Three: **Check the structure.**

In addition to context clues, the Regents' Test contains words whose meanings can be recognized through the use of structural analysis. Knowledge of common Greek and Latin prefixes, roots, and suffixes is extremely useful. Prefixes appear at the beginning of words while suffixes appear at the end of words. Roots are the basic parts of words and appear either independently or with prefixes and/or suffixes. Familiarity with a few word parts can help a student determine the meanings of many unknown words. Below is a list of word parts which occur frequently in English.

Root or Affix	Meaning	Example
ab-	away (from)	absent
ad-	toward	adhere
ambi-	both	ambivalent
anthrop-	man, mankind	anthropology
anti-	against	antipathy
archy, cracy	rule	patriarchy
archaeo-	old	archaeology
bene	good, well	benign
bio	life	biography
contra-	against, opposite	contrast
com-, con	together	committee
cred	believe	incredible
dic, dict	say	dictation
equ, equi	equal	equilateral
eu	good	euthanasia
ex-	out	exit
extra-	over, above	extraneous
gamy	marriage	monogamy
graph	write	monograph
inter-	between	interstate
-ist, -er, -or, -ant	one who	pianist
-less	without	pitiless
-logy	study of	biology
mal	bad	maladjusted
meter	measure	thermometer
mono	one	monotone
mort	death	mortuary
multi	many	multitude
non-, in-, im	not	immobile
omni	all	omnipresent
-ous	full of	bounteous
phil	love	philosophy
poly	many	polygamy
port	carry	portable
post-	after	posterior
pre-	before	predestination
spect	see, look	speculate
sub-	under	submarine
super-	over, above	superior
sym-, syn-	same	synonym
ten	hold	tentacle
terre	earth	terrestrial
theo	god	atheist
-tion	act of	distribution
trans-	across	transport

Exercise 2 Just for fun, use structural analysis to "define" the following underlined nonsense words.

1. If you dare to attend a current horror film, you will certainly see <u>multimorts</u> in gruesome color.

2. The couple made a <u>transterre</u> trip to celebrate their <u>benegamy.</u>
   Cross   good love

3. Always be an <u>ambispectator</u> when crossing the street, especially on the college campus.
   both look = Look both

4. Advise your friends to do a great deal of <u>gamology</u> before taking the big step.
   Study of Love

5. No matter what I say, I can always count on you to <u>contracred.</u>
   go against

6. He is so still and quiet as he reclines in his chair that I feel the need to check him with a <u>biometer.</u>
   life two measure

7. The starry-eyed couple looked at each other with <u>philous</u> expressions.
   full of love

8. My composition teacher often accused me of <u>malagraphics.</u> writing
   Bad writing Bad Writing

9. Fortunately my speech teacher delighted in my <u>eudiction.</u> good speaking

10. Baggage handlers who <u>polyport</u> pieces of luggage all day are probably <u>extramuscular.</u>
    carry many   big

Exercise 3 In the following sentences, determine the meanings of the words by utilizing context clues and structural analysis.

1. Our writing should be concise; we want to avoid the use of <u>extraneous</u> verbiage and say what we mean with a few well-chosen words.

<u>extraneous</u> means: _____

(extra) above full of_____ (ous) ___full of_____

2. A beautiful <u>eulogy</u> was delivered at the funeral for the <u>philanthropist;</u> he was much loved for his generosity to others.

<u>eulogy</u> means: _____

(eu) _good_____ (logy) ___Study_____

<u>philanthropist</u> means: _____

(phil) _love_____ (anthrop) _man_____ (ist) _one who____

16

3. She was sure everything in her life had been determined before her birth; she was a believer in predestination.

predestination means: _____

(pre) _before_ (destiny) _going to happen_ (tion) _act of_

4. A child who wants to please his parents will try not to contradict them too often.

contradict means: _opposite say - say the opposite_

(contra) _opposite_ (dict) _say_

5. Alan had begun to believe that George was indeed a malicious ghost whose evil surpassed his imagination.

malicious means: _____

(mal) _bad_ (ous) _full of_

Exercise 4 Integrating both context clues and structural analysis, work through the exercises presented below. Try to locate and highlight any key words, phrases, or word parts which aid you in determining the meanings of the underlined words.

1. In most cases high school graduation is a prerequisite for college.

   prerequisite _before_

2. When wearing gloves, your fingernails are not conspicuous.

   conspicuous _are not seen_

3. U.S. involvement in the conflict in Vietnam started slowly, built gradually, and finally escalated into a full-scale war.

   escalated _increased_

4. Acupuncture instead of anesthesia has been observed in some cases to make the patient impervious to the pain of surgery.

   impervious _num - immune_

5. Farmers usually plant corn in rows, whereas homeowners disperse grass seed randomly on the lawn.

   disperse _through out_

   randomly _anywhere, not in order_

6. The baby grabbed my finger and held on so tenaciously I had difficulty pulling away.

   tenaciously _tight_

17

7. Workers who are not paid well and who work under substandard conditions are being <u>exploited</u> by <u>ruthless</u> employers.

exploited _____ out _____

ruthless _____ without _____

8. A few <u>garrulous</u> classmates can dominate every discussion to the <u>detriment</u> of the other students who never get to participate.

garrulous _____ full of _____

detriment _____ harm _____

9. When a tumor is found, the patient is always relieved to hear that it is <u>benign</u> and horrified if it is diagnosed as <u>malignant.</u>

benign _____ good _____

malignant _____ bad _____

10. The lawyer was not suggesting politely that the defendant remain in town, but she was <u>exhorting</u> him not to leave the country.

exhorting _____ out _____

11. We often <u>speculate</u> about other people's lives, wondering if their experiences and feelings are similar to ours.

speculate _____ guest _____

12. In Greek mythology, the gods were <u>endowed</u> with all the knowledge and power, <u>omniscience</u> and <u>omnipotence,</u> to <u>intervene</u> in the lives of mere <u>mortals.</u>

endowed _____ last _____

omniscience _____ all _____

omnipotence _____ 911 _____

intervene _____ inside _____

mortals _____ dead _____

13. On our nature trek through the woods, the variety of <u>flora</u> growing in abundance was breathtaking.

flora _____ flower _____

14. The unusual <u>fauna</u> of Australia, native or <u>indigenous</u> to the outback, seems <u>forlorn</u> in an <u>urban</u> zoo.

fauna _____

indigenous _____

forlorn _____

urban _____

15. The African-American woman felt <u>ambivalent</u> about being in South Africa. She had conflicting feelings about her experience.

ambivalent _____

16. The hardened criminal who expresses no <u>remorse</u> over his crime is the most difficult to <u>rehabilitate</u>.

<u>remorse</u> _Sorrow_____

<u>rehabilitate</u> _To do over_____

17. The usually very <u>composed</u> and <u>meticulously</u> groomed Mrs. Almond appeared flustered and disheveled when the police were questioning her.

<u>composed</u> _together_____

<u>meticulously</u> _full of_____

18. Mrs. Jones and I have a <u>tentative</u> lunch date for Friday; she is to call and confirm it on Thursday.

<u>tentative</u> _?_____

19. During the interrogation, the prisoner's face remained <u>impassive</u> concealing the emotion that any but the most <u>inured</u> criminal would probably feel.

<u>impassive</u> _____

<u>inured</u> _____

20. <u>Anthropologists</u> tell us that people in all cultures try to <u>modify</u> their appearances by decorating their bodies with cosmetics or jewelry.

<u>anthropologists</u> _One who is mankind_____

<u>modify</u> _make over_____

21. Large houses, green lawns, and an occasional Mercedes distinguished the <u>affluent</u> neighborhood.

<u>affluent</u> _rich, well to do_____

Practice Passages

Exercise 5 Read the following passages and answer the vocabulary questions using context and word structure clues.

Passage One

Any brand or <u>faction</u> of Puritans was <u>anathema</u> to King James. Though not much interested in <u>theology.</u> he distrusted any religion that did not fit in with his own ideas of relations between church and state. In his estimation the Puritans, by <u>repudiating</u> the episcopal system of church government, were threatening to pull down one of the chief pillars of <u>monarchy</u> itself. Refusal to submit to the authority of bishops appointed by the king was identical in his mind with disloyalty to the sovereign. For this reason he regarded the Puritans as the <u>equivalent</u> of traitors and threatened to "harry" them out of the land. He showed little more wisdom or <u>discretion</u> in his dealings with the Catholics. For the most part, he favored them, though he could not resist the temptation to levy fines upon them from time to time for violating the severe code which came down from the Reformation. In 1605 a group of <u>fanatical</u> adherents of the

Roman faith organized the Gunpowder Plot. They planned to blow up the Parliament building while the king and the legislators were assembled in it, and in the resulting confusion, seize control of the government. The plot was discovered, and parliament enacted even more stringent laws against the Catholics. James, however, allowed the measures to go unenforced. Needless to say, his persistent leniency antagonized his Protestant subjects and made him more unpopular than ever.

Burns, Western Civilizations, *pp. 468-469.*

1. The underlined word <u>faction</u> means
   1. victory.
   2. group.
   3. problem.
   4. ritual.

2. <u>Anathema,</u> underlined in the passage, means
   1. something that is hated.
   2. something that is trusted.
   3. something that is valued.
   4. something that is understood.

3. The underlined word <u>theology</u> means
   1. theory.
   2. study of philosophy.
   3. study of God.
   4. ideas.

4. As used in the passage, <u>repudiating</u> means
   1. supporting.
   2. attacking.
   3. ignoring.
   4. rejecting.

5. The underlined word <u>monarchy</u> means
   1. government by a few people.
   2. rule by a king or absolute one.
   3. government by all the people.
   4. rule by the church.

6. As used in the passage, <u>equivalent</u> means
   1. different from.
   2. worse than.
   3. having the same morals.
   4. having the same effect.

7. As used in the passage, <u>harry</u> means
   1. resist or retard.
   2. harass or annoy.
   3. carry or transport.
   4. beg or plead.

8. As used in the passage, <u>discretion</u> means
   1. judgment. ✓
   2. approval.
   3. courage.
   4. trust.

9. The underlined word <u>fanatical</u> means
   1. faithful.
   2. peaceful.
   3. extremist. ✓
   4. disloyal.

10. As used in the passage, <u>stringent</u> means
    1. scarce.
    2. tense.
    3. generous.
    4. strict. ✓

11. As used in the passage, <u>leniency</u> most nearly means
    1. anger.
    2. harshness.
    3. tolerance. ✓
    4. wisdom.

12. <u>Antagonized</u>, underlined in the passage, means
    1. angered. ✓
    2. pacified.
    3. rewarded.
    4. alarmed.

Passage Two

Cave-man art throws a flood of light on many problems relating to <u>primitive</u> mentality and folkways. To a certain extent it was undoubtedly an expression of a true <u>aesthetic</u> sense. Cro-Magnon man did obviously take some delight in a graceful line or <u>symmetrical</u> pattern or brilliant color. The fact that he painted and tattooed his body and wore ornaments gives evidence of this. But his chief works of art can scarcely have been produced for the sake of creating beautiful objects. Such a possibility must be <u>excluded</u> for several reasons. To begin with, the best of the paintings and drawings are usually to be found on the walls and ceilings of the darkest and most <u>inaccessible</u> parts of the caves. The gallery of paintings at Niaux, for instance, is more than half a mile from the entrance of the cavern. No one could see the artists' creations except in the <u>imperfect</u> light of torches or of <u>primitive</u> lamps, which must have smoked and sputtered badly, for the only illuminating fluid was animal fat. Furthermore, there is evidence the Cro-Magnon man was largely <u>indifferent</u> toward his work of art after it was finished. Numerous examples have been found of paintings or drawings <u>superimposed</u> upon earlier ones of the same or of different types. Evidently the important thing was not the finished work itself, but the act of making it.

Burns, Western Civilizations, p. 11.

13. Primitive, as used in the passage (sentence one), most nearly means
    1. crude.
    2. sophisticated.
    3. archaic.
    4. superstitious.

14. Aesthetic, underlined in the passage, means
    1. philosophical.
    2. having a love of beauty.
    3. historical.
    4. having a love of God.

15. As used in the passage, symmetrical means
    1. mixed.
    2. disorganized.
    3. beautiful.
    4. harmonious.

16. The underlined word excluded means
    1. expelled.
    2. disregarded.
    3. considered.
    4. confirmed.

17. As used in the passage, inaccessible means
    1. easy to reach.
    2. hard to reach.
    3. unavoidable.
    4. uncomfortable.

18. As used in the passage, imperfect means
    1. flawed.
    2. dim.
    3. impure.
    4. incomplete.

19. As used in the passage (sentence nine), primitive means
    1. crude.
    2. sophisticated.
    3. archaic.
    4. superstitious.

20. Indifferent, underlined in the passage, means
    1. neutral.
    2. unbiased.
    3. biased.
    4. disinterested.

21. As used in the passage, <u>superimposed</u> most nearly means
    1. opposed to.
    2. placed over.
    3. hidden under.
    4. based on.

Passage Three

Mars has long been the planet of greatest interest to scientists and nonscientists alike. Its interesting appearance as a reddish object in the night sky and some past scientific studies have made Mars the <u>prime</u> object of <u>speculation</u> as to whether or not <u>extraterrestrial</u> life exists there.

In 1877, the Italian astronomer Giovanni Schiaparelli published the results of a long series of telescopic observations he had made of Mars. He reported that he had seen <u>canali</u> on the surface. When this Italian word for "channels" was improperly translated into "canals," which seemed to <u>connote</u> that they were dug by intelligent life, public interest in Mars increased.

Pasachoff, *Astronomy: From the Earth to the Universe*, p. 167.

22. As used in the passage <u>prime</u> means
    1. most valuable.
    2. most perfect.
    3. chief.
    4. earliest.

23. <u>Speculation</u>, underlined in the passage most nearly means
    1. wonder.
    2. risk taking.
    3. visualization.
    4. calculation.

24. <u>Extraterrestrial</u>, underlined in the passage, means
    1. fashion.
    2. outside the earth.
    3. unknown.
    4. primitive.

25. The underlined word <u>canali</u> means
    1. canals.
    2. rivers.
    3. channels.
    4. ditches.

26. As used in the passage <u>connote</u> means
    1. imply.
    2. mean.
    3. deny.
    4. reveal.

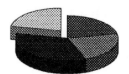

Unit Four

Literal Comprehension

Literal comprehension questions require the student to recognize information or ideas directly stated in the text. Such questions test recognition of facts, concepts, or events. They also include the recognition of a sequence of events and the identification of referents. Literal comprehension questions and answers do not always utilize the exact words stated in the passage; however, the ideas, concepts, or information are explicit in the text. In other words, the answer will be stated specifically in the text.

This unit will discuss the different kinds of literal comprehension questions a student will encounter on the Regents' Reading Test. They may be identified as follows:

Literal Comprehension of Details
Literal Comprehension of Relationship Patterns
    Comparison and Contrast
    Cause and Effect
    Definition
    Illustration and Examples
Comprehension of Referents

Literal Comprehension of Details

Specific details or facts often support the main idea. For the Regents' Reading Test, the student is required to recognize these supporting details or facts. Identifying significant stated details is a literal level of reading. Generally, the answers appear directly in the passage, and if necessary, the student could point out the specific words which answer the test questions. For these types of questions the student may scan the passage to validate his responses.

Read the following passage:

> Settlement of the Plains and the West involved the greatest migration in American history. Between 1870 and 1900, more acres were settled and put under cultivation than in the previous 250 years. Between 1860 and 1910, the number of farms tripled, from 2 million to over 6 million. During the 1870s alone, Kansas gained 350,000 new settlers; and in the 1880s Nebraska's population increased by 250,000. California and Texas grew 216 and 273 percent respectively between 1870 and 1890. Males accounted for the majority of migrants to new agricultural areas, out-numbering women by about six to five--a ratio above the national average but below that of the mining states.
>
> Norton, et. al., *A People And A Nation,* p. 481.

Exercise 1A Write the main idea.

Settlement of the Plains & the West involved the greatest migration.

1B What details illustrate that the Plains and the West had the greatest migration in American history?

Write them here: <u>More acres were settled and put under</u> <u>cultivation, 1860 to 1910 farms tripled, 1870 Kansas</u> <u>gained 350,000</u>
_____

Scanning a passage for details will help the reader locate the answer quickly and save time for other questions. To scan for specific information, follow these strategies:

1. Quickly look through the article remembering the question being asked. Visualize the question before you start scanning.
2. Notice key words or phrases in the question stem that may suggest the location of the answer and underline or circle these question words. This will emphasize them.
3. Now look carefully for word/words that answer the question. Search for key words, numbers, or capital letters to help in locating the information quickly.
4. Read the sentence that mentions the information sought. Once you find the specific information, stop reading and mark your answer sheet.

Although detail questions can be worded many different ways, some common question stems asking for specific information usually begin with the following *wh* question words:

Where
When
Who
What number (e.g., dates, times), name (e.g., people, places, things)

(Note: the *wh* question words why, what for and how are usually associated with inferential comprehension.)

Literal Comprehension of Relationship Patterns

Questions in this area test a student's ability to recognize organizational structure and to see relationships. To answer the questions correctly, the student must understand the structure of the passage and must recognize organizational patterns such as sequence of events, comparison/contrast, cause and effect, definition, and illustration and example.

Sequence

The student is required to identify the **order of events** stated in a reading passage. Information may not be listed in the order of occurrence. This type of question asks for **chronological order** and sometimes requires the student to re-order the occurrences. Clues may be the use of words such as *then, next, before, finally, in the first place, subsequently,* and *thereafter.* These *time words* are the best indicators that the passage is developed around some kind of chronological order. Questions may be stated as:

Which was the most recent?

The first thing that happened was....

Of the following, which had the most immediate result?

In what order did the events in the story take place?

Exercise 2 Read the following passage and note the sequence. Then answer the questions.

> Between 1603 and 1715 England experienced the most tumultuous years of its long history. In this period Puritan resistance to the Elizabethan religious settlement merged with fierce parliamentary opposition to the aspirations to absolute monarchy of the Stuart kings. During these years no fewer than three foreigners occupied the English throne, and between 1649 and 1660 England was without a king altogether. Yet by the end of this century of crisis England provided a model to Europe of limited monarchy, parliamentary government, and measured religious toleration.
>
> Kagan, et al., *The Western Heritage Since 1648*, p. 49-50.

A. During which period was England without a king?
1. 1603–1715
2. 1649–1660
3. 1660–1715
4. 1603–1649

B. The English government was a model to Europe
1. in 1603.
2. while England was without a king.
3. between 1649-1660.
4. by the end of the century.

Comparison and Contrast

For comparison-contrast passages the student is asked to identify likenesses or differences among periods, events, characters, philosophies, actions, or ideas. Key words and phrases indicating comparison (likeness) are:

similarly
like
alike
in the same way
likewise
just as
furthermore
in addition

Words to look for which may indicate contrast (differences) are:

but
however
on the other hand
different(ly)
in contrast to
unlike
contrarily

27

Exercise 3 Read the following example of a comparison and contrast passage and then answer the questions.

The differences in ideals and in religious and social attitudes were perhaps more fundamental. The Egyptian culture was predominantly ethical, the Mesopotamian legalistic. The Egyptian outlook on life, except during the Middle Kingdom, was generally one of cheerful resignation, comparatively free from the cruder superstitions. By contrast, the Mesopotamian view was gloomy, pessimistic, and enthralled by morbid fears. Where the native of Egypt believed in immortality and dedicated a large part of his energy to preparation for the life to come, his Mesopotamian contemporary lived in the present and cherished few hopes regarding his fate beyond the grave. Finally, the civilization of the Nile valley embodied concepts of monotheism, a religion of love, and of social equalitarianism; that of the Tigris-Euphrates was more selfish and practical. Its religion seldom evolved beyond the stage of primitive polytheism, and its arts bore few of the natural and personal qualities of the Egyptian.

On the other hand, there were similarities too striking to be ignored. Both civilizations made progress in ethical theory and in concepts of social justice. Both had their evils of slavery and imperialism, of oppressive kings and greedy priests. Both had common problems of irrigation and land boundaries; and, as a result, both made notable progress in the sciences, especially in mathematics. Finally, rivalry among small states led eventually to consolidation and to the growth of mighty empires, especially in the case of Mesopotamia.

Burns, *Western Civilizations,* pp. 49-50.

A. In what way were the Egyptian and the Mesopotamian cultures alike?
1. They were pessimistic in their outlook.
2. They believed in monotheism.
3. They had benevolent kings.
④. They made progress in the sciences.

B. Which of the following is NOT a difference between the Egyptians and the Mesopotamians?
1. outlook on life
2. religious views
③. views on slavery
4. ideals

Cause and Effect

In cause and effect relationships, the student is asked to identify the reason or reasons for events, actions, decisions, or the outcomes of an event, action, or decision. This pattern is often found in social studies or science texts. In this pattern there is a cause and a result or effect of that cause. Key words often used to indicate cause and effect are:

consequently
because
therefore
resulting
thus
for
this
reason

so
ergo
so
that
hence

Example:

The terrible drought caused the farmer to lose most of his crops.
cause: drought
effect: lost crops

Exercise 4 Read the following passage and answer the questions. Look for the cause and effect relationship.

Most migrants came from one of two places of origin: the eastern states and Europe. In fact, several western states opened immigration bureaus in the East and in Europe to lure settlers westward. Land-grant railroads were especially aggressive, advertising cheap land at $2-8 per acre, arranging credit terms, offering reduced fares, and promising instant success. Railroad agents--often former im-migrants--greeted newcomers at eastern ports and traveled to Europe to recruit prospective settlers. In California, fruit and vegetable growers imported Japanese and Mexican laborers to work in the fields and canneries.

Most migrants went west because opportunities there seemed to promise a better life. Between 1870 and 1910 the nation's population rose from 40 million to 92 million, and the total urban population swelled by over 400 percent. As a result, demand for farm products grew rapidly. Meanwhile, scientific advances were enabling farmers to use the soil more efficiently. Agricultural experts developed the technique of dry farming, a system of plowing and harrowing that prevented precious moisture from evaporating. Scientists perfected varieties of "hard" wheat whose seeds could withstand northern winters, and millers invented an efficient process for grinding these tougher new wheat kernels into flour. Railroad expansion made remote farming regions more accessible, and grain-elevator construction eased problems of shipping and storage.

Norton, et. al. *A People And A Nation,* pp. 481-483.

A. The demand for farm products grew rapidly between 1870 and 1910 because
   1. land was cheap.
   2. the population grew.
   3. techniques for growing crops improved.
   4. storage and shipping of crops improved.

B. The passage states the migrants did NOT move West because
   1. the land was cheap.
   2. of easy credit terms.
   3. wheat would grow easily.
   4. they were promised instant success.

Definition

Thoughts of the writer may be organized by defining or classifying a difficult or complex concept or term. An object or idea may be defined by identifying the general class to which it belongs and isolating that object within that class or by describing how it differs from other elements in the same category. The author may further expand by restating or giving examples. This pattern is often used in psychology, in the sciences, and in any area where the reader may encounter unfamiliar terms.

Exercise 5 Read the following passage and then answer the question.

To understand what made Athens work, we must begin with what the Athenians thought about human nature. Greeks generally understood that there was within human nature a certain tendency toward baseness, toward material comfort, toward concern with the needs and wants of the body. But they believed that human nature had another, more exalted dimension—one that reached toward the gods. Through cultivation and breeding, through careful education, and through the sheer force of character, they believed that man was capable of realizing a natural potential for human excellence— that he could find the means of bringing forth the very best of human capacity. Their term for this quest for excellence was <u>arete.</u>

Fox and Pope, *American Heritages,* p. 16.*

Arete, as defined by the author, means
1. tendency toward baseness.
2. search for fulfillment.
3. concern for material comfort.
4. human nature.

Examples and Illustrations

This pattern of organization uses specific examples or illustrations to develop an idea or point. Often the author who begins with the phrase "For example" will support her ideas with illustrations. Frequently a key idea will be stated first and a series of examples or illustrations will be used to develop or clarify the author's point, as done in the selection below.

Exercise 6 Read the passage and then answer the question.

Static electricity is all around us. We see it in lightning, or we may receive electric shocks when we walk on a nylon rug on a dry day and touch something (or someone). We can see sparks fly from a cat's fur when we pet it in the dark. When we rub a balloon on a sweater and the balloon sticks to the wall or ceiling, this is evidence of static electricity. Our clothes may even cling together when we take them from the clothes dryer due to the effect of static electricity. This happens because there is a buildup of one of the two kinds of electrical charge, either positive or negative....

All of the following are mentioned as having static electricity except
1. walking on a nylon rug.
2. clothes cling together.
3. rubbing a sweater.
4. lightning.

* From *American Heritage* by Frank Fox and Clayne Pope. Copyright © 1990 by Kendall/Hunt Publishing Company. Used with permission.

Comprehension of Referents

The student must recognize the referent(s) for which a word or group of words has been substituted. This includes identifying referents for pronouns such as *he, she, we, they, this, these, that, those,* and *it.* (You is rarely if ever utilized.) Also, the student may be asked to identify the terms or phrases which are represented by noun phrases such as *the former, the latter,* (or any specific phrases) which are used to point the reader back to their "specific meanings."

Exercise 7 Read the following passage and determine the answer to the question by identifying the referent.

It is the custom among many historians to distinguish between historic and prehistoric periods in the evolution of human society. By the <u>former</u> they mean history based upon written records. By the <u>latter</u> they mean the record of man's achievements before the invention-of writing. But this distinction is not altogether satisfactory. It suggests that human accomplishments before they were recorded in characters or symbols representing words or concepts were not important. Nothing could be farther from the truth....

Burns, *Western Civilization,* p. 5.

As underlined in the passage, <u>former</u> refers to
1. prehistoric periods.
2. human society.
3. historic periods.
4. historians.

Practice Passages

Exercise 8 Read the passages below and answer the questions that follow each.

The difference between "an historical event" and "a dramatic event" is well illustrated by the stories of the Stevens Party and the Donner <u>Party</u>. The <u>former</u> is historically important, and the pioneers who composed it brought the first wagons to California and discovered the pass across the Sierra Nevada that serves still as the chief route for railroad, highway telephone, and airlines. The Donner Party, however, is of negligible importance historically, but the story has been told and retold, published and republished, because of its dramatic details of starvation, cannibalism, murder, heroism, and disaster. Again, every American who knows of the one, a thousand must know of the other. As a kind of final irony, the pass discovered by the Stevens Party has come to be known as Donner Pass.

Yet, actually the two parties have much in common. They were groups of Middle Westerners, native and foreign-born, migrating to California. Both included women and children, and traveled overland in ox-drawn covered wagons. Over much of the way they followed the same route. Both were overtaken by winter, and faced their chief difficulties because of snow. Some of the Donner Party spent the winter in a cabin built by three members of the Stevens Party....

Stewart, *The Smart Ones Got Through,* p. 60.

1. As underlined the <u>former</u> refers to
   1. the Stevens Party.
   2. the Donner Party.
   3. an historical event.
   4. a dramatic event.

31

2. All are true of the Donner and Stevens Parties except
    1. they were Middle Westerners.
    2. they were migrating to California.
    3. they included women and children.
    4. they traveled in horse-drawn wagons.

3. Which of the following represents the story of "an historical event"?
    1. Middle Westerners
    2. Donner Party
    3. Stevens Party
    4. Americans

4. <u>Party</u> as used in the passage refers to
    1. a social gathering.
    2. a political group.
    3. a legal proceeding.
    4. a gathered group.

Exercise 9 Now try this passage and questions.

Soft coal is found in Western Pennsylvania; hard coal in Eastern Pennsylvania. All the coal in this state was formed in the same geological period. Why, then, are these two coals so different? A study of the coal beds reveals that those in the hard coal region are buckled into tight folds, while those in the soft coal area are nearly horizontal. We infer from this and from many other evidences in other lands, that high pressure and high temperatures associated with the crushing and folding of the beds changed the soft coal, which is classified as sedimentary rock, into hard coal, which is classified as metamorphic rock.

Hard coal is not only harder than soft, it is more lustrous; it breaks into smooth-surfaced, irregular fragments instead of rectangular blocks; it has a higher percentage of carbon in it; it is harder to start burning--as our colonial forefathers discovered.

Blough, et al, *Elementary School Science and How to Teach It,* p. 122.

1. Soft coal is turned into hard coal by
    1. high temperature.
    2. high pressure.
    3. crushing and folding of the coal beds.
    4. all of the above.

2. Soft coal is also known as
    1. metamorphic rock.
    2. tight fold coal.
    3. sedimentary rock.
    4. irregular coal.

3. All of the following are differences between hard coal and soft coal except
    1. hard coal is harder.
    2. hard coal is found in Western Pennsylvania.
    3. hard coal is more lustrous.
    4. hard coal has higher carbon.

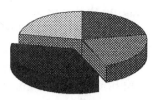

Unit Five

Inference

Inference questions usually comprise about one-third of the Regents' Reading Test. For this reason, it is very important for the reader to understand what is required in order to draw accurate inferences. Perhaps the best way to explain inferential comprehension is to contrast it with literal comprehension. Unit Four dealt with the identification of specific or literal information stated in the passage. The answers to questions could even be pinpointed. With inferential comprehension, however, the answers are not stated in the passage. They are not given directly.

Look at the pictures below. What can be inferred from the illustrations?

Team A.
Picture 1 inference

_____

Team B.
Picture 2 inference

_____

How does a reader know that Team B did not win? He or she probably used clues such as: the players are not smiling, they are not jumping up and down, they are not hugging each other, or the cheerleaders are hanging their heads, and so forth. All of these are **clues** that allow the reader to make the correct inference, "Team B lost the game." The name of the losing team is not directly stated anywhere in the picture. It must be **inferred**.

Inference is often referred to as "reading between the lines." Carrying this idea further, try to imagine that you are a private investigator, and the ability to arrest the criminal is based on clues and evidence. You did not see the criminal committing the crime (literal comprehension), thus you must put together the evidence you have discovered and come up with a solution to the problem: "Who committed the crime?" (inferential comprehension). You want to be very sure of your decision; however, you know that total certainty is not possible. Therefore, you make the most accurate guess possible. You make a reasonable inference. This is a crucial part of drawing inferences: **the more actual evidence you can gather, the more accurate your inference is likely to be.** A logical conclusion must be based on supportive evidence, not speculation, imagination, or personal opinion.

Example 1: Consider the pictures below. Use the visual images to determine the relationship between the man and the woman. Write the kind of relationship you think exists for each picture in the space provided.

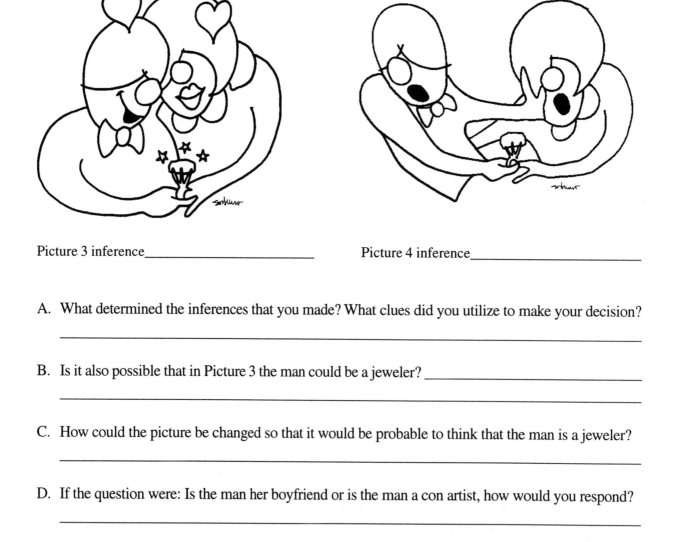

Picture 3 inference_____   Picture 4 inference_____

A. What determined the inferences that you made? What clues did you utilize to make your decision?
   _____

B. Is it also possible that in Picture 3 the man could be a jeweler? _____
   _____

C. How could the picture be changed so that it would be probable to think that the man is a jeweler?
   _____

D. If the question were: Is the man her boyfriend or is the man a con artist, how would you respond?
   _____

E. For which answer do you have the most actual evidence? _____

Example 2: Make inferences using any clues in the illustrations. Write "Yes" if you can make the inference, and "No" if you cannot.

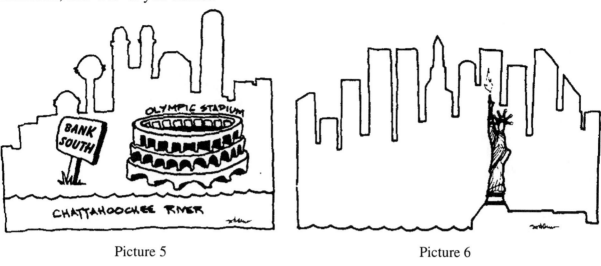

Picture 5   Picture 6

____ 1. Both pictures show large cities.
____ 2. Both cities are in the northern United States.
____ 3. The city in Picture 5 has a sports team.
____ 4. Picture 6 is New York City, New York.

This ability to detect clues in pictures is similar to detecting clues in paragraphs. Instead of looking for visual images, you look for words, phrases, or sentences that give clues as to what can be inferred. Authors provide hints through the words they choose. The words may have negative or positive feelings or connotations that will help the reader make the intended inferences. Scan the following paragraph to find clues and determine who killed Duncan the King:

> Macbeth had a wife, to whom he communicated the strange prediction of the weird sisters.... She was a bad, ambitious woman, and so as her husband and herself could arrive at greatness, she cared not much by what means. She spurred on the reluctant purpose of Macbeth, who felt compunction at the thoughts of blood, and did not cease to represent the murder of the king as a step absolutely necessary to the fulfillment of the flattering prophecy.
>
> Lamb's *Tales from Shakespeare*

Exercise 1 List any parts of this paragraph which provide clues that help identify the murderer:

Macbeth   *Lady Macbeth*

_____   _____

_____   _____

_____   _____

According to the hints given in this paragraph, the prime suspect is Macbeth's wife: "bad," "ambitious," "she cared not much by what means," and "the murder of the king as a step absolutely necessary." The characterization of Macbeth, though scanty, is apparent through these phrases: "reluctant," "felt compunction at the thoughts of blood." Presented with only this paragraph, the most accurate inference made with confidence is "Lady Macbeth murdered the King." Even though you may know the play *Macbeth,* and you may know Macbeth (not Lady Macbeth) killed Duncan the King, based on the information in this paragraph, the answer is still Lady Macbeth.

Exercise 2 While reading this excerpt, focus on Jo and the type of person she is.

> "Jo does use such slang words!" observed Amy, with a reproving look at the long figure stretched on the rug. Jo immediately sat up, put her hands in her pockets and began to whistle.
> "Don't Jo, it's so boyish!"
> "That's why I do it."
> "I detest rude, unladylike girls!"
> "I hate affected, niminy-piminy chits!"
>
> Alcott, Little Women

Inferences about Jo: _____

Clues: _____

Exercise 3 Given the following description of the husband of Mary, Queen of Scots, what three inferences can you make about his character? Highlight the clues.

> Her marriage with Darnley in 1565 concentrated every element of opposition in the country. He was a Roman Catholic, and a Catholic reaction was feared, without very much reason.... The leaders of the Protestant lords had rebelled when the marriage took place; Darnley, jealous and resentful of what he considered Mary's neglect of his advice and of his claim, entered into a plot along with the exiled lords who were his natural enemies. The conspirators intended not only to murder Mary's secretary Rizzio, whose influence over the Queen was resented by her husband, but also to deprive Mary of any share in the government of the realm. When the first object had been attained [the murder of Rizzio] Darnley, perceiving that his allies were not likely to submit to his own ascendancy, deserted and betrayed them.
>
> Rait, History of Scotland, pp. 71-72.

Inferences: 1. _____
                    2. _____
                    3. _____
                    Other: _____

Exercise 4 It is also possible to make inferences about information of a more scientific nature. Read the passage below and then answer the multiple-choice inference questions.

> In the third article of this chapter, Joseph Schneider addresses the question "How did drunkenness become a disease?" Using a historical approach, the author is able to show that the belief that "alcoholism is a disease" is more the result of social and political forces than the result of scientific discovery. At first, the Church had jurisdiction over drunkenness and, hence, it was defined as sin. Then, the State gained authority over defining and regulating drunkenness and it was summarily defined as criminal. More recently, interest groups such as Alcoholics Anonymous gained sufficient political influence to transform drunkenness from being criminal to being ill. With this historical approach, Schneider is suggesting that the path of drunkenness from sin to criminal to disease must be understood against the background of social and political forces.
>
> Ward, David A. Alcoholism, p. 6.

1. Joseph Schneider suggests that
    1. separate models of the nature of alcoholism are inadequate.
    2. Alcoholics Anonymous is the best model for the treatment of alcoholism.
    3. social and political forces are irrelevant to a discussion of alcoholism.
    4. the Church has been the most successful at controlling the problem of alcohol abuse in this country.

2. The author of this article would probably agree with which of the following statements?
    1. Political and social forces cannot determine what happens in societies.
    2. In order to understand the problems of present day society, we must consider what happened when alcohol was illegal.
    3. To better understand the different theories of alcoholism, one needs to consider the influence of social and political forces.
    4. Alcoholism can never be abolished.

Exercise 5 Read the following paragraph and answer the following inference questions.

According to Eric Berne, a renowned psychoanalyst, there are many similarities between fairy tale characters and real people. In fact, Berne suggests that a person may "script" her life based on a fairy tale which attracted her as a child. In other words, the child (who has been in her childlike way trying to determine who she is) upon hearing a story may say to herself "that's just like me." Perhaps we have many Cinderellas and Snow Whites walking this earth waiting to be rescued by their princes. If we as adults look at the fairy tale with a different and hopefully adult perspective, maybe we can determine how we have, in fact, "scripted" our lives. It is even possible that we may divert some aspects of disaster or at any rate change some self-destructive behaviors. Consider the excerpt taken from Berne's *What Do You Say After You Say Hello?* (pp. 43-44) below. It is a humorous and telling version of what the characters in Little Red Riding Hood (LRRH) were really up to:

One day LRRH's mother sent her through the woods to bring food to her grandmother, and on the way she met a wolf. What kind of a mother sends a little girl into a forest where there are wolves? Why didn't her mother do it herself, or go along with LRRH? If grandmother was so helpless, why did mother leave her all by herself in a hut far away? But if LRRH had to go, how come her mother had never warned her not to stop and talk to wolves? The story makes it clear that LRRH had never been told that this was dangerous. No mother could really be that stupid, so it sounds as if her mother didn't care much what happened to LRRH, or maybe even wanted to get rid of her. No little girl is that stupid either. How could LRRH look at the wolf's eyes, ears, hands, and teeth, and still think it was her grandmother? Why didn't she get out of there as fast as she could? And a mean little thing she was, too, gathering up stones to put into the wolf's belly. At any rate, any straight-thinking girl, after talking to the wolf, would certainly not have stopped to pick flowers, but would have said to herself: "That son of a _____ is going to eat up my grandmother if I don't get some help fast." Even the grandmother and the hunter aren't above suspicion.

1. Berne seems most interested in
    1. revealing the good traits of the mother.
    2. understanding the motives and behaviors of the characters.
    3. showing how the wolf was mistreated.
    4. expressing sympathy for the grandmother.

2. The author's opinion about the influence of fairy tales is that
    1. they may be detrimental.
    2. they promote personal growth.
    3. they should be read at a very early age.
    4. they have intriguing plots and characters.

3. Berne implies that LRRH and her mother are similar in that, in both, they
    1. desire to be good.
    2. are guilty to a degree.
    3. fear the wolf.
    4. loved flowers.

Drawing Conclusions

Analyzing a passage in order to predict an outcome entails the same process used in drawing inferences while reading. An efficient way to predict outcomes is to highlight clues and write them down. The actual writing of clues may give insights into patterns being developed. It may even be possible to map out the information. Thus, a conclusion, made with a high degree of confidence, may emerge from this kind of effort. For example, if my friend tells me that her sister has been performing poorly in school, that she changed friends, that she is out very late at night, that she looks nervous, and so forth, I may conclude with confidence that her sister is having personal problems and may need help. I may not, however, conclude that she is using alcohol or that she is consuming drugs; there is no evidence on which to base such a conclusion.

Exercise 6 Scan the pictures below and write a conclusion for each set of illustrations.

Conclusion _____

_____

Conclusion _____

Conclusion _____

Transferring these skills to passages may be easier if, while reading, key ideas or pattern words are highlighted or ''imaged'' in the mind.

Exercise 7 First, highlight the key events. Next, draw a picture of what you have ''imaged'' in the space provided. Finally, write a conclusion for the passage. Practice this process using the following paragraph.

He heard something behind him, the brush of feet. Turning he saw over the prostrate columns another figure; then before he was aware, another was at hand on the right, under a trilithon, and another on the left. The dawn shown full on the front of the man westward, and Clare could discern from this that he was tall, and walked as if trained. They all closed in with evident purpose. Her story then was true! Springing to his feet, he looked around for a weapon, loose stone, means of escape, anything.

Hardy, *Tess of the D'Urbervilles*

Drawing:

Conclusion _____

Exercise 8 Using the information given in the paragraph, try to predict an outcome.

    Pure ozone is an unstable, faintly bluish gas with a characteristic fresh, penetrating odor. It is the most chemically active form of oxygen. Ozone is formed in the ozone layer of the stratosphere by the action of solar ultraviolet light on oxygen; this layer plays an important role in preventing most ultraviolet and other high-energy radiation, which is harmful to life, from penetrating to the earth's surface. Some environmental scientists fear that certain man-made pollutants, e.g., nitric oxide, may cause a drastic depletion of stratospheric ozone.

                                          Levey & Greenhall, *The Concise Columbia Encyclopedia,* p. 634.

Scientists say _____

If what scientists say is true, then _____

_____

_____

Inferring the Main Idea

    The main idea of a passage is one statement which summarizes and covers all major ideas presented. In some writing, the main idea may be directly stated in the first sentence or another sentence; however, for the Regents' Reading Test the student will most likely be required to infer the main idea. As in drawing any inference, the main idea will be arrived at by putting together the clues given. For inferring the main idea, the clues will be the major ideas within the passage. Because you are allowed to write on your test booklet, it is possible for you to mark the major ideas as you read. After marking these, you should be able to write or choose a statement which is a "coverall" for the passage.

Look at Picture 7. What do you think the main idea is? _____

Exercise 9 Read this paragraph, marking the most important words and phrases as you read. Looking at the phrases you marked, compose a main idea for the passage.

Picture 7

Formed in the best proportions of her sex, Rowena was tall in stature, yet not so much so as to attract observation on account of superior height. Her complexion was exquisitely fair. . . . Her clear blue eyes, which sat enshrined beneath a graceful eyebrow of brown sufficiently marked to give expression to the forehead, seemed capable to kindle as well as melt, to command as well as to beseech.... Her profuse hair, of a colour betwixt brown and flaxen, was arranged in a fanciful and graceful manner in numerous ringlets.... She wore bracelets on her arms, which were bare. Her dress was an under-gown and kirtle of pale sea-green silk, over which hung a loose robe, which reached to the ground, having very wide sleeves, which came down, however, little below the elbow.

When Rowena perceived the Knight Templar's eyes bent on her with an ardour that, compared with the dark caverns under which they moved, gave them the effect of lighted charcoal, she drew with dignity the veil around her face, as an intimation that the determined freedom of his glance was disagreeable.

Scott, *Ivanhoe*

A. Main Idea: _____

B. How is this paragraph different from Picture 7? _____
_____

C. How is this paragraph similar to Picture 7? _____
_____

Exercise 10 For this exercise *draw* the major ideas. If you are not a great artist, just use stick figures. After you finish the drawing, try to write a main idea for the passage.

'James the Second that had the fire-mark in his face' recognized the existence of a grave menace to the monarchy, and possibly to the dynasty, and he acted with vigour and without scruple. He sent Douglas a safe conduct and invited him to Stirling Castle. The Earl, on a Monday evening in February 1452, passed to the castle and spoke with the King, who behaved pleasantly toward the Earl. The next day the King called him to dinner. They both thoroughly enjoyed the meal. After supper, King James charged his guest with being connected to a traitorous band . . . and started suddenly at the Earl with a knife, and struck him in the collar, and slit him down the body.

Rait, *History of Scotland,* p. 56.

A. Characterization:

41

B. Main idea: _____

_____

Exercise 11 Read the passages and then choose the correct answer.

Drinking in seventeenth and eighteenth century America was normative and although disapproved, drunkenness was far from rare.... If anything was "bad" about drinking it was not drink itself, which even prominent clergy called a "good creature of God." Churches and drinking houses, as social centers of the community, were often close together. Concern about public drunkenness was expressed by a small few scholarly, aristocratic church leaders who warned against the sin of drunken excess, sometimes attributed to the work of the Devil. Punishment was initially a clerical admonition, followed by the extreme sanction of suspension, and finally by excommunication as the ultimate, although probably infrequently used, religious control. Civil authorities affirmed the church's judgment and meted out various forms of public degradation: fines, ostracism, whippings, and imprisonment....

Ward, *Alcoholism*, p. 29.

A. This passage primarily focuses on
    1. drinking in the seventeenth and eighteenth centuries.
    2. punishments for drunkenness.
    3. drinking and the view of the Church.
    4. the Church's view on drinking, drunkenness, and punishment.

Katharine, the Shrew, was the eldest daughter of Baptista, a rich gentleman of Padua. She was a lady of such an ungovernable spirit and fiery temper, such a loud-tongued scold, that she was known in Padua by no other name than Katharine the Shrew. It seemed very unlikely, indeed impossible, that any gentleman would ever be found who would venture to marry this lady, and therefore Baptista was much blamed for deferring his consent to many excellent offers that were made to her gentle sister Bianca, putting off all Bianca's suitors with this excuse: that when the eldest sister was fairly off his hands, they should have free leave to address young Bianca.

Lamb, *Tales from Shakespeare*

B. The best statement of the main idea of this passage is
    1. Bianca had a better personality than Katharine.
    2. Katharine was so mean that no one wanted to marry her.
    3. Baptista wanted his eldest daughter to marry first.
    4. Baptista liked Bianca better than Katharine.

Figurative Language

Understanding how to draw inferences helps the student recognize and appreciate figurative language. Appreciating figurative language also involves utilizing an active imagination. For instance, you may think that your girl/boyfriend has really skinny legs. One day when you are describing these legs, you might say, "My boyfriend has chicken legs," or "My boyfriend's legs are as skinny as toothpicks," or "My boyfriend's legs are as thin as rails." You have already helped the person you are talking to visualize your boyfriend's legs. You have likened him to three totally different entities, but the pictures you have placed in the person's mind are graphic.

In written passages the author also might use figurative language to help the reader get a picture of what is being described. The writer may use key words such as "like" or "as" or s/he may merely describe. Consider this description of sharks:

> Though amid all the smoking horror and diabolism of a sea-fight, sharks will be seen longingly gazing up to the ship's decks, like hungry dogs round a table where red meat is being carved, ready to bolt down every killed man that is tossed to them; and though, while the valiant butchers over the deck-table are thus cannibally carving each other's live meat with carving-knives all gilded and tasseled, the sharks, also, with their jewel-hilted mouths, are quarrelsomely carving away under the table at the dead meat;...
>
> Melville, *Moby Dick*

Exercise 12 Looking back at the paragraph, determine what comparisons are being made through the use of figurative language.

1. Sharks are like _____

2. Ship's decks are compared to _____

3. The men in the sea-fight are likened to _____

4. The sharks' teeth are like _____

Exercise 13 After each excerpt below a noun is given. After reading the excerpt, write what the given noun is being figuratively compared to. Write your answer in the space provided. Then write the words or phrases which led to your answer.

> A. But their counsels and entreaties could not alter Hamlet's determination . . . And he felt as hardy as a lion, and bursting from them, who did all they could to hold him, he followed whithersoever the spirit led him.
>
> Lamb, *Tales from Shakespeare*

Hamlet: _____

Words/phrases: _____

B. Her aunt pushed something into Joan's hand. Joan looked down. It was a locket, and when she opened it, she thought at first that she was looking at a tiny version of herself. The girl looked back at her with catlike gray eyes surrounded by dusky, black lashes--the high, intelligent forehead, the soft, lengthy mane, wild and plentiful.

Joan: _____

Words/phrases: _____

C. The first objects that assume a distinct presence before me, as I look far back, into the blank of my infancy, are my mother with her pretty hair and youthful shape, and Peggotty with no shape at all, and eyes so dark they seemed to darken . . . her face, and cheeks and arms so hard and red that I wondered the birds didn't peck her in preference to apples.

Dickens, *David Copperfield*

Peggotty: _____

Words/phrases: _____

D. As the caravan approached, the weary could see Kenilworth Castle against the rainstreaked horizon--a blaze of fiery red splashed against a golden sea of sky.

Kenilworth Castle: _____

Words/Phrases: _____

Identifying Inference Question Stems

On the Regents' Reading Test the following types of question stems in regard to inference may appear.

Drawing conclusions and making generalizations:

♦ According to the passage, the reader might conclude that

♦ Based on the writer's ideas presented in the passage, the reader can conclude that

♦ The passage implies that

♦ This passage suggests

Identifying the main idea:

♦ The best statement of the main idea of this selection is

♦ This passage deals primarily with

♦ This passage focuses primarily on

♦ The author's main point is

♦ What is the main idea of the passage?

♦ Which of the following statements best expresses the central idea of the passage?

♦ The best title for this passage is

44

Identifying relationships and understanding the author's beliefs:

♦ The reader can infer that _____ is probably

♦ It can be inferred from this passage that _____ is

♦ The author suggests in the passage that

♦ The author seems to believe that

♦ The author would probably agree that

♦ The author implies that

Applying ideas presented to new situations:

♦ The author's ideas would make him most closely related to

♦ With which of the following statements would the author most likely agree?

Practice Passages

Exercise 14 Read the passages and answer the multiple-choice questions.

Passage One

The chamber looked such a bright little place to me as the sun shone in between the gay blue chintz window curtains, showing papered walls and a carpeted floor, so unlike the bare planks and stained plaster of Lowood, that my spirits rose at the view. Externals have a great effect on the young: I thought that a fairer era of life was beginning for me, one that was to have its flowers and pleasures, as well as its thorns and toils . . . I rose; I dressed myself with care: obliged to be plain--for I had no article of attire that was not made with extreme simplicity--I was still by nature solicitous to be neat. It was not my habit to be disregardful of appearance, or careless of the impression I made: on the contrary, I ever wished to look as well as I could, and to please as much as my want of beauty would permit. I sometimes regretted that I was not handsomer: I sometimes wished to have rosy cheeks, a straight nose, and small cherry mouth; I desired to be tall, stately, and finely developed in figure;

Brontë, *Jane Eyre*

1. The statement: "I thought that a fairer era of life was beginning for me, one that was to have its flowers and pleasures, as well as its thorns and toils . . ." in the first paragraph is
   1. literal.
   2. objective.
   3. academic.
   4. figurative.

2. The passage implies that the narrator's outlook is
   1. optimistic.
   2. pessimistic.
   3. depressed.
   4. unfeeling.

3. Jane was
    1. tall and rosy cheeked.
    2. a little pale but ordinary.
    3. fat but jovial.
    4. anorexic and short.

4. It can be inferred that Jane
    1. thought fondly of Lowood.
    2. thought of Lowood as an uninteresting place.
    3. considered Lowood a stately manor.
    4. didn't know where Lowood was.

5. The passage suggests that Jane
    1. was unrealistic.
    2. was realistic.
    3. was stupid.
    4. was timid.

6. The passage implies that Jane
    1. cared about her appearance.
    2. was careless about her appearance.
    3. preferred plain clothes.
    4. was satisfied with her looks.

Passage Two

The Union of the Kingdoms of England and Scotland in 1707 put an end to the existence of a legislative assembly of which there attaches considerable historical interest. Throughout the Middle Ages, there was little room in Scotland for debate of any kind, and none for the formal debates of an assembly to which the word "representative" could be applied. The Parliament of Scotland was apt to be the tool of a strong king or of the clique of nobles who were in the ascendancy when there was no strong king.

The real founder of the Scottish Parliament as a representative assembly was King Robert the Bruce. Before the time of The Bruce, the Parliament was the feudal Great Council composed solely of the great tenants-in-chief, lay and clerical. The Lords Spiritual were there: bishops, abbots, and priors, for they were tenants who held their ecclesiastical possessions directly from the Crown. "Lesser" men such as the burgesses had no place in the Great Council of David I or of William the Lion or of the Alexanders. The right of attendance was claimed only by the great men of the realm.

However, when King Robert The Bruce held a Parliament at the Abbey of Cambuskenneth, within sight of the field of Bannockburn, he summoned to it burgesses as well as "other free tenants of the kingdom." King Robert's object was very practical. This Parliament was called to settle the pecuniary relationships between the King and his people and to make provision for the expenses of war.

Rait, *History of Scotland,* pp. 225-227.

1. It is suggested by the passage that King Robert was different from rulers before him because
    1. he wanted all his people to be great tenants-in-chief.
    2. he allowed the Lords Spiritual to play a role in government.
    3. he had a pecuniary relationship with his people.
    4. he was the only king in his time to invite the burgesses to Parliament.

2. It is implied that in the time of David I, William the Lion, and the Alexanders that the right of attendance to Parliament was claimed by all of the following except
    1. great tenants-in-chief.
    2. royalty.
    3. Lords Spiritual.
    4. the common man.

3. It can be inferred that when there was no strong king Scotland was ruled by
    1. men of the Church.
    2. the queen.
    3. the nobles.
    4. the commons.

4. It can be inferred that the word ecclesiastical as used in this passage relates to
    1. kings.
    2. men of the Church.
    3. nobles.
    4. burgesses.

5. It is suggested that burgesses had no voice in government because
    1. they had no land.
    2. they were not spiritual.
    3. they were under the domination of the king.
    4. they were not great men of the realm.

Unit Six

Analysis of a Passage

The Regents' Reading Test includes **analysis** items to evaluate the student's ability to determine *why* and *how* a passage was written. A skillful analyst can dissect a passage and draw inferences about the writer's style, purpose, and organization. Recognizing the author's organization of ideas depends largely upon the reader's ability to recognize the functional relationships of the author's words, phrases, and sentences. Before studying these structural elements, read the following excerpt by Senator Edward Kennedy from an article in *Current History* about gun control.

> In 1975, the total gun murder rate in the United States was 6.2 per 10,000 population. And the handgun murder rate was 4.9. Thus, even the United States handgun murder rate was 62 times the rate in Scotland, Japan, the Netherlands, and Great Britain, 31 times the rate for Denmark, France, Sweden, and Switzerland, and 20 times the rate in New Zealand, Germany, and Italy.... Over 25,000 Americans die each year because of shooting, accidents, suicides, and murders caused by guns, primarily because too many Americans possess firearms. A brief review of the conditions involving firearms in this country makes it clear that the proliferation of firearms, particularly handguns must be halted.... When guns are available, they have proven to be a far too easily accessible tool for the destruction of human life.... Because of the senseless deaths and injuries caused by guns I strongly support the public demand for legislation to provide a uniform nationwide system to control the abuse and misuse of firearms.
>
> Kennedy, ''The Need for Handgun Control,'' p. 26-27.

Having background information about Senator Kennedy would help the reader to better understand the author's style, the author's purpose, the author's bias and attitude; however, on the Regents' Test, the reader must make inferences about *why* and also *how* the author writes *based only on the content* of the test passages. *How* did Kennedy write about gun control? Was he emotional? Did he use facts? Did he show cause and effect? *Why* did he write? Obviously, the tone of a passage directly affects how the reader interprets and responds to it. Even though many of Kennedy's statements are factual, the facts support his stance on gun control. The last part of the passage reveals the speaker's tone. What words does Kennedy use to convey his tone?

Author's Style

Readers may identify an **author's writing style** by examining various aspects of a passage:

A   the author's **tone** or attitude toward what is being written.

B   the writer's **point of view** or perspective about the subject.

C   the author's **type of language** (formal, humorous, dramatic, satirical, argumentative, etc.), or choice of words.

D   and the writer's use of **literary devices,** such as fact and opinion, analogy, and other methods of presentation.

Author's Tone

Tone is the manner in which a writer expresses or conveys his feelings. It is the emotional message behind his words. A writer may express his attitude by writing in a serious tone, an angry tone, a humorous tone, a sympathetic tone, a persuasive tone, and so forth.

When the reader discovers the tone of the author, he may make more valid inferences about the passage. The words listed below may be used to describe authors' tones and may be typical of the answer options to tone or attitude questions on the Regents' Reading test.

angry	depressing	hysterical	pessimistic
alarmed	distressed	impartial	respectful
anguished	enthusiastic	insulting	sincere
assertive	fearful	jovial	subjective
authoritative	gloomy	lonely	sympathetic
bitter	hateful	miserable	sarcastic
compassionate	hopeful	nostalgic	scornful
condescending	hostile	objective	serious
defensive	humorous	optimistic	threatening

Exercise 1 The following passage is an example of how an author may use tone to communicate his attitude to the reader:

> If a drunk driver kills my [child], how dare I hate him? We all know alcoholism is a disease and that no one gets a disease on purpose. But if I do hate him, if I'm out of my mind with rage and I kill the driver, you can't be angry with me. After all, wasn't I suffering from temporary insanity? (That's a brief disease like the flu.)
>
> Beaber, ''Stress and Other Scapegoats''

1. The author's tone may be characterized as
    1. impartial.
    2. sarcastic.
    3. compassionate.
    4. authoritative.

2. What specific words and phrases help to distinguish this tone?_____

Author's Point of View

The author's tone or attitude reveals point of view and represents the perspective from which he or she writes.

For example, it is easily observed in the drunk driver passage above that the speaker's tone is one of anger and that he is very much involved in the events he is relating. Therefore, you may determine readily that he is an involved participant and vehemently against drunk drivers.

An author's bias (personal beliefs and ideas) influences his views on a subject. These may be the result of upbringing, educational and professional background, or life experiences. Information which a writer includes in a passage is chosen because of his or her position or point of view. For example, one of the most controversial issues in America today is the topic of abortion. It is written about daily from many different viewpoints.

The point of view of each of the following authors is revealed by the specific information each chooses to cite.

Exercise 2 Read these paragraphs and state the authors' position.

1. Excerpt from a longer article:

"Jane Roe v. Henry Wade" -- An anonymous pregnant woman against the district attorney of Dallas County, Texas -- A simple case caption in the annals of the law -- And a tragic choice between fetal life and individual liberty. The divide is vast. To those who speak of the right to life, "Roe" is a diabolical license to murder. To those of the right-to-choose persuasion, "Roe" is a glorious symbol of women's freedom. Either way, to both factions, "Roe v. Wade" is merely a political result to be agreed or disagreed with -- rather than a judicial decision to be assessed on its own narrower terms. Is it good constitutional law or bad? For most anybody with an opinion on abortion, the answer reached flows solely from the outcome desired.

Kaplan, D.A. *Newsweek*, p. 49

Assuming that the writer's position (as presented in the longer article) is the same as the opinions he or she has chosen to cite, what is the writer's position concerning abortion?

_____

2. Excerpt from a longer article:

"Abortion has run into trouble. In June, the High Court ruled that women do not necessarily have a right to public funds to pay for abortions. Unless the states provide the money, thousands of poor women may have unwanted children this year, and whatever state money is saved on abortions will be more than paid out for welfare."

Sterling, J.C. *The Women's Movement: Revolution and Evolution*, p. 18

Assuming that the writer's position (as presented in the longer article) is the same as the opinions he or she has chosen to cite, what is the writer's position concerning abortion?

_____

3. Excerpt from a longer article:

Abortion is a human-rights/racism issue: "An insidious attempt being made to control a segment of our population by killing children," says Bishop Rene Gracida. Further, "Abortion is a violent, degrading event...nothing more than mechanical rape," according to Olivia Gans who heads a group called American Victims of Abortion...This is not just an argument about comparative mortality; it goes to the heart of how women see their lives. Helen Alvare, a sophisticated young lawyer, argues, "It is a sexist response that leads women to abortion clinics in the first place."

Adler, J. & McCormick, J. *Newsweek*, p. 44-47

51

Assuming that the writer's position (as presented in the longer article) is the same as the opinions he or she has chosen to cite, what is the writer's position concerning abortion?

Exercise 3 Read the following passage to identify the author's attitude and point of view about Will Rogers.

Will didn't go to the Mount to speak his sermon nor did he speak in parables. Like a folk song, fresh from the heart of the people, he said things that they want to say but do not know how to put into words. Their inarticulate voice has been spoken many times in verities of Christ and Lincoln and Woodrow Wilson and many others. Their immovable courage kept these men going. Nevertheless, Will's phrasings of their longings was even closer because he was more a part of them. He knew only too well that the granite fibers out of which democracy has been built come from them. Perhaps that is the reason why, without any hullabaloo or advertising, over twelve hundred people a day drop their tears at the Will Rogers Memorial at Claremore, Oklahoma, thousands of others leave his old ranch house at Santa Monica, California, stilled and hushed.

Day, *The Autobiography of Will Rogers,* p. 2

1. The author writes from the point of view of
    1. an admirer of Will Rogers.
    2. one who questions the sincerity of Will Rogers.
    3. an objective observer.
    4. a scornful acquaintance.

2. The tone expressed in the passage reflects
    1. anger.
    2. indifference.
    3. sarcasm.
    4. respect.

Type of Language

The author's unique choice of language creates the "personality" of the passage. Words can be manipulated in order to communicate with an expected audience. For example, if the author is expecting an educated reader, he is likely to make his sentences long and the vocabulary difficult; if the writer is expecting a more general audience, he may use language rich in slang and a very informal style of writing. Argumentative language may be chosen if the writer wishes to convince a reader that his particular stand on an issue is the best one. Humorous language is found in the description of U.S. Presidential doctors by Will Rogers, the great American humorist:

Exercise 4 Now try this paragraph.

Mr. Harding has had quite a little sick spell lately from which he is recovering. I sorter think it's these Doctors these Presidents have. They are promoted from a Horse and Buggy trade in the country to an Admiral in the U.S. Navy, or a Major General in the U.S. Army so quickly that I really believe they have to give so much time trying to learn to salute and to getting their uniform on proper side forward that they haven't the time to devote to our President's health. So, with our next President, I hereby start a movement to let his Doctor keep his bagged-kneed breeches and his old slouch hat.

Day, *The Autobiography of Will Rogers,* p. 73.

Test items following this passage might include the following:

1. The tone of this passage may best be described as
    1. argumentative.
    2. formal.
    3. impersonal.
    4. humorous.

2. What is the author's attitude toward the presidential doctors?
    1. respectful and admiring
    2. trusting and proud
    3. indifferent and accepting
    4. sarcastic and annoyed

3. Which of the following best describes the language of this passage?
    1. informal
    2. formal
    3. academic
    4. romantic

Literary Devices

An author may use literary devices to more effectively communicate with the reader and these devices may include the author's use of (1) fact and opinion, (2) irony, and (3) analogy.

Facts (objective statements) can be checked for accuracy, i.e., they may be quantified, validated, measured, or observed. When Edward Kennedy says, "In 1973, the total gun murder rate in the United States was 6.2 per 10,000 population and the handgun murder rate was 4.9 . . . ," he is stating facts or making **objective** statements. These statements can be validated by consulting documented evidence. Objective material often appears in textbooks, scientific journals, news reports, and legal documents. Opinions, on the other hand, are **subjective** statements which reveal the writer's beliefs, judgments, attitudes, or feelings. They cannot be proven or evaluated as either true or false. When Will Rogers says, ". . . I really believe they have to give so much time trying to learn to salute and to getting their uniforms on proper side forward that they haven't the time to devote to our President's health . . . ," he is stating his opinion (in this case using humor and sarcasm). A writer may seek to strengthen an argument by providing facts on which opinions are based. Subjective writing can be found in newspaper editorials, book and movie reviews, advertisements, and literary criticism.

Readers must distinguish fact from opinion in order to determine if the information is presented objectively or in a biased (prejudiced or slanted) manner (subjectively). Phrases which may indicate an opinion include *I believe, I suggest, I feel, I conclude, I surmise, you should, I think,* and *in my opinion.* Descriptive adjectives and judgmental words and phrases also indicate author's opinions. The careful reader recognizes qualifying words and phrases and considers them while encoding the printed page.

Exercise 5 Read the following selection by James Burns about John F. Kennedy's presidency to note the author's use of opinion.

> The job of the next President [John Fitzgerald Kennedy] will be the hardest since Roosevelt, and I think Roosevelt had the hardest of all except Lincoln and perhaps Washington. The job will be tremendous, and a great responsibility centers on the President.... He serves as a catalyst, an energizer, the defender of the public interest against all the narrow private interests which operate in our society. Only the President can do this, and only a President who recognizes the true nature of this hard challenge can fulfill this historic function.... Congress is quite obviously not equipped to make basic policy, to conduct foreign relations, to speak for the national interest in the way that a President can and must.... I ... believe that in the next two or three decades there will be greater demands upon the President than ever before--and the powers are there, if the man will use them.
>
> Burns, *John Kennedy: A Political Profile*, p. 29.

1. Which of the following statements could be a fact and NOT an opinion?
    1. The job of the next President will be the hardest since Roosevelt, and I think Roosevelt had the hardest of all.
    2. I believe that in the next two or three decades there will be greater demands upon the President than ever before.
    3. He serves as an energizer, the defender of the public interest against all the narrow private interests which operate in our society.
    4. Congress is quite obviously not equipped to make basic policy, to conduct foreign relations.

2. Which of the following best describes the language of this passage?
    1. technical
    2. casual
    3. humorous
    4. serious

3. The author's attitude toward the presidential responsibilities may be described as one of
    1. condescension.
    2. disdain.
    3. indifference.
    4. high regard.

Irony is a literary device which may illustrate differences between what a character expects or deserves and actually experiences or between what a character says and means. Sarcasm, a form of irony, is used to attack a person or a belief by cutting remarks that mean the opposite of what is said.

Authors may use figurative expressions to express irony. **Understatements** may be utilized to deliberately make something appear smaller in size or degree of seriousness than it actually is. The opposite of this is **hyperbole** through which an author intentionally exaggerates something to create an effect (overstatement).

Exercise 6 The following selection on motivation from a *Business Horizon's* article illustrates a writer's use of irony to teach a difficult concept in a management textbook:

> Once upon a time there were six donkeys hitched to a wagon pulling a heavy load up a steep hill. Two of the donkeys were not achievement oriented and decided to coast along and let others do most of the pulling. Two others were relatively young and inexperienced and had a difficult time pulling their share.

54

One of the remaining two suffered from a light hangover from consuming fermented barley the night before. The sixth donkey did most of the work. The wagon arrived at the top of the hill. The driver got down from his seat, patted each of the donkeys on the head, and gave six carrots to each. Prior to the next hill climb, the sixth donkey ran away.

McConkey, " 'The Jackass Effect' in Management Compensation,'' p. 81

The story is a satire and includes **personification**, a figurative expression (giving traits of living persons to animals, things, or inanimate objects). The irony of this incident is that the driver intended to motivate the donkeys to work for rewards. However, by rewarding all donkeys in the incident equally instead of rewarding only the hard-working cooperative donkey, he lost his only worker. The outcome was opposite to that which he expected (irony).

The short selection about the donkeys also illustrates the use of **analogy**, another literary device. This technique may be used by an author when anticipating that the reader may not understand a difficult or unfamiliar concept being presented. A familiar, but not totally different idea or concept may be compared or contrasted to the unfamiliar concept. The following questions are illustrative of literary devices used by authors:

1. The outcome of the story is an example of which of the following literary devices?
   1. metaphor
   2. irony
   3. understatement
   4. hyperbole

2. Which of the following does the author primarily use to develop his concept of motivation?
   1. personal experience
   2. narration
   3. historical analysis
   4. facts

3. What was the irony expressed by this story?
   1. Donkeys do not need to be motivated.
   2. Managers reward the hardest workers.
   3. The driver's motivation strategy drove away his only worker.
   4. Light hangovers interfere with workers' performance.

Author's Purpose

Another element of analysis is identification of the author's purpose for writing. Most authors usually write with a definite overall purpose or intention in mind: to inform, to entertain, or to persuade a particular audience with reference to a particular topic. The purpose may be discerned through the technique of presentation or organization of ideas, i.e., chronology, cause and effect, comparison, contrast, definition, or illustrations and examples, as well as in the tone, point of view, or style of writing. Description, sensory images, facts, statistics, or opinions may also be used to achieve specific purposes. The writer rarely says in an introduction, "I intend to inform you" or "I intend to entertain you" or "I intend to dissuade you to…" But if, for instance, the purpose is to inform or to instruct, the writer may choose a straightforward, explanatory style of writing. This type of writing is referred to as **expository** writing. The following example illustrates this:

The most important set of glands activated by your endocrine system is the adrenal. Your adrenal produces the hormone adrenaline as well as a family of related hormones called corticoid. You can no doubt recall a news account of an accident in which a rescuer at the scene (frequently a parent) lifts a heavy object off someone pinned beneath it (frequently a child). In a "normal" situation the parent would be totally incapable of lifting that great a weight. This very temporary increase in muscle power is brought about by the actions of the adrenal. The increased secretion of adrenaline helps prepare your body to be on guard against whatever threat it is experiencing.

Johnson, *Psychology Today*, p. 31.

Exercise 7 The following analysis questions might appear on the Regents' Test to evaluate the student's ability to recognize the author's purpose in the above passage. Please circle your answer.

1. The author's purpose in writing this passage is to
   1. entertain his audience.
   2. persuade his readers.
   3. inform his readers.
   4. explain differing points of view.

2. Which of the following does the author primarily use in this passage?
   1. personal experiences
   2. cause and effect
   3. comparison
   4. statistics

If an author's desire is to entertain, he may choose **narration**. Narration is a type of writing in which the author tells a story or recounts a series of events in chronological order. It may also include dialogue. Narrative writing is more subjective and may include personal feelings and emotions and might utilize figurative language or language with a sensory appeal. It may even paint a verbal picture, as does Pat Conroy in this selection from *The Lords of Discipline:*

As I walked the streets I listened to the conversations and murmurings of families on verandas. I walked slowly through the city of the four-year test, the city of exquisite, measureless beauty, smelling the wet flowers shimmering with aroma in the secret gardens behind high brick walls. All around me was the smell of sweetbay and jasmine, loquat and wisteria, and the stammering of insects among the daphne and tea olive.

I had come to Charleston as a young boy, a lonely visitor slouching through its well-tended streets, a young boy, lean and grassy, who grew fluent in his devotion and appreciation of that city's inestimable charm. I was a boy there and saw things through the eyes of a boy for the last time. The boy was dying and I wanted to leave him in the silent lanes South of Broad. I would leave him with no regrets except that I had not stopped to honor his passing. I had not thanked the boy for his capacity for astonishment, for curiosity, and for survival. I was indebted to that boy. I owed him my respect and my thanks. I owed him my remembrance of the lessons he learned so keenly and so ominously. He had issued me a challenge as he passed the baton to the man in me: He had challenged me to have the courage to become a gentle, harmless man. For so long, I had felt like the last boy in America and now, at last, it was time to leave him. Now it was the man. The man was the quest.

Conroy, *The Lords of Discipline*, pp. 494-495.

Exercise 8 Based on the passage, answer these questions.

1. Which of the following does the author use in relating the events?
    1. argumentation
    2. narration
    3. exposition
    4. definition

2. The author's primary purpose of this passage is to
    1. persuade his readers to adopt his point of view.
    2. inform the reader by providing factual data.
    3. entertain the reader through descriptive narration.
    4. alarm the audience of impending doom.

3. The statement, ''The boy was dying and I wanted to leave him . . .'' is meant to be
    1. factual.
    2. figurative.
    3. academic.
    4. literal.

4. In the first paragraph of the passage, the author uses
    1. deductive logic.
    2. factual narration.
    3. sensory appeal.
    4. inference.

Often a writer's purpose is to argue a point of view or to persuade the reader. **Argumentation** and **persuasion** may be found in all types of writing. For example, an advertising copy editor may write in an amusing style in order to capture readers' interests and persuade them to purchase a product. Newspaper editorials are often aimed at gaining public support for a political position. **Argumentation** is used to convince the reader that a particular statement or idea is true and seeks to bring about a change in the opinion of the reader. The writer may use statistics, comparisons, contrasts, quotations, and expert opinions to support his position.

The following statement taken from the introductory excerpt by Senator Kennedy uses facts to support his argument in favor of gun control: ''Over 25,000 Americans die each year because of shooting, accidents, suicides, and murders caused by guns, primarily because too many Americans possess firearms.''

Persuasive writing goes one step further than argumentation and attempts to change the behavior of the reader by asking for a commitment or action on the reader's part.

Exercise 9 Senator Kennedy, in the statements below, argues persuasively for national hand gun control. Read this excerpt and then circle the correct answer.

> Because of senseless deaths and injuries caused by guns, I strongly support the public demand for legislation to provide a uniform nationwide system to control the abuse and misuse of firearms. A brief review of the conditions involving firearms in this country makes it clear that the proliferation of firearms, particularly handguns must be halted . . .''

1. The primary purpose of this paragraph is to
   1. describe the abuse and misuse of firearms.
   2. explain the problems of firearms ownership.
   3. criticize Congress for lack of firearm legislation.
   4. persuade the reader to support efforts to obtain gun control legislation.

2. In the excerpt above, Senator Kennedy supports his idea that national handgun control is urgently needed by using
   1. comparison and contrast.
   2. definition.
   3. appeal to emotions.
   4. statistics.

3. The author's tone is
   1. pessimistic.
   2. sentimental.
   3. neutral.
   4. serious.

4. The language used by Senator Kennedy in this passage is
   1. casual.
   2. poetic.
   3. technical.
   4. forceful.

The reader must look for clues in the language and in the tone which indicate the author's purpose--whether his intention is to persuade, inform, or entertain. A critical reader is as interested in *how* and *why* something is written as in *what is* written. He is likely to ask first, "Why did the author write this?"

Exercise 10 The selection below from a history textbook was written with a definite purpose. Please answer the questions.

> Tobacco was native to America. The Indians had taught the Spaniards to use it, and the Spaniards had taught the rest of Europe. At first it was valued only as a medicine, said to cure any affliction from the waist up. But by the end of the sixteenth century people were smoking for the fun of it, much to the distress of those who knew better, including King James, and much to the joy of Spanish tobacco merchants. The Indians of Virginia smoked a native variety, coarse and unpalatable. John Rolfe, who later gained greater fame by marrying Pocahontas, tried planting the West Indian species in 1612, just as other settlers were experimenting with other Spanish products. The West Indian variety grew extraordinarily well in Virginia, and the settlers turned enthusiastically to growing it. By 1617 they were able to ship twenty thousand pounds to England.
>
> Blum, *The National Experience*, p. 79.

1. The author has written this passage primarily to
   1. tell a story about John Rolfe.
   2. alarm the audience about tobacco use.
   3. persuade the reader that tobacco is harmful.
   4. explain tobacco usage and its rapid growth and popularity in the New World.

2. How does the author organize his ideas about tobacco?
    1. comparison and contrast
    2. cause and effect
    3. order of importance
    4. chronological order

3. The tone of the author toward the subject of tobacco is
    1. cynical.
    2. objective.
    3. condescending.
    4. suspicious..

Functional Relationships

In addition to recognizing the author's purpose and technique of organization in a passage on the Regents' Reading Test, a student must be able to identify **functional relationships** between words, phrases, sentences, or paragraphs that make up a passage. In other words, the reader must understand the way in which parts relate to the whole or the relationship between the items that are being connected. The author may use **transition words** or **phrases**, such as *while, although, as long as, in the meantime, consequently, while, although, as long as, certainly, until, however, in other* words, *likewise, as a result, indeed, furthermore, on the contrary, in fact,* etc. to provide a smooth and logical connection between the parts of the passage. Transitional words or phrases permit the writer to show connections between ideas, to transfer from one idea to another, to show clarification of ideas, to show enumeration or to prioritize ideas, and to shift the focus from one emphasis to another.

The question stems on the Regents' Reading Test might be similar to those that follow:

1. The function of the second paragraph is to....

2. Consider the purpose of the last sentence of the passage and choose the word or phrase that could logically be used at the beginning of this sentence:

3. In the last paragraph, the author gives examples of ... in order to support the idea that....

4. The author's main idea is best supported by the statement that....

5. Which of the following details given in the passage best illustrates the author's idea that.... ?

Exercise 11 An excerpt from the handgun control passage by Senator Edward Kennedy illustrates the functional relationship between one part of his argument to another.

Over 25,000 Americans die each year because of shooting, accidents, suicides, and murders caused by guns, primarily because too many Americans possess firearms. A brief review of the conditions involving firearms in this country makes it clear that the proliferation of firearms, particularly handguns must be halted.... When guns are available, they have proven to be a far too easily accessible tool for the destruction of human life....

Because of the senseless death and injuries caused by guns, I strongly support the public demand for legislation to provide a uniform nationwide system to control the abuse and misuse of firearms.

These questions might follow this passage to test for recognition of functional relationships:

1. Consider the purpose of the clause that begins "I strongly support the public demand for legislation to provide a uniform . . ." and choose the word that could logically be used after "I" at the beginning of this clause.
   1. therefore
   2. because
   3. nevertheless
   4. in addition

2. Which of the following details is the most convincing for gun control legislation?
   1. Twenty-five thousand Americans die each year because of shooting, accidents, suicides, and murders caused by guns.
   2. This country has a proliferation of guns.
   3. Too many Americans possess firearms.
   4. Guns are too accessible.

Practice Passage

The questions that follow this passage about the cerebellum will test the analysis skills you have developed in this chapter.

The cerebellum, one of three major parts of the brain, (literally "little brain") is located adjacent to the back surface of the brain stem. It is a relatively large and deeply folded structure. The cerebellum is involved in the coordination of movement and is also critical to our sense of equilibrium, or physical balance. Although the commands for muscular movements may come from higher brain centers, the cerebellum plays a key role in the execution of these commands. It is your cerebellum that allows you to hold your hand out to the side and smoothly bring your finger to a stop on your nose. This is a useful roadside test for drunken driving because the cerebellum is one of the structures first depressed by alcohol. Damage to the cerebellum disrupts fine motor skills, such as those involved in writing, typing, or playing tennis.

Weiten, *Psychology Themes and Variations,* p. 15.

1. The primary purpose of this passage is to
   1. argue that drunken drivers aren't responsible for their conditions.
   2. define "cerebellum" and illustrate its importance.
   3. report a scientific finding.
   4. reveal the differences between the brain parts.

2. Consider the purpose of the sentence that begins "It is your cerebellum that allows you to...." and choose the word or phrase that could logically be used at the beginning of this sentence.
   1. similarly
   2. for example
   3. nevertheless
   4. on the other hand

3. The language used in this passage is
   1. entertaining.
   2. informative.
   3. persuasive.
   4. argumentative.

4. Which of the following best describes the author's tone?
   1. negative
   2. dramatic
   3. objective
   4. subjective

5. Which of the following does the author primarily use to support his point about the cerebellum?
   1. comparison-contrast
   2. chronology
   3. definition
   4. narration

6. Which of the following literary devices does the author use to define the cerebellum?
   1. propaganda
   2. personification
   3. analogy
   4. factual information

7. Which of the following statements drawn from the passage could be an opinion?
   1. Damage to the cerebellum disrupts fine motor skills.
   2. The cerebellum is one of the three major parts of the brain.
   3. The cerebellum is a relatively large and deeply folded structure.
   4. Bringing your finger to your nose is a useful roadside test for drunken driving.

The Reading Test
Practice Test One
Diagnostic

DIRECTIONS

This is a test of reading comprehension. It is designed to measure your understanding of the material that you read.

The test contains 10 passages. Following each passage is a set of questions about the passage. There are 60 questions on the test.

For each question following a passage, choose the *best* response on the basis of the content of the passage.

Your response to each question must be marked on the separate answer sheet in the row that has the same number as the question. Mark you answers clearly on the answer sheet. Do not mark more than one answer for each question. If you need to erase, do so carefully and cleanly. You must not make any other marks on your answer sheet. Write any notes that you wish to make on this test booklet, but make sure that your responses are marked on the separate answer sheet.

Do not spend too much time on any one question. If a question seems very difficult, make the most careful guess you can. *Your score is the number of correct answers that you give;* there is no added penalty for wrong answers.

You will have *60 minutes* to complete the test.

DO NOT OPEN THIS BOOKLET UNTIL YOU ARE TOLD TO DO SO

Communism is based on the belief that man is so weak and inadequate that he is unable to govern himself, and therefore requires the rule of strong masters.

5   Democracy is based on the conviction that man has the moral and intellectual capacity, as well as the inalienable right, to govern himself with reason and justice.

Communism subjects the individuals to arrest
10   without lawful cause, punishment without trial, and forced labor as the chattel of the state. It decrees what information he shall receive, what art he shall produce, what leaders he shall follow, and what thoughts he shall think.

15   Democracy maintains that government is established for the benefit of the individual, and is charged with the responsibility of protecting the rights of the individual and his freedom in the exercise of his abilities.

20   Communism maintains that social wrongs can be corrected only by violence.

Democracy has proved that social justice can be achieved through peaceful change.

Communism holds that the world is so
25   deeply divided into opposing classes that war is inevitable.

Democracy holds that free nations can settle differences justly and maintain lasting peace.

These differences between communism and
30   democracy do not concern the United States alone. People everywhere are coming to realize that what is involved is material well-being, human dignity, and the right to believe in and worship God.

35   I state these differences, not to draw issues of belief as such, but because the actions resulting from the Communist philosophy are a threat to the efforts of free nations to bring about world recovery and lasting peace.

(Truman, 1948)

1. The author used which of the following to make his point?
    1. cause-effect.
    2. comparison-contrast.
    3. description.
    4. narrative.

2. Conviction as underlined, means
    1. accusation.
    2. charge.
    3. criminal.
    4. strong belief.

3. Chattel, as underlined, means
    1. property.
    2. official.
    3. leader.
    4. warden.

4. Which of the following is NOT a belief of Communism?
    1. Man is unable to govern himself.
    2. Man is able to govern himself.
    3. Individuals may be arrested without lawful cause.
    4. Information man receives should be controlled.

5. The tone of the passage is best described as
    1. argumentative.
    2. neutral.
    3. nostalgic.
    4. sarcastic.

6. The author's primary purpose is to
    1. show parallels between democracy and communism.
    2. explain the philosophy of communism.
    3. show that communism is a threat to freedom.
    4. build support for the United States.

Henry and Margaret were in many respects a most ill-suited pair. In contrast to his ineffectual, other-worldly nature she was a tigress, quick-tempered, courageous and passionate both in

5 her likes and dislikes. She cannot have found Henry a very attentive husband. In the early years of their marriage the rumor was that the King's confessor and councillor was responsible for dissuading him from having "his sport" with

10 the Queen, advising Henry not to go near her. Given Henry's prudish views, it is doubtful whether he needed much persuading. When he recovered from his first madness he himself expressed bewilderment at the birth of his son,

15 who, he said, must have been conceived by the Holy Ghost.

Notwithstanding their incompatibility, the Queen was a powerful force in the world of politics. Henry was putty in her hands when she

20 wanted something done, and she developed a fierce loyalty to his chief ministers: first Suffolk, whom she treated as a father; then Somerset, who was accused of being her lover.

Equally fierce was Margaret's dislike of York

25 whom she saw as an arrogant aggressor intent on destroying herself, her husband and her son. She was, as it happened, proved absolutely right, but it was her own implacable hostility towards York which converted him to hatred.

30 With the King clearly unfit to rule there was nothing Margaret or Somerset could do to prevent York's appointment as Protector in March 1454. Somerset was arrested (in the Queen's apartments), impeached and committed

35 to the Tower.

(Fraser, 1975)

7. Margaret is called a "tigress, quick-tempered, courageous...." This statement is meant to be
   1. factual.
   2. academic.
   3. figurative.
   4. logical.

8. According to the passage, Margaret was close to
   1. York and Somerset.
   2. Somerset and Suffolk.
   3. Suffolk and York.
   4. Henry and York.

9. Which of the following is a reason the King was NOT a good ruler?
   1. He was irrational and mad.
   2. He loved Margaret too much.
   3. He was not loyal to the nobles.
   4. He had no heirs.

10. The author states that York's feelings toward Margaret
    1. were totally unfounded.
    2. were induced by Margaret's hostility.
    3. were born out of jealousy.
    4. were fiercely loyal.

11. The passage implies that
    1. Henry would have promoted Somerset.
    2. York became Margaret's lover.
    3. Henry was aggressive.
    4. York feared Somerset.

12. As used in the passage, prudish means
    1. bold and unrestrained.
    2. modest and prim.
    3. arrogant and haughty.
    4. congenial and compatible.

There is certainly a good case for adopting an international language, whether it be English or Malaysian or Thraco-Phrygian. Translating is an enormously costly and time-consuming
5 business. An internal survey by the European Community in 1987 found that it was costing $15 a word, $500 a page, to translate its documents. One in every three employees of the European Community is engaged in translating papers and
10 speeches.... Every time a member is added to EC, as most recently with Greece, Spain, and Portugal, the translation problems multiply exponentially. Under the Treaty of Rome each member country's language must be treated
15 equally, and it is not easy even in multilingual Brussels to find linguists who can translate from Dutch into Portuguese or from Danish into Greek.

A more compelling reason for an international language is the frequency and gravity of
20 misunderstandings owing to difficulties of translation. The 1905 draft of a treaty between Russia and Japan, written in both French and English treated the English control and French contrôler as synonyms when in fact the English
25 form means "to dominate or hold power" while the French means simply "to inspect." The treaty nearly fell apart as a result. The Japanese involvement in World War II may have been inadvertently prolonged when the Domei news
30 agency, the official government information service, rendered the word mokusatsu as "ignore" when the sense intended was that of "reserving a reply until we have had time to consider the matter more carefully."

(Bryson, 1990)

13. It can NOT be concluded from the passage that adopting an international language would

    1. promote international goodwill.
    2. save money.
    3. encourage everyone to learn English.
    4. aid the drafting of peace treaties.

14. The Russia-Japan treaty was almost destroyed because

    1. the English translation was much stronger than the French.
    2. the French translation was much stronger than the English.
    3. no one could interpret the treaty.
    4. French and English are inferior languages.

15. The author believes that the most important reason for adopting an international language is that

    1. inadequate translations lead to too many misunderstandings.
    2. multiple languages cost too much money.
    3. no one is being treated fairly.
    4. no one can learn all these languages.

16. As used in the passage, rendered means

    1. omitted.
    2. created.
    3. translated.
    4. ignored.

17. According to the author, one-third of all employees of the European Community are

    1. businessmen.
    2. writers of treaties.
    3. speakers of English.
    4. linguists.

18. Which of the following does the author primarily use in this passage?

    1. persuasion
    2. narration
    3. personal experiences
    4. comparison/contrast

They moved along the bank of the river, going south. Montag tried to see the men's faces, the old faces he remembered from the firelight, lined and tired. He was looking for a brightness, a
5   resolve, a triumph over tomorrow that hardly seemed to be there. Perhaps he had expected their faces to burn and glitter with the knowledge they carried, to glow as lanterns glow, with the light in them. But all the light had come from the
10 campfire, and these men had seemed no different than any others who had run a long race, searched a long search, seen good things destroyed, and now, very late, were gathered to wait for the end of the party and the blowing out
15 of the lamps. They weren't at all certain that the things they carried in their heads might make every future dawn glow with a purer light, they were sure of nothing save that the books were on file behind their quiet eyes, the books were
20 waiting, with their pages uncut, for the <u>customers</u> who might come by in later years, some with clean and some with dirty fingers.

   Montag squinted from one face to another as they walked.
25   "<u>Don't judge a book by its cover,</u>" someone said.

   And they all laughed quietly, moving down-stream . . .

                                        (Bradbury, 1987)

19. The men's attitudes toward the future can best be described as

   1.   hopeful.
   2.   uncertain.
   3.   indifferent.
   4.   objective.

20. The narrator's impression of the men is that they

   1.   are extremely weary.
   2.   are very intelligent.
   3.   are returning from a celebration.
   4.   are excited about sharing their ideas.

21. In the passage, the maxim, "<u>Don't judge a book by its cover,</u>" means

   1.   beware of these men.
   2.   pay no attention to these men.
   3.   don't evaluate books by their covers.
   4.   don't judge a man's knowledge by his appearance.

22. Just prior to this scene in the book

   1.   something unforgettable had happened.
   2.   something insignificant had happened.
   3.   the men had been fishing.
   4.   the men had been at a party.

23. The passage implies that

   1.   tomorrow would dawn brightly.
   2.   each man possessed knowledge waiting to be shared.
   3.   the river would carry them home.
   4.   death awaits them.

24. It can be concluded from the passage that the <u>customers</u> are

   1.   fellow journeymen.
   2.   enemies.
   3.   future generations.
   4.   librarians.

25. The author implies that

   1.   Montag was well acquainted with the men.
   2.   Montag disapproved of the men.
   3.   Montag was concerned by what he saw in the men's faces.
   4.   Montag was afraid for the men's futures.

In 1902 novelist Owen Wister published *The Virginian,* and the novel took the country by storm. It told of the adventures of a new sort of American hero, the cowboy, who rode alone with
5 his trusty horse and his six-gun, who settled matters of right and wrong with dramatic finality, who inhabited the West and all that it stood for, and who breathed the pure air of freedom.

Before the advent of the cowboy as romantic
10 hero, Americans had rarely looked backward. They had spoken with enthusiasm of Progress and leaned eagerly into the future. Now they seemed possessed by a new feeling of <u>nostalgia.</u> The world of the cowboy was, after all, the world
15 of Jefferson and Jackson, of the opening of the frontier, and of the brash and haughty American adolescence. Moreover, the cowboy bore a certain curious relationship to the evils of the Gilded Age. Where Americans seemed to be
20 under the thumb of giant institutions and mired down in bureaucracy, the cowboy answered only to himself. Where Americans had ever greater trouble comprehending the world around them, the world of the cowboy was simplicity itself--all
25 he had to do was catch the rustlers and everything would be settled. Where Americans had increasing difficulty sorting out the right and wrong of things, the cowboy knew precisely which was which. And where Americans seemed
30 to fear the increasing loss of freedom, the cowboy always cantered into the sunset of his own heart's desire.

Fascination with the cowboy and his <u>idyllic</u> life quite likely masked a growing fear of change
35 and where that change was leading. To many, American democracy was becoming corrupt and degenerate. The market economy was leading toward rapacious monopoly. Important traits of the American character--virtue, rationality, self-
40 governance--appeared to be weakening. And advanced thinkers like Darwin, Freud, and Marx were giving all sorts of plausible reasons why. In symbolic ways, the cowboy represented an older, simpler, nicer world--a world that Americans
45 feared was fast slipping away.

26. In the second paragraph the author uses
    1. cause-effect.
    2. comparison/contrast.
    3. narrative.
    4. statistics.

27. The novel, *The Virginian,* was
    1. a look at America's future.
    2. based on a character from Virginia.
    3. unpopular with the public.
    4. popular with the public.

28. The passage implies that the cowboy
    1. took the law into his own hands.
    2. preferred a lawful government.
    3. lived in groups.
    4. was a brash adolescent.

29. <u>Nostalgia</u>, underlined, means
    1. homesickness.
    2. longing for something of long ago.
    3. a general idea.
    4. a quantity added to another.

30. Americans seemed to admire the cowboy because
    1. he was a free spirit.
    2. he was simplistic.
    3. he did not know right from wrong.
    4. he exemplified progress.

31. As used in the passage, <u>idyllic</u> means
    1. tumultuous.
    2. picturesque.
    3. amoral.
    4. virtuous.

The creative designer observes the universe with sensitivity, absorbing impressions from all around. These impressions drop into the subconscious mind like cells that divide and
5 combine to form new entities that could never be constructed by conscious effort. Often when one least expects it, one becomes aware of new relationships and, seeing them in terms of a unique vision, works to give them a form that will make
10 them apparent to others. This, in essence, is the phenomenon known as inspiration.

Since inspiration is nourished by impression, it becomes imperative that the artist absorb through the senses as much of the world as
15 possible. One designer may find motivation in travel to other lands, another in films of space flight, yet another in the sight of a familiar weed. Some artists draw their ideas directly from their own memories and experiences. Generally
20 speaking, the more one is exposed to sights, sounds, smells, and textures, the more one learns of the arts of theater, dance, poetry, and music; and the extent to which one attempts to understand the workings of science and
25 technology--the better will be the likelihood of one's arriving at designs that will awaken response in a variety of people.

The New Mexico-based artist Georgia O'Keeffe has <u>executed</u> a series of paintings
30 based on flowers. Here <u>the artist's inspiration</u> was a natural form, but she brings to the subject her unique viewpoint.

(Bevlin, 1977)

32. As used in the passage <u>executed</u> means
    1. killed.
    2. produced.
    3. proclaimed.
    4. denied.

33. The author states that inspiration comes when
    1. urged by conscious effort.
    2. made apparent to others.
    3. expected least.
    4. the mind is uncluttered.

34. The primary purpose of the first paragraph is to explain
    1. the phenomenon of inspiration.
    2. observations of a creative designer.
    3. the many kinds of impressions.
    4. sources of artists' motivations.

35. The author's style is
    1. sarcastic.
    2. argumentative.
    3. informative.
    4. ironic.

36. With which of the following statements would the author most likely disagree?
    1. An artist must absorb a variety of impressions through the senses.
    2. It is possible to receive an impression of the world by reading a book or watching a film.
    3. An artist with a broad background of knowledge is more likely to create art which appeals to many people.
    4. Artists must travel to other lands to gather impressions.

37. In the last sentence, <u>the artist's inspiration</u> refers to
    1. a series of paintings.
    2. flowers.
    3. impressions.
    4. a unique viewpoint.

The importance of using the entire campus as a learning lab can best be understood by reviewing the various reasons students come to college. You may be seeking to increase your
5　earning power, to gain training for a good job, or simply to enjoy social activities. Many students have always assumed they'd go to college because their parents didn't have an opportunity to get a college education when they were young.
10　Others feel that in today's society you just "have to have a college diploma."

All these reasons for attending college are good ones, but why are you *really* in college? Believe it or not, I discovered the real reasons
15　students attend college while attending a rock concert. During intermission, the famous rock star had granted the customary interviews, and a reporter asked what characteristics were needed to be successful in the entertainment industry.
20　The star replied <u>candidly</u> and without hesitation: "First, as I was growing up I found out everything I could about the music and entertainment industry. Second, I developed skills so I could use the knowledge I acquired. As a result, I can
25　play over twenty musical instruments. I have written dozens of songs. In other words, I can *apply the knowledge* I have acquired in a productive manner."

(Gardner, 1989)

38. As used in the passage, <u>candidly</u> means
    1. timidly.
    2. straightforwardly.
    3. boastfully.
    4. arrogantly.

39. The purpose of the passage is
    1. to promote music as a career.
    2. to show reasons for attending college.
    3. to show that rock stars are well educated.
    4. to show that students attend college to advance social relationships.

40. The author uses which of the following to get his point across?
    1. contrast
    2. cause-effect
    3. example
    4. sequence

41. The passage most likely appeared in
    1. a rock magazine.
    2. a college recruitment brochure.
    3. a college freshman orientation manual.
    4. an education journal.

42. According to the passage, all are reasons students may attend college except
    1. for the social life.
    2. in today's society everyone is expected to have a college diploma.
    3. to gain training for a good job.
    4. for the inherent value of learning.

Mother's ambition, passed on to me like a disease, was that we both wanted to become writers. It was a defect that, as Southern women, we sought to overcome--she, by submission to appearances, I, through early marriage and motherhood. We had observed that Carson McCullers, Flannery O'Connor, Margaret Mitchell, and her creation of Scarlett O'Hara had all been punished for their ambition by illness, death, or the loss of love. My favorite story--a true one--was that of a woman in Washington, Georgia, during the nineteenth century who, accused of the murder of her husband, had been condemned to death by Jurors whose jealous wives insisted upon it; she had gone to her hanging in the streets of the town known for its antebellum beauty wearing her prettiest silk gown. After hearing and reading stories of what had happened to exceptional Southern women, I shivered: was this the fate that awaited every woman who craved more than the traditional feminine role?

(Rose, 1965)

43. The author implies that extraordinary Southern women
    1. became well known.
    2. were punished for ambition.
    3. were criminals.
    4. were devious.

44. The author tried to conquer her need to write by
    1. keeping up appearances.
    2. losing her desire to write.
    3. marrying early and becoming a mother.
    4. appearing very smart.

45. Scarlet O'Hara was a character in a book by
    1. Margaret Mitchell.
    2. Flannery O'Connor.
    3. Carson McCullers.
    4. the author.

46. Which of the following is NOT implied about the jurors?
    1. They were all men.
    2. They were pressured into finding the woman guilty.
    3. They had jealous wives.
    4. They were right in their condemnation of the woman.

47. The woman was convicted because
    1. she was exceptional.
    2. she was beautiful.
    3. she lost her love.
    4. she was a traditional woman.

48. The author implies that writers like Margaret Mitchell, Carson McCullers, and Flannery O'Connor
    1. submitted to the traditional feminine role.
    2. committed crimes for which they were condemned.
    3. lived lives clouded by misfortune.
    4. knew only the success created by hard work and ambition.

The vascular system, the circuit through which blood travels, consists of the blood vessels in your body.

The circulatory system consists of two loops.
5   The shorter loop begins at the right side of your heart, delivers blood to your lungs, and returns oxygenated blood to your heart. The longer loop begins at the left side of the heart, where it receives the blood that was oxygenated in the
10 lungs.

From the left side blood is pumped to tissues of your body through a sequence of smaller blood vessels; arteries branch into smaller arterioles, and the arterioles branch into tiny capillaries that
15 deliver blood to tissues. After the blood in the capillaries collects carbon dioxide and other waste products from the tissues, it begins its trip back to your heart via small venules and, eventually, veins. Blood circulates through your
20 liver and kidneys, where waste products are removed or processed, then returns to your heart.

The distribution of blood within blood vessels varies considerably with exercise and exposure
25 to heat and cold. During exercise, for example, the blood flow to active muscles is increased; after you eat, your stomach and intestines draw more blood to assist in the digestive process. Changes in the surrounding temperature also
30 affect the flow of blood; warmer temperatures produce increased flow to the outer layers of your skin (which helps you to dissipate heat); on the other hand, your body responds to cold by redistributing blood flow into the inner vessels in
35 order to conserve heat.

This flexible system is subject to a wide range of malfunctions. Some are the result of heart disorders; others occur because of disorders that directly affect the blood vessels, such
40 as diabetes.

(Larson, 1990)

49. The style of writing may be best characterized as
    1. objective.
    2. ironic.
    3. informal.
    4. persuasive

50. The major function of the circulatory system is
    1. to carry oxygenated blood to body tissues and remove wastes.
    2. to regulate body temperature and metabolism.
    3. to allow the body to exercise regularly.
    4. to control body weight.

51. Which of the following does not affect blood circulation?
    1. food intake
    2. change in body temperature
    3. diabetes
    4. carbon dioxide

52. It is stated in the passage that
    1. there is an increased blood flow to the outer layers of the skin in warmer temperatures.
    2. blood flow is increased to the inner vessels to dissipate heat.
    3. during exercise, blood flow is decreased to the muscles.
    4. during the digestive process, less blood is necessary.

53. As used in the passage, dissipate means
    1. retain.
    2. collect.
    3. disperse.
    4. manufacture.

54. The primary purpose of this passage is to explain
    1. the variable distribution of blood vessels.
    2. the workings of the vascular system.
    3. that exercise is necessary for blood distribution.
    4. that blood removes the body's waste products.

A bureaucracy is a <u>hierarchical</u> form of social organization, best represented by the diagram of a triangle with a few people at the top and many below. A bureaucracy is an orderly or rational

5 kind of organization based on written rules. It is assumed that the few people at the top have most of the power, but also that they have it because they meet reasonable and specified requirements. The ways in which one moves

10 from the bottom of the pyramid to the top are also clearly specified, as are the relationships among all the members of a bureaucracy. Bureaucracies are slow to change and have no mechanism for adaptation to individual needs. If

15 it is not written down in the rules, it does not exist. The army is a good example of a bureaucracy. So are American governments . . . industry, schools, unions, even large religious denominations, are organized hierarchically.

20 Some people show great ability to understand bureaucratic structures. They can rise rapidly within the structures while fulfilling their needs. Most people, however, find their desires and needs inadequately fulfilled in

25 bureaucracies. Particularly common is the feeling of being manipulated and at the mercy of impersonal forces, even though the people at the top of the bureaucracy may have been elected to their positions by popular vote and can be

30 removed by proper procedures. As a result, there frequently grows up within the formal structure of the bureaucratic organization an informal structure which provides ways of <u>circumventing</u> the rules.

55. As used in the passage, <u>hierarchical</u> means

　　1. universally.
　　2. in rank order.
　　3. according to ability.
　　4. arbitrarily.

56. As used in the passage <u>circumventing</u> means

　　1. changing.
　　2. hiding.
　　3. advertising.
　　4. bypassing.

57. The author implies that

　　1. bureaucracies are the only type of organization.
　　2. many persons function well in bureaucracies.
　　3. rules are made to be broken.
　　4. to function successfully in a bureaucracy, one must "bend" the rules.

58. According to the passage

　　1. individual needs are not met in schools.
　　2. bureaucracies are vicious structures.
　　3. bureaucracies cannot be changed.
　　4. people who work in bureaucracies often feel exploited.

59. The passage states that people who hold top positions within the bureaucracy

　　1. cannot be removed.
　　2. are impersonal.
　　3. can sometimes be removed by proper procedures.
　　4. are manipulators.

60. The passage states that the hierarchical structure

　　1. is likely to change.
　　2. has a wide base and narrow top.
　　3. should be reexamined.
　　4. can get top-heavy.

The Reading Test
Practice Test Two

In the developing countries of Asia, Africa, and South America, both women and men associate the smoking of cigarettes with affluence, leisure, development, and Western
5 values. Advertising in many of these countries is unrestrained by the health conscious codes, laws and controls that shackle the North American and European tobacco advertisers. As a result, unaware of the long term health costs, the
10 developing countries' most affluent citizens take up smoking as an indicator of material success.

The transnational tobacco companies are currently engaged in aggressive development of the only market left--the developing countries. It
15 is recognized that the market in developed countries is saturated, and in many areas decreasing, while the market in developing countries is increasing markedly. The British American Tobacco Company, for instance,
20 reported in 1979 a drop of 1.2% in the North American market, but an increase in size of 2.1% in the developing world. The tobacco industry is not dying--rather, its challenge, which is being met, is to transfer both the growth, production,
25 and marketing to the developing countries. It is proving possible to create tobacco dependency in increasing numbers of women and men through canny advertising in countries yet to develop regulatory codes on the promotion, sales, and
30 manufacture of cigarettes.

Since the more affluent acquire the smoking habit first, more men than women currently smoke in the developing countries. However, the irony of "progress" for women is clear as the
35 women most liberated from restraining cultural and religious customs and beliefs in developing countries are also those most likely to smoke.

1. The primary purpose of the passage is to describe
   1. tobacco marketing techniques in Asia, Africa, and South America.
   2. a drop in the North American tobacco market.
   3. a growing tobacco market in developing countries.
   4. proportions of men and women smokers in developing countries.

2. The passage implies that the tobacco market is declining in North America and Europe because of
   1. the existence of health conscious codes, laws, and controls.
   2. the decreasing population.
   3. restrictive religious and cultural beliefs.
   4. unrestricted advertising.

3. What is the irony of "progress" for women in developing countries?
   1. Many women in South America smoke.
   2. Through advertising, tobacco dependency is increased.
   3. The most liberated women are most likely to smoke.
   4. The more affluent women acquire the smoking habit first.

4. As used in the passage canny means
   1. insensitive.
   2. weird.
   3. colorful.
   4. shrewd.

5. Which of the following statements drawn from the passage could be a fact rather than an opinion?
   1. The irony of "progress" for women is clear.
   2. More men than women currently smoke in developing countries.
   3. Canny advertising is creating tobacco dependency.
   4. Regulatory controls shackle the tobacco industry.

6. Which of the following describes the author's attitude toward smoking?
   1. Smoking is morally wrong.
   2. Smoking is an indicator of material success.
   3. Smoking is damaging to one's health.
   4. Smoking is a thing of the past in America.

From "The Tobacco Industry Weeding Women Out" by Greaves, Lorraine and Margaret L W Bulst In Women's Health by Nancy Worcester and Marianne Whatley (eds).

As he moved across Georgia, Sherman cut a path fifty to sixty miles wide; the totality of the destruction was awesome. A Georgia woman described the "Burnt Country" this way: "The
5 fields were trampled down and the road was lined with carcasses of horses, hogs, and cattle that the invaders, unable either to consume or to carry with them, had <u>wantonly</u> shot down to starve our people and prevent them from making
10 their crops. The stench in some places was unbearable." Such devastation diminished the South's material resources, and, more importantly, it was bound to damage the faltering Southern will to resist.
15   After reaching Savannah in December, Sherman turned north and marched his armies into the Carolinas. Wreaking great destruction as he moved through South Carolina into North Carolina, Sherman encountered little resistance.
20 The opposing army of General Johnston was small, but Sherman's men should have been prime targets for guerrilla raids and harassing attacks by local defense units. The absence of both led South Carolinas's James Chestnut, Jr.,
25 to write that his state "was shamefully and unnecessarily lost.... We had time, opportunity and means to destroy <u>him</u>. But there was wholly wanting the energy and ability required by the occasion." Southerners were reaching the limit of
30 their endurance.

(Norton et al.)

7. As used in the passage, <u>wantonly</u> means
    1. accidentally.
    2. humanely.
    3. mercilessly.
    4. carefully.

8. According to the passage, Sherman's army
    1. was damaged by guerrilla raids and local attacks.
    2. was opposed by an impressive army led by General Johnston.
    3. destroyed or took only what they could consume.
    4. devastated the will and ability of the South to resist.

9. As underlined, <u>him</u> refers to
    1. Sherman.
    2. Sherman's soldier.
    3. James Chestnut, Jr.
    4. General Johnston.

10. It is implied that Sherman and his men are likely to be remembered for their
    1. brilliant military strategy.
    2. brave battle exploits.
    3. fiery destructive march.
    4. ability to endure hardships.

11. Which of the following statements from the passage is a statement of fact and could not be an opinion?
    1. Sherman's men should have been a prime target for guerilla raids and harassing attacks by local defense units.
    2. The totality of his destruction was awesome.
    3. After reaching Savannah in December, Sherman turned north and marched his armies into the Carolinas.
    4. Such devastation was bound to damage the faltering Southern will to resist.

12. The author implies that
    1. Sherman was a skilled military strategist.
    2. Union soldiers had tremendous appetites.
    3. Sherman could have been beaten if the Southerners had wanted to fight.
    4. war is ironic.

13. It can be assumed that the author of the passage is
    1. an impartial observer.
    2. a Confederate sympathizer.
    3. a loyal Unionist.
    4. a military expert.

14. Which of the following does the author primarily use in this passage?
    1. comparison and contrast
    2. statistics
    3. sequence of events
    4. cause and effect

The Renaissance wrought a revolution in the fine arts. Both the humanistic enthusiasm for classical antiquity and the growing secularism of the age carried over into the realm of the arts.
5 Exploiting these new forces, and aided by technical advances, men of genius produced an extraordinary number of masterpieces. In particular, they released painting and sculpture from their subservience to architecture, "queen of
10 the arts" in the medieval West. In the era of the Romanesque and the Gothic, sculptors, the painters of altarpieces, and the superb craftsmen who made stained-glass windows, had all enhanced the glory of the cathedrals and other
15 splendid buildings. But at most they had made only a contribution to the beauty of the whole structure. In the Renaissance, architecture lost its old aesthetic prominence, and painting and sculpture came into their own, often still closely
20 allied with architecture, but often functioning as "free-standing" arts. The individual picture or statue won fresh importance as an independent work of art rather than as a part of a larger whole. The celebrated individualism of the
25 Renaissance was replacing the stamp of the community found in the medieval West.

Reflecting the classical revival, the fashion in building changed from the soaring Gothic to adaptations of the ancient Roman temple,
30 emphasizing symmetry and horizontal line. The contrast may be observed by comparing a Gothic cathedral like Chartres with a Renaissance monument like St. Peter's at Rome.

(Brinton, 1963)

15. According to the passage, the primary benefit of the Renaissance for painters and sculptors was the opportunity to
   1. enhance architecture.
   2. produce works which stood on their own merit.
   3. use new technologies.
   4. paint altar pieces.

16. By stating that painting and sculpture were released from their subservience, the author means that their relationship to architecture had been
   1. unusual.
   2. supportive.
   3. useless.
   4. inappropriate.

17. The author primarily makes his point through the use of
   1. personal opinion.
   2. argument.
   3. analogies.
   4. cause/effect.

18. The reader can infer that Gothic architecture
   1. was pre-Renaissance.
   2. flourished during the Renaissance.
   3. was the author's favorite.
   4. had not previously been well accepted.

19. According to the passage, during the Renaissance
   1. many artists were exceptionally productive.
   2. architecture was not directly affected.
   3. no cathedrals were built.
   4. architectural styles maintained their elaborate details.

20. As used in the passage, enhanced means
   1. diminished.
   2. created.
   3. increased.
   4. praised.

The presidency is today the preeminent institution in the national government of the United States. While the Founding Fathers had no intention that it be so, the office has become
5   the central energizer of government policy, the articulator of the national purpose, the principal symbol at home and abroad of the American political system, and the focus of the hopes (and fears) of countless individuals and groups. For
10 better or worse, we tend to think about American history in four-or-eight-year chunks corresponding to the term in office of a particular president. We invariably turn to the president when the times are out of kilter, demanding
15 remedial action from him and then either blaming him if improvements are not immediately forthcoming or praising him unduly if the burden of problems is eased. We depend on the president to set the legislative agenda for
20 Congress, to define national objectives in time of war and conflict, and to represent the United States before the world.

In these and in countless other ways, both symbolic and actual, the presidency embodies
25 the headship of the government, surely not a monarch, but just as surely more than "first among equals." I shall argue that the office has reached this position over the course of our history not because of random events or
30 usurpations of power, but because of certain developments in American capitalism.

(Greenburg, 1989)

21. The primary purpose of the passage is to
    1. support capitalism.
    2. list ways the president represents the headship of all U.S. government.
    3. belittle the ways Americans view their presidents.
    4. contradict the Founding Fathers.

22. The author uses the phrase for better or worse to imply that
    1. he has no opinion about the way Americans perceive presidential terms of office.
    2. he understands the seriousness of American government.
    3. Americans credit their presidents with good and bad times.
    4. Americans are committed to their presidents.

23. The passage states that the presidency would not have become the foremost institution in the U.S. if it had not been for
    1. the Founding Fathers.
    2. the American political system.
    3. American capitalism.
    4. national objectives.

24. What is meant by the statement that the president is surely more than "first among equals?"
    1. The president has equal rights.
    2. The president's office, though important, is balanced by other offices.
    3. Equal rights demand equal responsibility.
    4. The U.S. president has more power than other governmental officers.

25. The author believes that our attitude toward U.S. presidents
    1. has dangerous overtones.
    2. evolved over a period of time.
    3. borders on the ridiculous.
    4. is undemocratic.

26. Which of the following does the author primarily use to support his point?
    1. analogy
    2. historical narrative
    3. examples
    4. irony

Dependency in the male is equated with weakness, so much so that even normal amounts are often suppressed. There is little that makes a father prouder than to see his five or six-year-old son acting like a "little man."

If the mother tolerates or encourages dependency, she stands to be accused of emasculating him. Father, ever mindful of the competitive struggles of his everyday life, overreacts and sees his son's dependency as dangerous.

From early childhood on the boy learns that masculinity means not depending on anybody. His needs are bottled up and disowned. He reacts violently to those who lean on others and calls them "parasites." Dependency, in the typical male mind, spells disaster.

The male resistance to asking for help ties in closely with both his resistance to dependency and his resistance to passivity. As a boy he may struggle for hours over a problem or task because he is too embarrassed to ask for help. As an adult he may drive around lost for a half-hour, hoping to stumble on the right direction rather than to stop and ask for help. He hides his business and other worldly problems because he's convinced that no one can help him anyway. Others might, he thinks, even use his helplessness against him.

This resistance tends to devastate his relationships with intimates, spouse, friends, and children. If they love him, he believes, they will know what he needs--and he quietly resents it when they don't.

(Goldberg, 1977)

27. The author's purpose is to show that
    1. boys are dependent.
    2. dependency is an advantage in males.
    3. men equate dependency with weakness.
    4. others take advantage of weak, dependent men.

28. When a mother encourages dependency she is accused of
    1. emasculating the boy.
    2. good parenting.
    3. strengthening character.
    4. instilling values.

29. Men do not like to ask for help because they
    1. don't need other people.
    2. they view it as a sign of weakness.
    3. really don't want help.
    4. believe women will become dominating.

30. The author implies that the fear of dependency in males
    1. destroys relationships because there is no communication.
    2. helps relationships because some fear is healthy.
    3. encourages females to be maternal.
    4. leads men to commit suicide.

31. As underlined in the passage, parasites means
    1. insects.
    2. children.
    3. independent males.
    4. dependent people.

32. Which of the following is not specifically mentioned in the passage?
    1. father
    2. mother
    3. daughter
    4. son

The term fossil has been variously used, but is here interpreted to be an evidence, direct or indirect of existence of organisms in prehistoric time.... An exact definition as to what constitutes

5 a fossil, or an upper limit of prehistoric time, is difficult to establish. For example, are the hollow molds of a mule or a man buried in ash in the city of Pompeii fossils, or is the well-tanned and pickled Irish man buried in a peat bog in the 12th

10 century, a fossil? Are the remains (of a mastodon or hairy mammoth) fossils, when they are still well enough preserved that the meat can be eaten rather palatably, even though the animals lived in the Pleistocene? The upper fringe of

15 prehistoric time is a difficult and sometimes arbitrary area in the definition of the term fossil.

Evidence of fossils may range from exceedingly well-preserved forms like the mastodons frozen in the tundra of Alaska and Siberia, to less

20 well-preserved forms such as clam shells which have been replaced and re-crystallized. Direct evidence of fossils usually tell us much about the shape of the animal or plant, and commonly contain materials which were actually precipitated

25 by the life processes of the organism. Indirect fossils on the other hand, are normally only impressions, yet still suggestive of size and proportions. A track, a trail, a burrow-filling, a "stomach stone," or a coprolite are indirect

30 evidences of organic activity and tell us something about the organisms.

(Peterson, 1982)

33. As used in the passage, arrow means
    1. misused.
    2. debatable.
    3. unlearned.
    4. forgotten.

34. The remains of the mastodon present
    1. indirect fossil evidence.
    2. direct fossil evidence.
    3. an exact fossil definition.
    4. confusion among scientists.

35. Size and proportion of the organism is best indicated by
    1. indirect fossil evidence.
    2. direct fossil evidence.
    3. a track.
    4. a burrow filling.

36. The Irishman was buried in a peat bog during the
    1. 1200's.
    2. 1300's.
    3. 1100's.
    4. 1000's.

37. Precipitated, as used in the passage, means
    1. fallen from.
    2. caused to happen.
    3. condensed into rain.
    4. slowed down.

38. Which word or phrase could be used at the beginning of the last sentence, "a track, a trace, a burrow-filling . . ."?
    1. In addition
    2. For example
    3. However
    4. Although

A fearful man, all in coarse gray; with a great
iron on his leg. A man with no hat, and with
broken shoes, and with an old rag tied round his
head. A man who had been soaked in water, and
5   smothered in mud, and lamed by stones, and cut
by flints, and stung by nettles, and torn by briars;
who limped, and shivered, and glared and
growled; and whose teeth chattered in his head
as he seized me by the chin....
10   'Ha!' he muttered then, considering. "Who
d'ye live with--supposing you're kindly let to live,
which I han't made up my mind about?"
"My sister, sir--Mrs. Joe Gargery--wife of Joe
Gargery, the black-smith, sir."
15   "Blacksmith, eh?" said he. And looked down
at his leg.
After darkly looking at his leg and at me
several times, he came closer to my tombstone,
took me by both arms, and tilted me back as far
20   as he could hold me; so that his eyes looked
most powerfully down into mine, and mine looked
most helplessly up into his....
"You get me file," He tilted me again. "And
you get me whittles~ He tilted me again. "You
25   bring 'em both to me." He tilted me again. "Or I'll
have your heart and liver out." He tilted me again.
I was dreadfully frightened, and so giddy that
I clung to him with both hands, and said, "If you
would kindly please to let me keep upright, sir,
30   perhaps I shouldn't be sick, and perhaps I could
attend more." . . .
"You bring me, tomorrow morning early, that
file and them whittles. You bring the lot to me, at
that old Battery over yonder. You do it, and you
35   never dare to say a word or dare to make a sign
concerning your having seen such a person as
me, or any person sumever, and you shall be let
to live. You fail, or you go from my words in any
partickler, no matter how small it is, and your
40   heart and your liver shall be tore out, roasted and
ate. Now, I ain't alone, as you may think I am.
There's a young man hid with me, in comparison
with which young man, I am an Angel.
I am a keeping that young man from harming
45   you at the present moment, with great difficulty....
Now, what do you say?"

(Dickens, 1861)

39. According to the passage, what will happen
to the boy if he doesn't get the file and
whittles?
    1. The man will turn him upside down.
    2. The man will eat his last piece of bread.
    3. The man will kill him.
    4. The young man will become the boy's
       friend.

40. The author uses which of the following to get
his point across?
    1. contrast
    2. comparison
    3. description
    4. narration

41. The man looks at his leg after the boy
mentions that Joe is a blacksmith because
    1. he has an iron leg.
    2. he needs shoes for his horse.
    3. he wants to remove the shackles.
    4. he wants to make friends with the
       blacksmith.

42. The scene takes place
    1. outside the blacksmith's shop.
    2. over at the Battery.
    3. in a cemetery.
    4. near a river.

43. The reader can infer that the man in gray
mentions his companion in order to
    1. interest the narrator.
    2. frighten the narrator.
    3. offend the narrator.
    4. criticize the narrator.

44. It can be inferred that the man in gray is
    1. an angel.
    2. an escaped prisoner.
    3. a grave-robber.
    4. an injured sailor.

Radiant heating is a method of supplying heat, in the form of radiant energy (radiation), in automatically controlled amounts. The heat is generated, just as in any hot-water heating
5 system, by a boiler, and then <u>conveyed</u> by hot water pipes to surfaces, called panels, in the rooms.

In most cases, parallel rows of pipes or tubes, connected by return bends or headers, are
10 embedded in a concrete floor slab or in a plastered ceiling or wall. A circulating pump near the boiler forces the water through the piping system. The heat from the water is transmitted to the room through the embedding material; thus
15 the radiant heat does not actually come from the embedded piping, but from the surface of the panel.

Two advantages of such a system: Heat sources are invisible--no radiators, convector
20 cabinets, registers or grilles--and no floor space need be sacrificed for heating devices. When the system is operating, air is heated only as it comes in contact with the warm surfaces. Room-air temperatures, therefore are somewhat lower
25 than with conventional systems.

Radiant heating is most valuable in base-mentless houses where other types of heat cannot produce completely warm floors. The heat given off by the panels is absorbed by all other
30 room surfaces that are at lower temperatures than the panels and in direct line with the heat rays, so the floors can be warm even if the panels are in the ceiling.

(Reader's Digest, 1973)

45. The author's primary purpose is to
    1. show importance of radiant heating.
    2. tell disadvantages of radiant heating.
    3. explain heating systems.
    4. explain the radiant heating system.

46. <u>Conveyed</u>, as underlined, means
    1. carried.
    2. boiled.
    3. surfaced.
    4. streamlined.

47. Which of the following does the author use in paragraph two?
    1. comparison and contrast
    2. sequential order
    3. narration
    4. statistics

48. Of the following, which is NOT an advantage of radiant heating?
    1. Heat sources are invisible.
    2. Temperatures are higher.
    3. Floor space is not sacrificed.
    4. Houses without basements may be warmer.

49. According to the passage, radiant heated rooms are heated by
    1. radiators.
    2. grilles.
    3. panels.
    4. cabinets.

In the broadest sense the term "culture" refers to all aspects of human society that are either learned or man-made. The culture of a society includes such components as family structure, stock of capital equipment, and religious beliefs and values. Culture is also distinguishable into material and non-material aspects. Material culture is the objective dimension of culture and refers to the tangible elements that people have invented or built into the tools of its society, its technology, homes and factories, automobiles, infrastructure, communication facilities, hydroelectric power plants and medicine. In other words, all the things made by people are what comprise the material culture of human society.

By contrast, the non-material culture or the subjective dimension of culture refers to such intangibles as attitudes, beliefs, values, traditions, language, normative standards and more. Whereas material culture exists in concrete form in the real world and it can be perceived and touched, non-material culture exists in the minds of people. A culture is thus a way of life of a population, all their ways of doing things, all the kinds of behavior they have learned and transmitted to successive generations. While specifying these explicit attributes of culture, it is essential to indicate what it is not. Culture is not the result of biological inheritance. It is not genetically predetermined.

(Sarfo, 1988)

50. The primary purpose of the passage is to
    1. contrast materialism with non-materialism.
    2. compare cultures.
    3. list beliefs.
    4. describe culture.

51. Which of the following would be considered non-material culture?
    1. television
    2. transportation systems
    3. religion
    4. automobiles

52. Intangibles as underlined means
    1. necessities of life.
    2. objective dimensions.
    3. things people have invented.
    4. things incapable of being perceived by the senses.

53. The tone of the passage is best described as
    1. sentimental.
    2. informative.
    3. entertaining.
    4. enthusiastic.

54. What is the relationship between the first and second paragraph?
    1. The second contradicts the first.
    2. The second draws a conclusion presented in the first.
    3. The second continues the discussion of a concept introduced in the first.
    4. The second introduces a new concept.

55. Which concept is most important for understanding the meaning of the passage?
    1. Non-material culture is in the minds of people.
    2. Culture includes objective and subjective dimensions.
    3. It is difficult to study the various aspects of culture.
    4. Material culture is objective.

A corporation comes into being when the government issues a charter. In the United States, corporate charters are issued by state governments. Obtaining a charter is simple and
5 inexpensive, and the charter itself places very few restrictions on the operations of corporations. The charter authorizes the corporation to issue and sell shares of stock. The people who own these shares, the stockholders, are the owners of
10 the corporation. Also, the charter establishes the corporation as a "legal person," separate from the "real persons" who are the owners and the managers of the corporation.

As a legal person, the corporation can enter
15 into contracts and make commitments in its own name. Under the law, the corporation itself is responsible for these obligations. Neither the owners nor the managers are individually liable for its debts and obligations. If the corporation
20 does well, the stock holders reap the profits, but if corporate operations are not successful, a stockholder's loss is limited to the value of the shares owned. This limited liability feature of corporation greatly increases their ability to
25 accumulate large sums of money for the enterprise.

The legal person created by the corporate charter has perpetual or unlimited life, which means that the corporation itself does not have
30 to be reorganized every time individual persons enter or leave the ownership or management of the corporation. This stability is attractive to shareholders, who need not fear that their wealth will be tied up in endless legal battles, as may
35 happen in partnerships.

(Bronfenbrenner, 1987)

56. It can be inferred from the passage that
    1. corporation charters are designed to protect individual stockholders.
    2. corporations are more prevalent than partnerships.
    3. when stockholders lose their confidence in corporations, profits drop.
    4. corporations are never sued.

57. The author's primary purpose is to
    1. list the benefits of limited liability.
    2. explain the primary features of corporation charters.
    3. contrast corporations with partnerships.
    4. explain the structure of corporations.

58. The author states that the creation of the "legal person"
    1. prevents endless legal battles.
    2. ensures profitability.
    3. promotes corporation stability.
    4. lessens corporation liabilities.

59. The passage states that the "legal person" is the same as
    1. the corporation.
    2. the owners of the corporation.
    3. the managers of the corporation.
    4. the stockholders of the corporation.

60. This limited liability refers to
    1. a stockholder's level of responsibility for corporation losses.
    2. the "legal person's" mandated role.
    3. the "real person's" restricted privileges.
    4. large sums of accumulated profit which must be taxed.

The Reading Test
Practice Test Three

And when they were alone together, the spirit broke silence and told Hamlet that he was the ghost of his father. The ghost told Hamlet that he had been cruelly murdered and related the

5 manner of it. It was done by his own <u>brother's hand</u>. Claudius, Hamlet's uncle, hoped of succeeding to the Queen's bed and the crown and so murdered the King. One day as the King was sleeping in his garden (as was his custom in

10 the afternoon), the treasonous Claudius stole upon the King and poured the juice of poison into his ears. As swiftly as quicksilver the poison coursed through the veins of the King's body baking his blood. It spread a crustlike leprosy all

15 over his skin. Thus, by a <u>brother's hand</u>, the King was cut off at once from his crown, his queen, and life. He pleaded with Hamlet, if he did ever love his dear father, to please avenge the foul murder. And the ghost related that even though

20 his wife, the Queen, had fallen from virtue and proved false to the wedded love of her first husband, she was by no means to be harmed. Hamlet was to leave his mother to Heaven and to the <u>stings and thorns</u> of conscience. And Hamlet

25 promised to observe the ghost's direction in all things, and the ghost vanished.

(Lamb, 1807)

1. Who was murdered?
   1. Claudius
   2. the Queen
   3. Hamlet's father
   4. Hamlet's uncle

2. The method of the murder was
   1. stabbing.
   2. drowning.
   3. burning.
   4. poisoning.

3. What did the ghost want Hamlet to do?
   1. follow him
   2. avenge the murder
   3. murder the queen
   4. commit suicide

4. As used in the passage, <u>stings and thorns</u> means
   1. confusions
   2. illusions.
   3. pains.
   4. disappointments.

5. It is suggested by the passage that
   1. the queen will kill Claudius.
   2. Claudius will kill Hamlet.
   3. the queen will kill Hamlet.
   4. Hamlet will kill Claudius.

6. The passage implies that Hamlet
   1. was indifferent toward his father.
   2. loved his father.
   3. misunderstood his father.
   4. hated his father.

7. The <u>brother's hand</u> refers to
   1. Hamlet
   2. the King.
   3. Hamlet's brother.
   4. Claudius.

Dreams show a person's conceptions of obstacles that stand in the way of the <u>gratification</u> of his impulses. These obstacles are often prohibitions emanating from his conscience and

5   may be represented in dreams by such obstacles as walls, curbs, and locked doors, by acts of restraint such as putting on the brakes of a car, or by the appearance of authority figures who interrupt the dreamer's pleasure. If an impulse is

10 gratified, the dreamer may express his conception of the punishment that will be visited upon him for his transgression. He may be punished directly by another person, or he may be the victim of misfortune. In any event, the kinds of

15 obstacles and the kinds of penalties which appear in dreams are interpreted in order to throw light upon the nature of the conceptual system which is called the superego. This conceptual system which is assumed to be

20 detached from the ego contains the moral ideology of the person.

Perhaps the most important information provided by dreams is the way in which they illuminate the basic predicaments of a person as

25 that person sees them. Dreams give one an inside view of the person's problems, a personal formulation that is not so likely to be as distorted or as superficial as are the reports made in waking life. Since it is the way in which a person

30 conceives of his conflicts that determines his behavior, the inside view is a <u>prerequisite</u> for clear understanding of human conduct.

(Gibbons, 1970)

8. The conceptual system is called the
    1. ego.
    2. dream.
    3. superego.
    4. transgression.

9. The primary purpose of this passage is to explain
    1. why the walls, curbs, and locked doors act as restraints in dreams.
    2. how the conflicts and punishments appearing in dreams can be interpreted.
    3. the appearance of authority figures who interrupt the dreamers' pleasure.
    4. the significance of dreams in relationship to human behavior.

10. According to this passage, one's behavior is determined by
    1. the way one interprets his conflicts in life.
    2. the obstacles in the way of gratification.
    3. the punishment one receives for his transgressions.
    4. the parents that raised him.

11. As used in the passage, <u>prerequisite</u> means
    1. requirement following a fact.
    2. requirement as a prior condition.
    3. a function which is most important.
    4. a function which is clearly understood.

12. As used in the first paragraph, <u>gratification</u> means
    1. compelling force.
    2. over-indulgence.
    3. satisfaction.
    4. penalty.

The fact that the earth's atmosphere contains ozone, water vapor, and carbon dioxide causes it to act like a greenhouse. The earth receives many forms of energy from the sun, including
5 some ultraviolet light, visible light, and infrared light. The crust of the earth absorbs this energy and remits it, primarily in the form of infrared radiation. The atmosphere tends to absorb this form of radiation quite efficiently and so the earth
10 retains a large amount of heat; in fact, the earth's surface temperature would probably be 45° C cooler were it not for this "greenhouse" phenomenon. While we do not want to contemplate what the earth would be like without the
15 warming influence of the greenhouse effect, neither do we want to neglect to observe that we are introducing large amounts of carbon dioxide into the atmosphere, a by-product of burning fossil fuels. Some experts speculate that the
20 average temperature of the earth may increase by several degrees in the next 25 to 50 years, as a direct result of the increased release of carbon dioxide into the atmosphere. Even a small change in the average temperature would
25 produce melting in the polar caps, to the point of changing the coastlines associated with the oceans of the world. As educated citizens, we must both be aware of the dangers and be willing to participate in corrective measures.

(Dixon, 1989)

13. One result of the increase in atmospheric temperature would be
    1. creation of polar caps.
    2. more carbon dioxide.
    3. fewer fossil fuels.
    4 a change in the coast lines.

14. The author's purpose is to
    1. entertain.
    2. inform.
    3. argue.
    4. narrate.

15. Speculate, as used in the passage means
    1. know.
    2. disbelieve.
    3. disagree.
    4. predict.

16. If there were no "greenhouse" phenomenon,
    1. there would be no change in the earth's temperature.
    2. the earth's temperature would fluctuate.
    3. the earth's temperature would be cooler.
    4. the earth's temperature would be hotter.

17. Based upon facts presented in the passage, the reader may conclude that
    1. the earth will end in fifty years.
    2. if some measures aren't taken, we may see coastal flooding in about fifty years.
    3. if corrective measures aren't taken, the earth's air will become colder.
    4. the earth's atmosphere will disappear.

18. According to the passage, what are we doing to harm the greenhouse phenomenon?
    1. remitting infrared radiation into the atmosphere.
    2. changing the earth's temperature.
    3. changing the earth's coastlines.
    4. burning fossil fuels.

The grand cultural era of the Cro-Magnons was the Upper Paleolithic or late Old Stone Age. Just as each stage of man's physical development owed much to its predecessors, so
5 the Upper Paleolithic culture enjoyed a considerable heritage from earlier cultures. The men of the late Old Stone Age used ancient Oldowan-phase tools and techniques as well as the recent scallop-edged scrapers of the
10 Neanderthals. To this basic stock the men of the Upper Paleolithic added their own inventory of technology. In stone-work the most significant advances were the perfection of a stone tool shaped very much like the blade of a penknife
15 and in its own way almost as effective--and the introduction of an implement known as a burin. Often no more than a spur on the corner of a hand-held pebble, occasionally a long, slender stone like a carpenter's flat pencil, the burin was
20 similarly sharpened by removing chips from the working, or pointed end, and it served as a combination gouge and chisel. The burin's great virtue was that it made possible the much more controlled working of wood and bone; Upper
25 Paleolithic man could now manufacture better tools from these materials and also add artistic expression by carving and engraving the surfaces with patterns and designs that had previously been impossible.

(Severin, 1973)

19. The author's purpose is to explain
    1. how the Upper Paleolithic Age was helped by earlier cultures.
    2. the cultural era of the Cro-Magnons.
    3. Neanderthal heritage.
    4. the ancestors of the New Stone Age.

20. Predecessors as used in the passage means
    1. heirs.
    2. stage.
    3. forefathers.
    4. society.

21. Implement as used in the passage means
    1. club.
    2. stock.
    3. wood.
    4. tool.

22. The burin's greatest virtue was that it
    1. made possible more control over wood and bone working.
    2. made possible more carving and en-graving.
    3. was a tool shaped like a knife.
    4. increased the inventory of technology.

23. Of the cultural eras mentioned in the pas-sage, the most recent age was
    1. late Old Stone Age.
    2. pre-Cro-Magnons.
    3. Oldowan.
    4. Neanderthals.

If average untrained college-men and women are tested for physical fitness, the men are likely to appear to be more fit, particularly in the area of strength. These results fit with the assumption
5 that many make that women naturally have less physical potential than men. However, exercise physiologists find very different results. For example, men tend to have greater strength in both upper (back, arms, shoulders) and lower
10 body, but when the measurement is adjusted relative to body weight, the differences in lower body strength disappear. When untrained men and women begin to do weight-training, the women often progress much faster because they
15 are farther below their potential. Androgens are needed for muscle proliferation, so the fact that the average woman has lower levels of androgens than the average man means there is some limit on her muscle bulk. However, this
20 does not mean much in terms of strength limitations since women can increase greatly in strength without "bulking" (muscles increasing in size). Right now we have no idea what the strength capability of women is since women are
25 so undertrained in terms of strength.

Women have a great capacity for developing endurance. Leading women marathoners can beat all but the best male runners and would, in fact, have won many past Olympic men's mara-
30 thons with their current times. Women do even better in relation to men in ultramarathons (50 or 100 miles). Women hold many long-distance swimming records and compete directly with men.

35 When boys and girls are tested for physical performance, they are matched up to ages 10 to 12. In fact, girls are often faster than their male classmates in elementary school. After age 12, boys tend to increase in strength and
40 cardiovascular fitness more than girls. Exercise physiologists believe these differences may be more social than biological in origin. It is not hormones that make women weaker but social and cultural processes.

(Whatley, 1988)

24. The primary purpose of the passage is to
    1. inform the reader about the physical fitness of men and women.
    2. entertain the reader with examples of "muscle women" and "marathon men."
    3. persuade the reader that assumptions about male and female physical potential may be incorrect.
    4. explain the merits of muscle development.

25. Physiologists, used in the passage, means
    1. those who study the mind.
    2. those who study the body.
    3. those who are health professionals.
    4. those who study weight training.

26. The author would agree with which of the following statements?
    1. Women's muscles will not get as large as men's but we do not know how strong women can become.
    2. Girls increase their strength and cardiovascular fitness more slowly than boys after age 12 because of their bodily changes.
    3. Women naturally have less physical potential than men.
    4. Women develop less muscle because they have lower levels of androgens; therefore, they are incapable of building much muscle strength.

27. As used in the passage, proliferation means
    1. elasticity.
    2. tone.
    3. growth.
    4. strength.

28. Which one of the following statements is most relevant to the author's idea about women's fitness?
    1. Male socialization involves physical fitness.
    2. Androgens are necessary for muscle proliferation.
    3. Women's societal roles do not encourage physical strength.
    4. Relative to weight, average untrained men are biologically no stronger than women.

29. Endurance in women is evidenced by
    1. their performances in long-distance swimming.
    2. their development of muscle strength without "bulking. "
    3. their winning gold medals in past Olympic men's marathons.
    4. their superior progress in beginning weight training as compared with men's progress.

Four score and seven years ago our fathers brought forth on this continent a new nation, conceived in liberty, and dedicated to the proposition that all men are created equal.

5 Now we are engaged in a great civil war, testing whether that nation, or any nation so conceived and so dedicated, can long endure. We are met on a great battlefield of that war. We have come to dedicate a portion of that field as a

10 final resting place for those who here gave their lives that the nation might live. It is altogether fitting and proper that we should do this.

But, in a larger sense, we cannot dedicate, we cannot consecrate, we cannot hallow this

15 ground. The brave men, living and dead, who struggled here, have consecrated it far above our poor power to add or detract. The world will little note nor long remember what we say here, but it can never forget what they did here. It is for us,

20 the living, rather, to be dedicated here to the unfinished work which they who fought here have thus far so nobly advanced. It is rather the great task remaining before us; that from these hon- ored dead we take increased devotion to that

25 cause for which they gave the last full measure of devotion; that we here highly resolve that these dead shall not have died in vain; that this nation, under God, shall have a new birth of freedom; and that government of the people, by

30 the people, for the people, shall not perish from the earth.

(Lincoln, 1863)

30. As used in this passage, conceived means
    1. begun.
    2. erected.
    3. shaped.
    4. conquered.

31. The greater purpose of the speech is to
    1. honor the dead.
    2. uphold democracy.
    3. bury the dead.
    4. condemn the war.

32. The author's attitude is
    1. hopeful.
    2. pessimistic.
    3. objective.
    4. indifferent.

33. The speaker states that the war is a test of the nation's
    1. brave men.
    2. dedication to the continuation of govern- ment.
    3. devotion to those who have died on the battlefield.
    4. basic proposition of liberty.

34. The author would probably agree that
    1. war will solve the country's problems.
    2. the people who survive the war will be responsible for freedom afterwards.
    3. the dead died in vain.
    4. battlefields cannot be dedicated.

35. Lincoln believed that dedicating the battle field was
    1. appropriate.
    2. ridiculous.
    3. hard work.
    4. a sign of greatness.

A second way of viewing beliefs is to determine their degree of certainty. Some beliefs are fixed, while others are open to change, or are variable. Fixed beliefs are those that have been
5 reinforced throughout your life, making them central to your thinking. Obviously, many of your early childhood beliefs are fixed, such as "Bad behavior will be punished" and "If you work hard, you will succeed." Other beliefs become not only
10 fixed but anchored as well; especially as you grow older, such beliefs harden in your mind and are highly resistant to change. For example, as people grow older, they tend to vote along political party lines election after election; they
15 tend to purchase and drive the same kind of vehicles; they tend to believe that certain people and occupations are respectable and others are not; and they tend not to change religions or churches. Thus, the demographic variable of age
20 may indicate fixed beliefs. Fixed beliefs become habituated and can even be called stereotypes because we often generalize our fixed beliefs to larger groups. For example, we might say, "All Republicans are honest." "People who do things
25 like that should be arrested!" or "Never trust a German shepherd."

In contrast, variable beliefs are less well anchored in our minds and experiences. You might enter college thinking you are very well
30 suited by temperament and talent to be a chemist; then, after an instructor has praised your abilities in a composition class, you might see yourself as <u>predestined</u> to be a writer; next, you take a marketing class and find out that you
35 are very good at planning advertising campaigns. After that course, you go to the Advisement Center to change your major.

(Gronbecketal, 1989)

36. According to the passage, which of the following is an example of a variable belief?
    1. an adult's fear of failure
    2. an older person's voting along political party lines
    3. a young person's dreams of becoming a writer
    4. mature people tending to belong to the same religion

37. The author of this passage is primarily concerned with comparing
    1. youth and older adults.
    2. fixed and variable beliefs.
    3. bad beliefs and good beliefs.
    4. beliefs and habits.

38. The author makes his point primarily through the use of
    1. statistics.
    2. examples.
    3. persuasion.
    4. analogy.

39. According to the passage, fixed beliefs become stereotypes when
    1. unpleasant experiences occur.
    2. childhood memories emerge.
    3. peer groups agree with the fixed belief.
    4. beliefs become habitual and generalized.

40. As used in the passage, <u>predestined</u> means
    1. made impossible.
    2. established in advance.
    3. subjected to preview.
    4. selected by the professor.

41. The reader can conclude that older people are most likely to join organizations that
    1. offer interesting projects for its members.
    2. promote political activism.
    3. support the beliefs of the members.
    4. offer enjoyable leisure activities.

Whether they grow in deserts, water, grasslands, or forests, most plants synthesize their own organic molecules, but a few species known as **parasites** take nourishment from other plants
5 or from decaying vegetation. Parasites may obtain some or all of their nutrients from such "hosts." One example of a true plant parasite is the dodder, or "love vine," a gold-colored plant that lacks chlorophyll and lives by twining itself
10 around low trees and other <u>chaparral plants</u>. <u>It</u> then grows root-like structures that grow into the host plant and remove water, sugar, and other nutrients.

Mistletoe is often described as a parasite, but
15 it actually is only partially so because it synthesizes its own food while taking only water and minerals from its host plant. There are also parasitic plants that, like the dodder, do not contain chlorophyll yet appear to live independent
20 of other plants. Small clumps of the Indian pipe *(Monotropa uniflora)* arise ghostlike from the forest floor. The clumps survive because they are nutritionally connected to other plants in the vicinity by joining Into an association with soil
25 fungi whose filaments carry nutrients from the "host" plant to the Indian pipe.

42. The primary purpose of the passage is to
    1. compare mistletoe to Indian pipe.
    2. discuss the root systems of parasites.
    3. give examples of "host" plants.
    4. explain and define parasites.

43. <u>Chaparral plants</u> as used in the passage most likely means
    1. tall trees.
    2. low bushes.
    3. gold-colored plants.
    4. decaying vegetation.

44. <u>It</u> refers to
    1. a parasite.
    2. a plant.
    3. a chaparral plant.
    4. vegetation.

45. Unlike other parasites, mistletoe produces its own
    1. water.
    2. minerals.
    3. food.
    4. fungi.

46. With which statement would the author probably not agree?
    1. Parasites may derive nutrients from decaying vegetation.
    2. Mistletoe is not a true parasite.
    3. The dodder is completely dependent on the"host" plant.
    4. Indian pipe, unlike the love vine, contains chlorophyll.

47. The author makes his point primarily through the use of
    1. sequence.
    2. examples.
    3. opinions.
    4. statistics.

48. The function of the second paragraph is to
    1. give effects of causes listed in the first paragraph.
    2. summarize ideas presented in the first paragraph.
    3. contrast the ideas given in the first paragraph.
    4. give additional examples of a concept discussed in the first paragraph.

At the head of the Scottish Council was Lord Drummond of Stobshall. This noble was the father of the Lady Margaret who was passion-ately loved by James IV. It is evident that he
5   indulged the young monarch with the company of Margaret. Lord Drummond doubtless had full intention of raising his daughter to the throne of Scotland.

Most historians agree that James married the
10   Lady Margaret Drummond with all the cere-monies of the Roman Catholic Church; however, the marriage was concealed. Hence, James IV remained without an acknowledged Queen.

Because the Scottish nobles and clergy
15   wished the King to ally himself with an English bride, James IV and Margaret Tudor were affianced in 1500. Nevertheless, the evil day was still distant when the King of Scotland would be forced to reveal his secret marriage with
20   Margaret Drummond or dismiss her to make way for the English Princess.

Loving his wedded wife and resolved not to forsake her, James prepared to bring the matter to a crisis. He was willing to struggle against all
25   opposition from his realm. While waiting for the moment in which to confront the opposing force, James received tragic news. At Drummond Castle, along with her two sisters Lady Fleming and Sybella Drummond, Margaret had been
30   poisoned.

(Strickland, 1851)

49. Who was James IV's first wife?
    1. Margaret Tudor
    2. Lady Margaret Drummond
    3. Sybella Drummond
    4. Lady Margaret Fleming

50. It can be concluded that Lord Drummond wanted his daughter to marry the king because
    1. he wanted a queen in the family.
    2. he knew Margaret bred James.
    3. he wanted revenge.
    4. she was pregnant.

51. The reader can infer that
    1. James was a bigamist.
    2. Margaret Tudor was too young to marry.
    3. Margaret Tudor had met Margaret Drummond.
    4. the Scottish nobles and clergy were suspects in Margaret Drummond's death.

52. Which of the following conclusions can be drawn from the passage?
    1. Lord Drummond was removed from office.
    2. The Scottish nobles mourned the sisters' deaths.
    3. James was forced to marry Margaret Tudor for political reasons.
    4. James was forced to reveal his secret marriage.

53. The author makes her point by using
    1. comparison/contrast.
    2. narration.
    3. analogy.
    4. historical narration.

There was nothing of the giant in the aspect of the man who was beginning to awaken on the sleeping-porch of a Dutch Colonial house in that residential district of Zenith known as Floral
5 Heights.

His name was George F. Babbitt. He was forty-six years old now, in April, 1920, and he made nothing in particular, neither butter nor shoes nor poetry, but he was <u>nimble</u> in the calling
10 of selling houses for more than people could afford to pay.

His large head was pink, his brown hair thin and dry. His face was babyish in slumber, despite his wrinkles and the red spectacle-dents
15 on the slopes of his nose. He was not fat but he was exceedingly well fed; his cheeks were pads, and the unroughened hand which lay helpless upon the khaki-colored blanket was slightly puffy. He seemed prosperous, extremely married and
20 unromantic; and, altogether unromantic appeared this sleeping-porch, which looked on one sizable elm, two respectable grass-plots, a cement driveway, and a corrugated iron garage. Yet Babbitt was again dreaming of the fairy child, a
25 dream more romantic than scarlet pagodas by a silver sea.

For years the fairy child had come to him. Where others saw but George Babbitt, she discerned gallant youth. She waited for him, in
30 the darkness beyond mysterious groves. When at last he could slip away from the crowded house he darted to her. His wife, his clamoring friends, sought to follow, but he escaped, the girl fleet beside him....

(Lewis, 1922)

54. The author's primary purpose is to
   1. explain a day in the life of George Babbitt.
   2. defend George Babbitt's behavior.
   3. describe the real George Babbitt.
   4. illustrate the relationship between Babbitt and the fairy child.

55. George Babbitt's occupation is that of a/an
   1. building contractor.
   2. real estate salesman.
   3. architect.
   4. manager.

56. "Fairy child" refers to
   1. Babbitt's mistress.
   2. Babbitt's wife.
   3. a small child.
   4. a dream figure.

57. As used in the passage, <u>nimble</u> means
   1. agile.
   2. trained.
   3. clever.
   4. spry.

58. The statement, "For years the fairy child had come to him," probably means
   1. a small child visits him regularly.
   2. his mistress comes to see him often.
   3. the fairy waits for him outside the house.
   4. he habitually uses a dream to escape the mundane things in his life.

59. The fairy child makes Babbitt feel
   1. older.
   2. guilty.
   3. liberated.
   4. wealthy.

60. The passage implies that Babbitt
   1. is somewhat unscrupulous in his business.
   2. is leaving his wife.
   3. is a handsome man.
   4. is happily married.

The Reading Test
Practice Test Four

We all know the story--the ugly duckling
transformed into swan after years of liquid
protein, the virtuous but oppressed stepdaughter
whose fairy godmother appears with a pumpkin
5   and a lifetime membership in Weight Watchers.
Our fantasies of transformation are desperate,
thrilling; when women imagine changing our lives,
we frequently begin with our weight. "I always
feel as if real life will begin tomorrow, next week,
10 sometime after the next diet," said one friend, a
talented writer who has been cheerfully married
for 12 years and a mother of five. "I know it's
crazy, but I won't be happy until I lose these
fifteen pounds." So far her efforts--like 90 percent
15 of all diets--have been unsuccessful. A few years
ago, when public opinion pollsters asked
respondents to name their greatest fear, 38
percent said "getting fat," Even very slender
women believed that their lives would be better if
20 only they could take off five pounds, or three, or
two. In a recent survey conducted for *Glamour* by
Susan Wooley, an associate professor in the
psychiatry department of the University of
Cincinnati College of Medicine, 75 percent of the
25 33,000 women who replied said that they were
"too fat," including, according to Wooley, "45
percent who in fact were underweight," by the
conservative 1959 Metropolitan Life Insurance
Company Height and Weight Table. (By the
30 revised 1983 table, which set generally higher
levels of up to 13 pounds for desirable weights,
these women would be even more underweight.)
Wooley, who is also co-director of the University's Eating Disorders Clinic, sees our
35 contemporary obsession with weight in part as a
perversion of feminism. "This striving for thinness
is striving to have a more masculine-type body,"
she points out. "As we join men's worlds, we
shouldn't be cashing in women's bodies. We
40 have to reclaim the right to have female bodies
and still be respected. Thinness has become the
cultural symbol of competency--if we buy that
symbol and foster it ourselves, that's a very self-
mutilating stand to take."

(Sternhell, 1985)

1. The primary purpose of this passage is to
    1. discuss women's obsessions with being
        thin.
    2. ridicule women's desire to be thin.

3. compare statistics of overweight and
    underweight women.
4. to explain successes and failures of
    popular diets.

2. The author implies that women have been
    1. denied employment because of their
        weight.
    2. unconcerned about their bodies.
    3. conditioned to believe they're too fat.
    4. manipulated by diet companies.

3. As used in the passage, perversion means
    1. destruction.
    2. avocation.
    3. distortion.
    4. perturbation.

4. Like the imaginary characters at the begin-
    ning of the passage, women's fantasies of
    transformation focus on
    1. thinness.
    2. desperation.
    3. thrills.
    4. virtue.

5. A survey showed that 75 percent of women
    polled replied that they were too fat. Of
    these, 45 percent were, in fact, underweight.
    This is an example of
    1. propaganda.
    2. situational irony.
    3. personification.
    4. sarcasm.

6. Wooley views this female obsession with
    thinness as all of the following except
    1. a self-mutilating stand.
    2. an attempt to have a masculine body.
    3. a feminist stand.
    4. a cultural symbol of competency.

7. The passage implies that a true feminist
    viewpoint would be that
    1. a woman can never be too thin.
    2. if a woman competes with a man, she
        should look masculine.
    3. women should have the right to have
        female bodies.
    4. thinness and competence in women are
        synonymous.

In most of the European countries, such as England, Germany, Belgium, and Italy, the building of a high-grade gun proceeds in the following manner: a barrel maker will start a gun
5   by making the barrels and will stay on this job until they are completed, from the <u>forged</u> or bulldozed tubes until the barrels are assembled with the lug, ribs, etc., are fully bored, and the lug machined. An action fitter will make the complete
10 action, a stock fitter will fit the action into the stock and then shape and finish the stock, and so on for each part of the making and assembly of the gun. Each gun is an individual unit, with no parts being anywhere near interchangeable with
15 the same parts of other guns. This is one extreme in the theory of gun building and is the one followed by such famous firms as Purdey, Boss, Churchill, etc., in England.

    At the other extreme is the mass production
20 concept used by many low-priced gun manufacturers. All parts are carefully machined to close tolerances, but are made so that the parts fit together without hand filing or similar work but go together interchangeably with a
25 tolerance between parts of, let us say, about .005 of an inch.

(Johnson, 1961)

8. Which of the following does the author use in the first paragraph?
  1. cause-effect
  2. sequence
  3. enumeration
  4. statistics

9. The author feels that
  1. gun making methods are extreme.
  2. the best guns are made by Purdey.
  3. gun making requires precision.
  4. guns are made for violence.

10. It can be inferred that handmade guns
  1. must be filed to fit with other guns.
  2. go together with no filing.
  3. cost more than mass produced guns.
  4. are easier to shoot.

11. Handmade guns differ with mass produced guns in that handmade guns
  1. have high tolerances.
  2. have parts that cannot be interchanged with other guns.
  3. have parts that fit together without filing.
  4. must be built in Europe.

12. As used in the passage <u>forged</u> means
  1. advanced.
  2. increased.
  3. formed.
  4. written.

Roosevelt told his advisers to string out Japanese American talks to gain time--time to fortify the Philippines, and time to check the fascists in Europe. "Let us do nothing to

5 precipitate a crisis," the President told the cabinet in November 1941. But by breaking the Japanese code ("Operation Magis"), Americans learned that Tokyo had committed itself to war with the United States if the oil embargo was not lifted. In

10 late November the Japanese rejected American proposals that they withdraw from Indochina. On December 1 decoding experts informed the president that Japanese task forces were being ordered into battle. Why not attack first? asked

15 aide Harry Hopkins. "No," said Roosevelt, "we would have to wait until it came." Secretary Stimson explained later that the United States let Japan fire the first shot so as "to have the full support of the American people" and "so that

20 there should remain no doubt in anyone's minds as to who were the aggressors." Fearing that they could not win a prolonged war, the Japanese plotted a daring raid on Pearl Harbor in Hawaii. A flotilla of Japanese aircraft carriers

25 crossed three thousand miles of ocean, and on the morning of December 7, planes stamped with the Rising Sun swept down on the unsuspecting American naval base, killing more than 2,400 people, sinking several battleships,

30 and smashing aircraft.

Though Roosevelt was distressed that the navy, his proud navy, had been caught by surprise, like many Americans he felt relief from the weeks of insufferable tension.

(Norton, 1990)

13. <u>Precipitate</u> used in the passage means
    1. prolong.
    2. hasten.
    3. prevent.
    4. avoid.

14. The last sentence is an example of which of the following?
    1. irony
    2. sarcasm
    3. satire
    4. analogy

15. According to the passage, Roosevelt waited until the war came to the U.S. because
    1. he feared he could not win a prolonged war.
    2. he wanted the American people behind him when the U.S. joined the war.
    3. he had no confidence in the U.S. navy.
    4. the Japanese were adamant in rejecting American proposals to withdraw from Indochina.

16. The passage suggests that
    1. Roosevelt anticipated the Pearl Harbor attack.
    2. Japan was dependent on oil.
    3. the Philippines were unimportant to the U.S.
    4. the American people were aggressors.

17. According to the passage, Japan objected to the United States'
    1. use of war codes.
    2. oil embargo and Indonesian proposal.
    3. occupation of the Philippines.
    4. interests in Europe.

18. Roosevelt's delay tactics were designed to
    1. precipitate a crisis with Japan.
    2. find solutions to coded messages.
    3. gain time to fortify the Philippines.
    4. help plan a conspiracy for Pearl Harbor.

It was a dreary night--fall to a landsman's eye; though they who better understood the signs of the heavens, as they are exhibited on the ocean, saw little more than the promise of
5 obscurity, and the usual hazards of darkness in a much-frequented area.

"This will be a dirty night, observed John Effingham, "and we may have occasion to bring in some of the <u>flaunting vanity</u> of the ship, ere
10 another morning returns."

"The vessel appears to be in good handset, returned Mr. Effingham: "I have watched them narrowly; for, I know not why, I have felt more anxiety on the occasion of this passage than on
15 any of the nine I have already made."

As he spoke, the tender father unconsciously bent his eyes on Eve, who leaned affectionately on his arm, steadying her light form against the pitching of the vessel. She understood his
20 feelings better than he did himself, possibly, since, accustomed to his fondest care from childhood, she well knew that he seldom thought of others, or even of himself, while her own wants or safety appealed to his unwearying love.

25 "Father," she said, smiling in his wistful face, "we have seen more troubled waters than these, far, and in a much frailer vessel. Do you not remember the Wallenstadt and its miserable skiff? Where I have heard you say there was
30 really danger, though we escaped from it all with a little fright."

"Perfectly well do I recollect it, love, nor have I forgotten our brave companion, and his good service, at that critical moment. But for his stout
35 arm and timely <u>succor</u>, we might not, as you say, have been quit for the fright."

Although Mr. Effingham looked only at his daughter while speaking, Mr. Sharp, who listened with interest, saw the quick, retreating glance of
40 Eve at Paul Blunt, and felt something like a chill in his blood as he perceived that her own cheeks seemed to reflect the glow which appeared on that of the young man.

(Cooper, 1838)

19. Which of the following does the author use in this passage?
    1. deductive logic
    2. statistics
    3. narration
    4. chronology

20. As used in the passage, <u>succor</u> means
    1. vessel.
    2. thinking.
    3. protection.
    4. clothing.

21. All of the following can be inferred about the story except
    1. there are five characters.
    2. the action takes place aboard a ship.
    3. the father has made nine previous sea voyages.
    4. a feeling of mutual admiration is secretly enjoyed by Paul and Eve.

22. The overall tone of the passage is one of
    1. cautious anticipation.
    2. despair.
    3. nostalgia.
    4. amusement.

23. It can be inferred from the passage that
    1. Paul Blunt was a passenger on the Wallenstadt.
    2. Eve is afraid of Mr. Sharp.
    3. Mr. Effingham, Eve's father, is aware of Eve's feelings for Paul.
    4. Eve and Paul were secretly involved.

24. The author uses <u>flaunting vanity</u> to refer to
    1. the ship's crew.
    2. the captain of the proud ship.
    3. the sails of the ship.
    4. the passengers.

25. What is the relationship between paragraph 3 and paragraph 5?
    1. a contrast between two voyages.
    2. opposing viewpoints.
    3. cause and effect.
    4. argumentation.

26. The author's purpose in paragraph four is to
    1. illustrate how selfish the daughter is.
    2. show the father's love for his daughter.
    3. reveal the father's anxiety.
    4. emphasize the daughter's loyalty.

The most important of the Enlightenment philosophers, at least from the American point of view, was John Locke. For it was Locke who cast the philosophy of natural law into the form
5   Americans found most agreeable.

He was educated at Christ Church, Oxford, a student of Thomas Hobbes, and made his mark in science and medicine as well as philosophy. In his famous *Essay Concerning Human*
10 *Understanding,* he argued that the human mind was a blank slate, devoid of <u>innate</u> ideas, and therefore essentially incapable of moral thinking. <u>It</u> learned its lessons through the five senses, he said, and it shaped its knowledge very much
15 according to self-interest.

Still, the mind was eminently reasonable. And through its powers of reason--what Locke specifically called *right reason*--the mind could discern the truths of Nature. For Locke, Nature
20 was not wild, amoral, and disorderly, as it has been for his mentor, Thomas Hobbes, but on the contrary a thing of harmony and affirmation.

Accordingly, when men lived in a state of nature, back before the days of recorded
25 history, Locke supposed that they lived a reasonably happy existence. All were equal and independent, and none had the right to harm another in his "life, health, liberty, or possession." Natural law, in other words, accorded to men
30 certain *natural rights*--specifically the rights of life, liberty, and property.

It was in this situation, according to Locke, that men came together and created govern-ment. The reason they did so was to protect their
35 rights from those few ill-disposed persons that any society might produce. What was important to note in this process was the fact that gov-ernment was created by free men, not the other way around, and that it was created specifically
40 to protect their natural rights. Rights did not derive from government. They could not be altered by government or abolished by government.

27. The author's primary purpose is to
    1. analyze the tenets of Hobbes.
    2. give examples of Hobbes' philosophy.
    3. explain Locke's philosophy of natural law.
    4. argue against Locke's philosophy.

28. <u>Innate</u> underlined means
    1. inherent.
    2. fanciful.
    3. creative.
    4. self-interest .

29. Locke believed the "mind" learned its lessons through
    1. moral thinking.
    2. nature.
    3. inborn characteristics.
    4. the five senses.

30. Which of the following is a characteristic of Thomas Hobbes' theory of Nature?
    1. harmony
    2. reason
    3. wildness
    4. affirmation

31. <u>It</u> in paragraph two refers to
    1. an idea.
    2. the mind.
    3. knowledge.
    4. nature.

The early nineteenth century brought the flowering of Romanticism, a cultural movement that stressed emotion, imagination, and individualism. In part, Romanticism was a

5 rebellion against the Neoclassicism of the eighteenth century Age of Reason. Romantic writers broke away from time-honored conventions and emphasized freedom of expression. Painters used bolder, more brilliant

10 colors and preferred dynamic motion to gracefully balanced poses.

But Romanticism was too diverse and complex to be defined by any single formula. It aimed to broaden all human horizons and

15 encompass the totality of our experience. The romantic movement was international in scope and influenced all the arts.

Emotional subjectivity was a basic quality of Romanticism in art. "All good poetry is the

20 spontaneous overflow of powerful feelings," wrote William Wordsworth, the English Romantic poet. And "spontaneous overflow" made much Romantic literature autobiographical; authors projected their personalities in their work. Walt Whitman,

25 the American poet, expressed this subjective attitude beautifully when he began a poem. "I celebrate myself, and sing myself."

Of all the inspirations for Romantic art, none was more important than nature. The physical

30 world was seen as a source of consolation and a mirror of the human heart. Wordsworth, for example, thought of nature as "the nurse, the guide, the guardian of my heart, and soul."

Romantic sensitivity to nature is revealed in

35 landscape painting, which attained new importance.

(Kamien, 1980)

32. The primary purpose of the passage is to
    1. persuade the reader to read romantic literature.
    2. show the effects of Romanticism.
    3. define and illustrate Romanticism.
    4. evaluate Romantic art.

33. The Romantic artists viewed nature as
    1. too harsh to be beneficial.
    2. unimportant.
    3. terrifying.
    4. comforting.

34. The purpose of the first paragraph of the passage is to
    1. shock the reader.
    2. contrast Romanticism with Neoclassicism.
    3. discuss time-honored conventions.
    4. discuss color and motion.

35. As used in the passage, emotional subjectivity refers to
    1. judging art work.
    2. the expression of the artists' feelings in their art forms.
    3. tales of terror.
    4. a gothic revival.

36. Romanticism affected
    1. Europe only.
    2. the Middle Ages.
    3. art and literature only.
    4. all of the arts.

37. The style of the writer may be described as
    1. romantic.
    2. informal.
    3. entertaining.
    4. academic.

38. Romanticism grew in popularity during
    1. the 1800's.
    2. the 1900's.
    3. the Age of Reason.
    4. The Age of Neoclassicism.

The promise of a smooth career, which my
first calm introduction to Thornfield Hall
seemed to pledge, was not belied on a longer
acquaintance with the place and its inmates.
5 Mrs. Fairfax turned out to be what she appeared,
a placid-tempered, kind-natured woman, of
competent education and average intelligence.
My pupil was a lively child, who had been spoilt
and indulged, and therefore was sometimes
10 wayward; but as she was committed entirely to
my care, and no injudicious interference from any
quarter ever thwarted my plans for her
improvement, she soon forgot her little freaks,
and became obedient and teachable. She had no
15 great talents, no marked traits of character, no
peculiar development of feeling or taste which
raised her one inch above the ordinary level of
childhood; but neither had she any deficiency or
vice which sunk her below it. She made
20 reasonable progress, entertained for me a
vivacious, though perhaps not very profound
affection; and by her simplicity, gay prattle and
efforts to please, inspired me, in return, with a
degree of attachment sufficient to make us both
25 content in each other's society.

(Brontë, 1847)

39. As used in the passage, placid means

1. quiet.
2. hot.
3. quick.
4. slow.

40. The child's abilities can best be described as

1. well above average.
2. below average.
3. average.
4. profoundly below average.

41. According to the passage all of the following
are true about the child except that

1. she was lively.
2. she was teachable.
3. she was spoiled.
4. she was defiant.

42. The passage states that the relationship
between teacher and pupil

1. was detached and cool.
2. was somewhat affectionate.
3. was extremely loving.
4. was strained and difficult.

43. The primary purpose of the passage is to
show that

1. the child needed to be educated.
2. the child was spoiled.
3. the teacher had her hands full.
4. the teacher and the student have a
   successful relationship.

44. The writer of this narration is

1. an objective character.
2. a participant in the narration.
3. the pupil.
4. an observer of the narration.

The special senses of taste and smell are called chemoreceptive senses. Chemoreception simply means the receiving of chemical stimuli. Many of the lower animals have chemical
5 receptors that are used to locate food or to move away from some <u>noxious</u> substances. Such behavior in response to chemical stimuli is called chemotaxis. Some insects have extremely sensitive chemoreceptors on their antennae and
10 mouth parts. A species of hawk moths, for example, is some 200 times more sensitive than humans in detecting the taste of sucrose (table sugar). Taste receptors of fish and amphibians may be widely distributed in the skin. Many fish,
15 by tasting the water, can detect food or the presence of an enemy fish in the area.

In humans, the receptors for taste are located in the taste buds found mostly on the tongue. There are four basic tastes that we can
20 detect; sweet, sour, salty, and bitter. Sweet and salty are tasted mostly on the tip of the tongue, sour along the sides, and bitter at the back of the tongue. The various substances that we taste must be in solution. This is one of the functions
25 of saliva in the mouth. Taste impulses are transmitted from the taste buds along several cranial nerves to the brain. As we grow older, the taste buds tend to degenerate and we become less sensitive to various tastes or flavors.
30 The sense of smell varies considerably among animals. Most mammals have a highly developed sense of smell, whereas this sense is very poor in most birds. Some whales are believed to have no sense of smell at all. Various
35 forms of animal behavior are influenced by smell. Smell may be used by fish such as salmon to return to their spawning grounds. The mother seal smells her newborn infant and thus is able to recognize her pup from the others.
40 Our sense organs of smell are found in epithelial tissue lining the upper portion of the nasal cavities. Neurons called olfactory cells lie within the epithelium and are the actual sensory receptors of odors. Nerve impulses from the
45 olfactory cells are transmitted along the olfactory nerve (one of the cranial nerves) to the cerebral cortex, where they are interpreted as odor. We have millions of these olfactory cells, which are capable in many instances of detecting
50 thousands of different odors. It is interesting that

we remember odors quite well and recognize them if we smell them at a later time. This applies with equal emphasis to body odors or Chanel No. 5.

(Graham, 1987)

45. The primary purpose of this passage is to explain
    1. how many animals and humans receive and respond to chemical stimuli through taste and smell.
    2. various forms of animal and human responses.
    3. where the receptors for the four basic tastes are located in the taste buds.
    4. that chemoreception is the receiving of chemical stimuli, and chemotaxis is the behavior in response to it.

46. In humans the bitter taste impulses are transmitted from the
    1. tip of tongue, through cranial nerves, to brain interpretation.
    2. through saliva to top of tongue, to brain, through cranial nerves to interpretation.
    3. the back of the tongue, through cranial nerves, to brain interpretation.
    4. along sides of tongue, through cranial nerves, to brain interpretation.

47. The author uses which of the following?
    1. persuasion
    2. comparison
    3. irony
    4. examples

48. The sensory receptors of odor are the
    1. cranial nerves.
    2. cerebral cortex.
    3. nasal cavities.
    4. olfactory cells.

49. As used in the passage, <u>noxious</u> means
    1. unknown.
    2. salty.
    3. injurious.
    4. corrupting.

President Harry S. Truman's Address to
Congress, March 12, 1947

　　The people of a number of countries of the
world have recently had <u>totalitarian regimes</u>
5　forced upon them against their will. The
Government of the United States has made
frequent protests against coercion and
intimidation, in violation of the Yalta agreement,
in Poland, Rumania, and Bulgaria. I must also
10　state that in a number of other countries there
have been similar developments.

　　At the present moment in world history nearly
every nation must choose between alternative
ways of life. The choice is too often not a free
15　one.

　　One way of life is based upon the will of the
majority, and is distinguished by free institutions,
representative government, free elections,
guarantees of individual liberty, freedom of
20　speech and religion, and freedom from political
oppression.

　　The second way of life is based upon the will
of a minority forcibly imposed upon the majority.
It relies upon terror and oppression, a controlled
25　press and radio, fixed elections, and the
suppression of personal freedoms.

　　I believe that it must be the policy of the
United States to support free peoples who are
resisting attempted subjugation by armed
30　minorities or by outside pressures.

　　I believe that we must assist free people to
work out their own destinies in their own way.

　　I believe that our help should be primarily
through economic and financial aid which is
35　essential to economic stability and orderly political
processes.... I therefore ask the Congress for
assistance to Greece and Turkey in the amount of
$400,000,000.

50. When Truman discusses the ways of life, he
    uses

    1. definition.
    2. contrast.
    3. comparison.
    4. narrative.

51. All of the following are opinions except that

    1. help should be primarily through
       economic aid.
    2. it must be the policy of the U.S. to
       support free people.
    3. Truman asked Congress for assistance
       to Greece and Turkey.
    4. people must work out their own destinies
       in their own ways.

52. We can conclude that Truman believed that

    1. the U.S. was in danger.
    2. minorities are militaristic.
    3. every nation should have a choice
       between alternative ways of life.
    4. Congress had not planned an accurate
       budget.

53. The reader can infer that <u>totalitarian regimes</u>
    are

    1. democratic.
    2. communistic.
    3. coercive.
    4. socialistic.

54. Truman's primary purpose is to

    1. entertain.
    2. describe.
    3. sympathize.
    4. persuade.

55. Truman's attitude toward totalitarian regimes is

    1. optimistic.
    2. condemning.
    3. quizzical.
    4. dramatic.

Manatees inhabit saltwater coastal regions and freshwater rivers throughout the tropics and subtropics of Africa, Asia, and the Americas, where they graze on virtually any vegetation they
5   find.

Manatees prey on nothing but plants, which helps keep waterways from clogging with vegetation. And they have developed no defenses since nothing preys on them, except
10 humans, a reality for which they have not adapted. Manatees, believed to live up to sixty years, are gentle mammals not much brighter than a cow--a bad combination for survival. The Florida manatee can grow to more than thirteen
15 feet in length and weigh more than 3,000 pounds.... Fossils indicate that the North American manatee ancestor lived a million years ago.

Today their surviving relatives will face
20 hunters throughout much of their habitat. Especially in poor areas such as the Amazon River system and southeast Asia, manatees provide a bountiful and easy harvest of meat and leather. The hunt demands no more skill or effort
25 than would a foray into a cow pasture. And bone is another commodity: In Belize, vendors hawk letters and trinkets carved from manatee bone.

We have already lost the world's only coldwater manatee. Named Stellar's sea cow for
30 the naturalist who discovered it in 1741 in the Bering Sea, this largest of all manatees (at thirty feet long, it weighed more than three tons) met with extinction at the hands of hunters within twenty-seven years after its first sighting.
35 Explorers in the waters of present-day Alaska marveled at how easily they harpooned the giant, toothless mammals; the harmless sea cows actually swam up to their boats, and apparently out of curiosity, looked them right in the eyes and
40 into their gun sights.

(Kiely, 1991)

56. As used in the passage, the word <u>foray</u> means
    1. casual glance.
    2. venture.
    3. small gathering.
    4. picnic.

57. The only significant threat to manatees is
    1. other natural enemies.
    2. cold sea water.
    3. humans.
    4. inadequate vegetation.

58. From the passage, the reader can infer that
    1. manatees are dangerous to humans.
    2. manatees are intelligent creatures.
    3. manatees' ancestors are ancient mammals.
    4. manatees may be found in all waters of the earth.

59. To support the idea that manatees inspire feelings of camaraderie with humans, the author uses
    1. appeal to emotions.
    2. statistics.
    3. personal experience.
    4. comparison and contrast.

60. Which of the following statements drawn from the passage could be a fact and is NOT an opinion?
    1. The harmless sea cows swam up to their boats and out of curiosity looked them right in the eyes.
    2. Manatees are gentle mammals and not much brighter than a cow.
    3. The hunt demands no more skill or effort than would a foray into a cow pasture.
    4. We have already lost the world's only cold water manatee.

The Reading Test
Practice Test Five

Between 1870 and 1914, the major powers of Europe worked to maintain both domestic and international stability. Accomplishment of this goal was facilitated by continuing
5 industrialization. Despite periodic trade depressions, general prosperity increased for almost all classes of society at least until 1900. And prosperity, in its turn, helped to produce stability, allowing for the establishment in many
10 countries of social welfare systems designed to benefit workers and their families, and thus to gain their political allegiance.

At the same time, various factors operated to make the achievement of a generally stable
15 Western world difficult, and ultimately impossible. First, the process of nation-building, which had resulted in the dramatic creation of a modern Germany and Italy, left potential conflict in its wake. Second, although the majority of citizens in
20 most western European countries participated at least indirectly in the governance of their country and enjoyed certain guaranteed rights, heated debate continued as to the political usefulness of such arrangements. And across Europe,
25 socialists contended against the political strength of the middle classes.

Internal tension resulted as well from shifts in class structure and class consciousness. One of the most dramatic occupational changes to occur
30 in late-nineteenth-century Europe was the rapid growth of a lower-to middle-level, "white-collar" class of bureaucrats, employed in commerce and industry and in expanding government departments. The post office, the railways, the
35 police, and the bureaus charged with the task of administering various social welfare and insurance programs, all demanded growing numbers of recruits.

(Burns, 1973)

1. The primary purpose of this passage is to
   1. describe the prosperity of a divided Europe.
   2. contrast "white-collar" workers with "blue-collar" workers.
   3. explain how major European powers worked to maintain domestic and international stability.
   4. discuss various examples of European instability.

2. The second paragraph is chiefly developed through the use of
   1. listing.
   2. propaganda.
   3. analogy.
   4. comparison/contrast.

3. According to the passage, which of the following factors contributed most to the stability of Europe between 1870 and 1914?
   1. shifts in class structure
   2. socialism
   3. industrialization
   4. expanding government departments

4. The most important shift in European class consciousness was the
   1. creation of a new welfare system.
   2. emergence of new socialistic nations.
   3. development of a new "white-collar" class.
   4. bureaucratic liberalism.

5. The creation of modern Germany and Italy
   1. promoted peace.
   2. started a war.
   3. promoted unity.
   4. opened the way for national struggles.

6. As used in the passage, facilitated means
   1. curbed.
   2. halted.
   3. accelerated.
   4. made easier.

The connection between the mind (psyche) and the body (soma) is not completely understood, but we do know that tension in children can set the stage for psychosomatic disease
5 later on. Childhood tension and anxiety not only shape the child's later personality, they can produce specific organ diseases. High blood pressure and coronary disease have been linked with some certainty to an ambitious, hard-driving,
10 and stressful style of life. As another example of mind-body linkage, there is recent evidence to suggest that a susceptibility to infection may be closely associated with tension. In a preschool in Cambridge, Massachusetts, the teachers
15 reported that they could predict which fathers were writing theses and which mothers were taking exams by the number of infections that the children suffered. Even more obvious is the incidence of acute respiratory infections in
20 small children just as their parents are about to go away on a trip, or make a move to another city. This may simply be a matter of lowered resistance which results from tension in a household.
25 More serious are the organic complaints commonly associated with stress, such as asthma, eczema, stomach ulcers, and colitis. In an individual with one of these diseases, a particular part of the body (respiratory system,
30 skin, stomach, or large intestine) is vulnerable to stress. Pressure from the environment of any sort causes these organs to react with symptoms and a spiraling cycle of psychosomatic disease may result.

(Child Health Encyclopedia, 1978)

7. According to the passage, the connection between mind and body

1. is unlikely.
2. is not of interest to doctors.
3. Is not discussed In medical journals.
4. may be related to stress.

8. This article was probably written by a(n)

1. school teacher.
2. health professional.
3. childcare provider.
4. athletic coach.

9. A "spiraling cycle of psychosomatic disease" (last sentence) is one which

1. makes one dizzy.
2. lasts a long time.
3. recurs often.
4. effects several organs progressively.

10. It is implied that children may get respiratory disease when they

1. fear abandonment.
2. stay out in the cold air.
3. are around pollen.
4. cough.

11. Colitis occurs in the

1. lungs.
2. skin.
3. stomach.
4. large intestine.

12. A susceptibility to infection may be closely associated with

1. soma.
2. heart disease.
3. asthmatic symptoms.
4. tension.

Apart from its other claims to fame, the importance assigned by Classical Greece to individual achievement assures it a place among the great ages of man. There were earlier great
5 ages, but those periods were dominated for the most part by absolute rulers of monolithic states; the truly creative individuals who certainly existed in Egypt, Mesopotamia and Anatolia are almost entirely anonymous.

10 Classical Greece was different. We know the names of more than 20,000 individuals in Athens, alone, most of them recorded because of their participation in civic affairs. In many aspects of life, we find that the beginnings of the various
15 literary genres of the schools of philosophy, of the major artistic trends are all associated with individual men. Even in the crafts the individual stands out. Recent excavations in the heart of Athens have yielded over a thousand "ostraka"
20 (the potsherds, or pottery fragments), each bearing the name of some outstanding man-- Aristides, Themistocles, Pericles, and many others. The fine pottery made in Athens in the Sixth and Fifth Centuries B C. can be assigned to
25 some five hundred different masters, many of whom signed their products.

Each "ostraka" offers interesting proof that at some stage in their careers these men were suspected by their fellow citizens of aiming at
30 tyranny. These pottery fragments remind us that the Athenians were ever mindful of the need to maintain a balance between personal ambition and the civic interest.

(Bowra, 1965)

13. Classical Greece is compared to
    1. absolute rulers of monolithic states.
    2. earlier great ages.
    3. ostraka.
    4. individual achievement.

14. Greece was different from Egypt because
    1. Egyptians were more intelligent.
    2. creative individuals in Greece were repressed.
    3. Egypt has more people.
    4. creative individuals in Greece were not anonymous.

15. The passage suggests that
    1. the individual in earlier times was not considered important.
    2. the individual in Classical Greece was not important.
    3. the absolute rulers of monolithic states were creative.
    4. Athenians have always been obsessed with personal ambition.

16. Recent excavations in the heart of Athens have yielded
    1. the remains of Pericles.
    2. information on literary genres of the times.
    3. skeletons of 20,000 individuals.
    4. pottery fragments.

17. The word "ostraka" means
    1. potsherds.
    2. proof.
    3. balance.
    4. name.

18. The author of this passage would probably agree that
    1. the focus of Classical Greece was on the achievement of the individual.
    2. the main contribution of Classical Greece was the findings of the excavations.
    3. the major trend in Mesopotamia was to exalt the individual.
    4. truly creative persons did not exist in Egypt, Mesopotamia and Anatolia.

Few sculptors in history have been more skilled, more productive, or more representative of their age than Bernini, the genius of Italian Baroque art. Bernini carved his first statue, a
5 classical tableau of the infant god Zeus, when he was 17 or younger, and his last, a figure of Christ, when he was 81. In the six decades between, he not only helped to revolutionize sculpture but also became one of the most
10 sought-after architects in Rome, filling the city with spectacular churches, piazzas, and palaces for a succession of cardinals and popes.

The style that Bernini helped to originate cast off conventional restraints. Exuberant, theatrical,
15 yet often intensely personal, it attempted to destroy the boundaries between art and life; under Bernini's own masterful <u>chisel</u>, gripping hands often seemed about to move and marble tears to flow. Bernini perfected, and taught other
20 Baroque artists innumerable ways of creating the illusion of reality. Not only was he a master at reproducing the human form, but he captured the emotions of his subjects as well. Once . . . he was so carried away by his passion that, when
25 carving a figure of a saint martyred by burning, he put his own leg into a fire in order to study the agony on his face.

So convincing did his sculpture become that a Roman cardinal once pointed at a man who
30 had just finished posing for Bernini and said, "This is the portrait of Monsignor Montoya." Then, turning to Bernini's bust, the cardinal added, "<u>This is Montoya</u>."

(Barnouw, 1976)

19. Bernini was a(n)
    1. painter and sculptor.
    2. sculptor and architect.
    3. architect and painter.
    4. fresco artist.

20. The author views Bernini with
    1. objectivity.
    2. impartiality.
    3. skepticism.
    4. admiration.

21. Bernini's first statue was
    1. David.
    2. a piazza.
    3. Christ.
    4. Zeus.

22. It is suggested by the passage that Bernini
    1. was interested in religious motifs.
    2. was involved in creating pagan statues.
    3. was careful to follow established principles of art.
    4. was emotionally unstable.

23. In this passage <u>chisel</u> means
    1. chip.
    2. envision.
    3. instrument.
    4. carve.

24. What is implied by the following quote: "<u>This is Montoya</u>"?
    1. The Roman cardinal was extremely confused.
    2. The bust was a poor representation of the model.
    3. Montoya's features were like marble.
    4. Bernini's sculpture was very realistic.

The South is a land rich with historical continuity, a land of long days, bright in the sun and slow to cool in the evening shadows. On a summer's day the heat dances visibly along
5   macadamized highways and dusty country roads. The ubiquitous screen doors shut with loud report on hollow stillness. Soft Southern voices add to the muted effect.

Everywhere there is a sense of something
10 old and stable. Go west in North Carolina through the Great Smokies to Cherokee at twilight and watch Cherokee Indians from the nearby reservation act out the tragic story of their ancestors' trek across the "trail of tears" in the
15 days of Andrew Jackson.

New Orleans is a special South within the South. The gems of architecture of the French quarter are perhaps unmatched in this country. Eighty miles upriver is Baton Rouge, where Huey
20 Long built a skyscraper capitol.

The Gulf Coast makes a wide arc from Biloxi to the southern top of Florida's west coast, a coastal vacation land running down to the citrus groves and cattle farms and thriving tourist towns
25 of Florida.

For all the changes from state to state, when the midday sun has softened, when afternoon shadows dapple tree-shaded streets, when children return to play after their naps, there is
30 always Savannah or Charleston with red-brick sidewalks and colonial architecture and patio gardens to remind us of the unique beauty of the South.

(Runyan, 1955)

25. The author gets his point across primarily through the use of
   1. narration.
   2. examples.
   3. contrast.
   4. argument.

26. Muted in paragraph one means
   1. deaf.
   2. loud.
   3. softened.
   4. mutant.

27. The South is characterized as
   1. technologically advanced regions.
   2. backwards.
   3. industrial.
   4. old and unique.

28. The author's attitude toward the South can be described as
   1. condescending.
   2. ridiculing.
   3. skeptical.
   4. appreciative.

29. The phrase "a special South within the South" used when describing New Orleans means
   1. New Orleans is not geographically located in the South.
   2. New Orleans is not Southern.
   3. New Orleans is the only real Southern town.
   4. New Orleans has its own kind of Southern culture.

The development of horticulture led to various alterations in man's way of life in both the Old World and the New, but these changes came about gradually. Long after farming was first begun, hunting and gathering must have continued to be the main source of subsistence, with horticulture only a sideline. Even after farming became a major source of food, seminomadic conditions persisted when soil resources were depleted, forcing a shift to new quarters. For example, a Neolithic settlement in the Rhineland consisting of 21 households is estimated to have been occupied seven times during a 450-year period. Sites like this were inhabited for about ten years and then abandoned to give the soil time to <u>regenerate</u> itself. Nevertheless, the potential for permanent settlement based on food production was strengthened in the Neolithic period.

Horticulture also facilitated the <u>preservation</u> of food. Grain could now be stored for the future. Hunters have no special problem if their region is rich in game, but, if it is not and if they have no techniques for salting, drying, or preserving meat, they are out of luck. Perhaps the Eskimos were fortunate to live in the natural icebox in winter; their food could be cached out of reach of dogs and wolves for later consumption. The Blackfoot and other Indian tribes of the Plains pounded dried lean meat, sometimes mixed with berries and bone marrow, to make pemmican, which they stored in buffalo skin containers.

(Blitzer, 1967)

30. In paragraph one, the example of the Neolithic settlement in the Rhineland supports the idea that
    1. farming sites were abandoned when the soil was depleted.
    2. permanent settlements based on food production were strengthened.
    3. hunting and gathering societies persisted even after farming became a major source of food.
    4. the shift to horticulture occurred suddenly.

31. As used in the passage, <u>preservation</u> means
    1. protection.
    2. spoilage.
    3. storage.
    4. icebox.

32. The primary purpose of the passage is to explain
    1. how farming changed the way of life in the Old World and the New.
    2. the development of horticulture in the Old World.
    3. the techniques of food preservation in the Old World and the New.
    4. the problems in preserving meat in the Old World.

33. The author mentions the Eskimos and their natural icebox as an example of those
    1. who have problems preserving meat.
    2. whose region is rich in game.
    3. who can easily preserve game.
    4. who needed to preserve meat.

34. As a result of the development of horticulture
    1. people became seminomadic.
    2. food preservation methods were developed.
    3. hunting and gathering continued to be the only source of subsistence.
    4. hunters were out of luck.

35. As used in the passage, <u>regenerate</u> means
    1. reform.
    2. irrigate.
    3. respond to.
    4. renew.

James I set himself the task of restoring peace and order to the turbulent Highlands, and to this end he ordered a Parliament to assemble at Inverness. All the Northern Chieftains, not
5 daring to disobey, proceeded to Inverness. Immediately on entering Parliament Hall, no less than forty of them were arrested, loaded with irons, and cast into prison. Many of them were subsequently executed.

10 Angry about the severity and restraint imposed upon them, the nobles conspired against the King's person. The smoldering spirit of treason culminated in a plot to murder him, the time chosen being during the Christmas
15 festivities. The place chosen was the Monastery of Perth where the King and Queen were staying. There a bank of the rebellious nobles broke into the Royal bedchamber. In the presence of the Queen and her ladies, they seized and murdered
20 the King who was clad only in a nightshirt. He had no weapon of defense, but he made a desperate attempt to resist. He was literally hacked to death by his kinsmen, Sir Robert Graham and Sir Robert Stewart.

25 The Queen had made a brave attempt to save her husband, during which she herself was wounded by the assailants. The next day she hunted them down and executed them with a terrible vengeance. Graham was nailed alive to a
30 tree and so dragged through the city of Perth. Afterwards he was tortured with hot pincers, while his son was beheaded before his dying eyes.

(Francis, 1928)

36. This passage primarily focuses on
    1. the nobles of Scotland during James I reign.
    2. James I's accomplishments.
    3. the events surrounding the murder of James I.
    4. Scotland during Medieval times.

37. The person who tried to save the King was
    1. the Queen.
    2. one of the Queen's ladies.
    3. Sir Robert Graham.
    4. a kinsman of James.

38. As used in the passage, smoldering means
    1. open.
    2. deteriorating.
    3. repressed anger.
    4. smoke-filled.

39. The word culminated in paragraph two means
    1. began.
    2. boiled.
    3. ruminated.
    4. ended.

40. The passage implies that
    1. the King blamed the nobles for the country's unrest.
    2. Scotland was normally quite serene.
    3. The Queen was a smarter ruler than the King.
    4. Kings usually carry weapons.

41. The reader can conclude that
    1. Graham became King.
    2. the Queen took control after the King was murdered.
    3. the nobles overthrew the government.
    4. Robert Stewart became Regent of Scotland.

The shortage of managerial talent posed problems for the early entrepreneur. The salaried manager, i.e. those in the layer of management below entrepreneur, were usually illiterate
5 workmen promoted from the worker ranks because they evidenced a greater degree of technical skills or had the ability (often the physical strength) to keep discipline. They were paid only a little more than the other workers and
10 more often than not were attracted to the managerial position because it gave them the power to hire wives and children to work in the factory. Untrained in the intricacies of managing, the manager was left on his own to develop his
15 own leadership style. Problems were met and solved on an *ad hoc* basis, and only a few managers could learn from the experiences of others in solving factory problems or handling people. The general view of leadership was that
20 success or failure to produce results depended upon the "character" of the leader, upon his personal traits and idiosyncrasies, and not upon any generalized concepts of leadership.

Other sources of management talent
25 provided little enlightenment. Entrepreneurs used relatives in managerial positions frequently, presumably based on the assumption that they were more trustworthy or would act to preserve their potential inheritance. This device also
30 served as a training ground to secure ownership and control in the family for the next generation. Another source of talent was the "counting-house"; entrepreneurs recruited likely looking bank clerks and tellers, thinking they probably
35 had both business and financial acumen. For developing managers, the entrepreneurs relied on osmosis and experience on the job to furnish these recruits with the necessary knowledge.

(Wren, 1979)

42. The passage most likely appeared in a
    1. history text chapter.
    2. career guide.
    3. trade magazine.
    4. chapter in a management text.

43. As used in the passage, acumen most nearly means
    1. interests.
    2. keen insight.
    3. ambition.
    4. methods.

44. From the passage, it can be inferred that managerial leaders in early history were chosen on the basis of
    1. scientific data.
    2. graduating classes.
    3. technical skills.
    4. applicant lists.

45. The term intricacies as used in the passage means
    1. complexities.
    2. structures.
    3. labor forces.
    4. financial aspects.

46. The function of the second paragraph is to
    1. give results of the causes listed in the first paragraph.
    2. summarize ideas presented in the first paragraph.
    3. contrast the ideas given in the first paragraph.
    4. provide additional examples of a concept discussed in the first paragraph.

47. As used in the passage, entrepreneurs most nearly means
    1. laborers.
    2. managers.
    3. owners.
    4. businessmen.

48. The best title for the passage would be
    1. The Search for Managerial Talent.
    2. The Development of Managerial Talent.
    3. The Role of the Family in Early Management History.
    4. Characteristics of Early Entrepreneurs.

Modern Dublin sometimes seems blind to its heritage. Eighteenth-Century buildings, which in England or almost anywhere in Western Europe would be swathed with notices advertising their
5 history and times of opening, here remain tattered, patched, crudely adapted to new functions. All over the city, 18th-century facades are obscured, or their proportions mangled, by neon-lit plastic signs. Even the columned quad-
10 rant of the Rotunda is partly obliterated by brash advertisements for the films being shown within.

Over front doors, plaster saints or images of Pope John and President Kennedy (both of whom would be sainted instantly if it were left to
15 an Irish vote)--look out from semi-elliptical or rectangular fanlights whose designers would have deplored such visual clutter, let alone the religious sentiments. Old men in raincoats snore on iron seats skillfully wrought by Victorian
20 craftsmen. Beneath converted Victorian gas lamps, beside huge cast-iron post-boxes still bearing the letters VR, initials of the Queen under whose dominion they were erected, above cobbles and antique granite pavings--some of
25 them chipped away, flake by flake, by masons to accommodate decorative coal-hole covers-- Dublin passes unheeding. To the despair of aesthetic purists, Dublin refuses to turn herself into a museum. She is more heart than head,
30 and antiquarians can go hang.
(Lehane, 1978)

49. It can be inferred that Dubliners are blind to their heritage because
    1. they don't care about Dublin.
    2. they are not interested in preserving antiquities.
    3. they don't want to be compared to the English.
    4. it is too costly to renovate old buildings.

50. The Rotunda is now a
    1. memorial.
    2. historical monument.
    3. cinema.
    4. government building.

51. It is suggested that Dubliners
    1. admired John F. Kennedy.
    2. disliked Pope John.
    3. sympathized with Queen Victoria.
    4. voted for President Kennedy.

52. What were installed during Queen Victoria's reign?
    1. cobbles
    2. antiquarians
    3. masons
    4. mail boxes

53. Gas lamps were used
    1. when President Kennedy was in office.
    2. in Medieval Dublin.
    3. during the Victorian Age.
    4. to light the plaster saints.

54. As used in the passage, swathed means
    1. clothed.
    2. bound.
    3. displayed.
    4. trashed.

It was inevitable that the drama should decline after Shakespeare, for the simple reason that there was no other great enough to fill his place. Aside from this, other causes were at
5 work, and the chief of these was at the very source of the Elizabethan dramas. It must be remembered that our first playwrights wrote to please their audiences; that the drama rose in England because of the desire of a patriotic
10 people to see something of the stirring life of the times reflected on the stage. For there were no papers or magazines in those days, and people came to the theaters not only to be amused but to be informed. Like children, they wanted to see
15 a story acted; and like men, they wanted to know what it meant. Shakespeare fulfilled their desire. He gave them their story, and his genius was great enough to show in every play not only their own life and passions but something of the
20 meaning of all life, and of that eternal justice which uses the war of human passions for its own great ends. Thus good and evil mingle freely in his dramas; but the evil is never attractive, and the good triumphs as inevitably as fate. Though
25 his language is sometimes <u>coarse</u>, we are to remember that it was the custom of his age to speak somewhat coarsely, and that in language, as in thought and feeling, Shakespeare is far above most of his contemporaries.
30 With his successors all this was changed. The audience itself had gradually changed, and in place of plain people eager for a story and for information, we see a larger and larger proportion of those who went to the play because they had
35 nothing else to do. They wanted amusement only, and since they had blunted by idleness the desire for simple and wholesome amusement, they called for something more sensational. Shakespeare's successors catered to the
40 <u>depraved</u> tastes of this new audience.

(Long, 1945)

55. The author believes that Shakespeare was exceedingly skilled at
    1. writing for children.
    2. portraying current events of his day.
    3. writing wholesome amusement.
    4. revealing the meaning of life through the passions of his characters.

56. The author believes that the decline of the Elizabethan drama was partly due to
    1. people having no further interest in theater.
    2. the fact that no one could replace Shakespeare.
    3. inferior Elizabethan actors.
    4. the decline of patriotism.

57. <u>Coarse</u> as used in the passage means
    1. inferior quality.
    2. boring.
    3. vulgar.
    4. circumspect.

58. <u>Depraved</u> as used in the passage means
    1. corrupt.
    2. depressed.
    3. distant.
    4. impersonal.

59. In contrast to Shakespeare, playwrights who came later
    1. were plain people.
    2. were lazy and indifferent toward their audiences.
    3. pandered to morally corrupt audiences.
    4. avoided the triumph of good.

60. Which of the following words could be used at the beginning of the second paragraph?
    1. Because
    2. In other words
    3. However
    4. Similarly

The Reading Test
Practice Test Six

In the course of my life, I have discovered a success principle that has enabled me to accumulate tens of millions of dollars while maintaining a constant state of happiness,
5 emotional balance, and zest for life. Success with money, family, relationships, health, and careers is the ability to reach your personal objectives in the shortest time, with the least effort and with the fewest mistakes. The goals you set for
10 yourself and the strategies you choose become your blueprint or plan.

Strategies are like recipes: choose the right ingredients, mix them in the correct proportions, and you'll always produce the same predictable
15 result: in this case, financial success. The success strategies for managing money and building wealth are called Money Strategies. By learning to use Money Strategies as a part of your day-to-day life, financial frustration and
20 failure will become a thing of the past. Why then, do so many people find it so difficult to accumulate wealth and, more importantly, to enjoy the journey? There are two reasons: not being clear about what they are after and not
25 knowing the strategies for achieving it.

. . . The two most important words in managing money and building wealth are "take control." No one will ever watch your money or your financial future as well as you--no broker,
30 financial planner, or insurance agent. Control begins with your written plan and is exercised through your choice of money strategies. The correct strategies turn wealth building, like walking, into a series of easy-to-accomplish
35 steps.

(Givens, 1988)

1. According to the author, the two most important factors in achieving success are
   1. money and happiness.
   2. money and more money.
   3. goals and strategies.
   4. goals and money.

2. The expression "strategies are like recipes" is an example of
   1. analogy.
   2. expository writing.
   3. argumentation.
   4. satire.

3. The passage suggests that
   1. the author was once poor.
   2. the author took control of his life.
   3. the author thinks building wealth is not easy.
   4. only a few can ever be wealthy.

4. By comparing wealth building to walking, the author is implying that
   1. walking is difficult.
   2. making money is difficult.
   3. anyone can make money.
   4. making money is not for everyone.

5. The author of this article would probably agree with which of the following?
   1. Most people are not intelligent enough to build wealth.
   2. Most financial planners are incompetent.
   3. Ultimately people are responsible for themselves.
   4. People should trust insurance companies.

All this happened, as on the previous afternoon, in the forest, under a lean-to used by
clogmakers. Its walls were of straw, and it had a
roof so low that they had to stoop. They sat close
5   together on a bed of dry leaves.

From that day forward, they wrote to one
another regularly every evening. Emma took her
letters to the end of the garden and hid them in a
crack of the terrace, close to the river. Rodolphe
10 fetched them, and left his own in the same
hiding-place. Always she found <u>them</u> too short.

One morning, when Charles had gone out
before it was light, the whim took her to see
Rodolphe without a moment's delay. It was
15 possible to reach LaHuchette quickly, spend an
hour there, and be back in Yonville before its
inhabitants were awake. The very thought of
such an expedition set her panting with desire,
and she was soon half-way across the meadows,
20 walking fast, and not once looking back.

Day was beginning to break. From far off
Emma recognized her lover's house by the two
fan-tailed vanes which stood out black in the half-
light.

25 Beyond the farmyard stood a solid mass
which could only be the Chateau. She entered it
as though the walls at her approach had opened
of themselves. A great staircase rose in a single
flight to the upper corridor. She turned the handle
30 of a door, and at once, on the far side of the
room, saw the figure of a man asleep. It was
Rodolphe. She uttered a cry.

'You!' he said: and again, 'you!--how on earth
did you get here?. . . Your dress is all wet!'

35 'I love you!' she replied: and threw her arms
about his neck.

This first bold stroke having succeeded,
Emma got into the way, whenever Charles left
the house early, of dressing quickly and creeping
40 <u>stealthily</u> down the terrace steps to the
waterside.

(Flaubert, 1881)

6. As underlined, <u>them</u> refers to
   1. her love affairs.
   2. letters.
   3. their visits.
   4. Chateau walls.

7. Emma was trying to hide her secret love from
   1. Charles.
   2. Rodolphe.
   3. servants.
   4. the village.

8. <u>Stealthily</u> as used in the passage means
   1. soundly.
   2. secretly.
   3. relevantly.
   4. intensely.

9. Emma lived in
   1. La Huchette.
   2. Yonville.
   3. the forest.
   4. a chateau.

10. In the last paragraph, "got into the way" most
nearly means
   1. created a burden.
   2. established a purpose.
   3. developed a routine.
   4. become a pest.

A Type A personality, either male or female, is characterized by intense drive, aggressiveness, ambition, competitiveness, and the habit of competing with the clock. He or she
5 may give an impression of iron control, or wear a mask of easy geniality, but the strain glints through.

By contrast, Type B's manner is more genuinely easy. He is open. He is not glancing at
10 his watch nor preoccupied with achievement. Type B is less competitive and even speaks in a more modulated style.

Most people are mixtures of Type A and Type B, of course, and Rosenman and Friedman
15 have sharpened their interviewing techniques to the point where they recognize four distinct subdivisions of each group, ranging from A-1, the most virulent, down to B-4, the mildest. The ways the answers are spoken are as important as the
20 responses to the interview question. An impatient subject, who shows his impatience, is probably an A, no matter what he says. Some questions even call for a pretense of stammering on the part of the interviewer. An A intrudes into the
25 stammer, while B waits quietly.

The extreme Type A is the person who, while waiting to see the dentist, is on the telephone making business calls. He speaks in staccato, and rushes through a sentence. He frequently
30 sighs faintly between words which is a sign of emotional exhaustion. He rarely goes to a doctor; indeed, many Type A's die of otherwise recoverable heart attacks simply because they wait too long to call for help.

(McQuade, 1975)

11. The author has written this passage primarily to
    1. narrate an incident.
    2. argue a point.
    3. persuade the reader.
    4. inform the reader.

12. How can Type A personalities be described?
    1. uptight
    2. senseless
    3. unhappy
    4. undisturbed

13. Virulent as used in the passage means
    1. hostile.
    2. moderate.
    3. harmless.
    4. benign.

14. In paragraph one "a mask of easy geniality" means that the person is really most likely to be
    1. intensely controlled.
    2. fond of practical jokes.
    3. friendly and relaxed.
    4. easy going and accepting.

15. According to the passage Type A's
    1. visit the doctor when they need to.
    2. think doctors are useless.
    3. wait too long to see a doctor.
    4. never visit the doctor.

16. Which of the following is not mentioned as a characteristic of a Type B personality?
    1. open
    2. patient
    3. ambitious
    4. less competitive

Every man, woman, and child in the United States generates four pounds of trash a day. Most of us have only vague ideas--and often misconceptions--about what trash contains. But as landfill space shrinks and the cost of dumping trash rises, we need to know exactly what it is that we're throwing out so we can decide how best to manage it. With hands-on knowledge of our trash, the Garbage Project has calculated percentages of different materials in landfills.

Perhaps the biggest surprise is the amount of paper we dispose of. Computers haven't saved us from a paper avalanche; they've added to it with mountains of printouts. In 1970 paper took up 35 percent of landfill space; today it takes up 50 percent.

Telephone directories such as the one retrieved from the landfill in New York City are among the fastest growing paper components. Newspapers are the largest single item in landfills, taking up as much as 18 percent of the space. Contrary to popular opinion, they do not biodegrade significantly--The Garbage Project finds legible copies that have been buried for 40 years.

Used by 85 percent of U.S. babies, disposable diapers are increasingly perceived as a serious trash concern. The nation's yearly load of more than 16 billion disposable diapers weighs some 1.5 million tons but takes up 0.8 percent of landfill space.

Polystyrene foam--thermal cups, for example--makes up nearly one percent. A bigger problem is construction and demolition debris, which accounts for 15 percent.

Recycling can reduce much of our trash load. The U.S. Environmental Protection Agency (EPA) estimates that we already recycle 13 percent. Aggressive recycling and creating markets for recycled materials could increase that figure to 45 percent, say some experts.

(Rathje, 1991)

17. As used in the passage, generates means
    1. destroys.
    2. uses.
    3. produces.
    4. reduces.

18. The primary purpose of this passage is to explain
    1. how much trash is generated by the United States.
    2. the composition of trash.
    3. methods of trash disposal.
    4. the need for recycling trash.

19. What is ironic about disposable diapers?
    1. They are used by 85 percent of the babies in the U.S.
    2. They are increasingly seen as a serious trash problem.
    3. Sixteen billion disposable diapers weigh approximately 1.5 million tons.
    4. They take up 0.8 percent of landfill space.

20. The largest single item in a landfill is
    1. newspapers.
    2. computer printouts.
    3. construction debris.
    4. polystyrene foam cups.

21. The author mentions the "avalanche" of computer paper to support his point that
    1. computers actually save paper in the long run.
    2. there are often misconceptions about what our trash contains.
    3. we have less paper in our landfills today than in 1970.
    4. paper is easily recyclable.

22. It can be concluded from the passage that
    1. Americans dispose of too much trash.
    2. new landfill space is limited to certain parts of the country.
    3. the trash problem could be reduced significantly by recycling.
    4. the use of disposable diapers and polystyrene cups should be banned.

John F. Kennedy, Inaugural Address

We observe today not a victory of party but a celebration of freedom, symbolizing an end as well as a beginning, signifying renewal as well as change. For I have sworn before you and Almighty God the same solemn oath our forebears prescribed nearly a century and three-quarters ago.

The world is very different now. For man holds in his mortal hands the power to abolish all forms of human poverty and all forms of human life. And yet the same revolutionary belief for which our forebears fought is still at issue around the globe, the belief that the rights of man come not from the generosity of the state but from the hand of God.

We dare not forget today that we are the heirs of that first revolution. Let the word go forth from this time and place, to friend and foe alike, that the torch has been passed to a new genera-tion of Americans, born in this century, tempered by war, disciplined by a hard and bitter peace, proud of our ancient heritage, and unwilling to witness or permit the slow undoing of those human rights to which this nation has always been committed, and to which we are committed today at home and around the world.

Let every nation know, whether it wishes us well or ill, that we shall pay any price, bear any burden, meet any hardship, support any friend, oppose any foe to assure the survival and the success of liberty.

This much we pledge--and more.

23. What vision of the U.S. is Kennedy trying to inspire in his listeners?

    1. survival of the fittest
    2. rebellion against government
    3. defender of freedom
    4. commitment to party goals

24. Kennedy's main purpose in his inaugural address is to

    1. compare.
    2. inspire.
    3. narrate.
    4. describe.

25. The word tempered, as used in the passage, means

    1. honored.
    2. tempted.
    3. punished.
    4. toughened.

26. What tone does Kennedy use in his speech?

    1. pessimism
    2. optimism
    3. sympathy
    4. skepticism

27. Kennedy believes that human rights are

    1. determined by government.
    2. debatable.
    3. disciplined by a hard and bitter peace.
    4. God given.

28. What basic assumption(s) about his listener's values does Kennedy make?

    1. They are party loyalists.
    2. They are conservatives.
    3. They believe in human rights.
    4. They are hard workers.

29. As used in the passage, forebears means

    1. heirs.
    2. ancestors.
    3. brothers.
    4. friends.

What are these stars that we see as twinkling dots of light in the nighttime sky? The stars are <u>luminous</u> balls of gas scattered throughout space. All the stars we see are among the 100

5 billion <u>stellar</u> members of a collection of stars and other matter called the Milky Way Galaxy. The sun, which is the star that controls our planet is so close to us that we can see detail on its surface, but it is just an ordinary star like the rest.

10 Stars are balls of gas held together by the force of gravity, the same force that keeps us on the ground no matter where we are on the earth. Long ago, gravity compressed large amounts of gas and dust into dense spheres that became

15 stars; the dust vaporized, and balls of gas remained.

Stars generate their own energy and light. Energy from the original gravitational contraction that formed the stars heated the interiors of the

20 gaseous spheres until they were hot enough for nuclear fusion to begin. It has been less than 50 years since the realization that the stars shine because of the energy they generate by nuclear fusion....

25 We see only the outer layers of the stars; the interiors are hidden from our view. The stars are gaseous through and through; they have no solid parts. The outer layers are not generating energy by themselves, but are merely glowing because

30 of the effects of energy transported outward from the stellar interiors.

(Pasachoff, 1983)

30. As used in the passage, <u>luminous</u> means
    1. deadly.
    2. glowing.
    3. solid.
    4. liquid.

31. The style of the passage is best described as
    1. humorous.
    2. argumentative.
    3. informative.
    4. informal.

32. <u>Stellar</u>, as used in the passage means
    1. planet like.
    2. star like.
    3. outstanding.
    4. heated.

33. The primary purpose of the passage is to
    1. describe the Milky Way.
    2. compare the sun to other stars of lesser magnitude.
    3. describe the characteristics of stars.
    4. illustrate the rapidity with which stellar research has taken place.

34. The Milky Way Galaxy may be referred to as all of the following *except*
    1. 100 billion stellar members.
    2. luminous balls of gas.
    3. twinkling dots of gas.
    4. vaporized dust.

35. A characteristic which is common to stars *and* the earth is
    1. self generation of light.
    2. gravity.
    3. interior nuclear fusion.
    4. no solid parts.

Eleven years after Lee surrendered to Grant at Appomattox Court House in Virginia, major-league baseball was born with the formation of the National League. In little more than a decade, independent minor leagues were flourishing. Pennsylvania, Ohio, Kansas, and Montana all had their own. Others were scattered from new England to the Pacific Northwest. For most towns, particularly those in the still isolated West, having a team was <u>tantamount to</u> being part of the nation's growth and progressive spirit.

5

10

"Salt Lake City has for a number of years fostered the game of baseball," said the *Salt Lake Daily Tribune* in 1887. "In fact, our city would not be up to modern ideas did <u>she</u> not do so. In these times baseball clubs are almost an imperative necessity."

15

For a long time the minor leagues were sovereign entities, competing for fans with the National and American leagues. Some players spent their entire career of 20 years or more in the minors. Then, in 1919, Branch Rickey became manager of the St. Louis Cardinals, a team so poor they wore shoddy mended uniforms for spring training and held it that year in St. Louis instead of Florida. Rickey decided that since the Cardinals couldn't afford to buy players, they would have to raise their own. Over the next 20 years he got control of 32 minor-league teams, and the minors became what they are today--a farm system, subsidized by major-league teams needing a pool of young talent to compete in an industry that has room at the top for only 650 men.

20

25

30

(Lamb, 1991)

36. <u>She</u> as underlined (line 15) refers to
    1. *Salt Lake Daily Tribune.*
    2. the game of baseball.
    3. a baseball fan.
    4. Salt Lake City.

37. As used in the passage, <u>tantamount to</u> means
    1. different from.
    2. equivalent to.
    3. incompatible with.
    4. inessential to.

38. The primary purpose of the passage is to show
    1. how Salt Lake City acquired a team.
    2. the formation of the National League.
    3. the development of the minor leagues.
    4. the birth of major league baseball.

39. Approximately how many years after Lee surrendered to Grant did the minor leagues begin to flourish?
    1. eleven years
    2. a decade
    3. ten years
    4. twenty-one years

40. The author mentions Salt Lake City to support his point that historically
    1. having a baseball team was evidence of progress and growth.
    2. Salt Lake City was not up to modern ideas.
    3. baseball teams were a major economic support for large cities.
    4. the minor leagues were sovereign entities.

Shooting, pillaging and burning, the 16th century adventurers known as the "Conquistadores" destroyed the mountain empire of the Incas. They melted down the Incas' treasure,
5 executed their leaders, and enslaved the people in an orgy of destruction and avarice. But the last of the Incas escaped deeper into the same mountains, to build a city as impressive as any that the Spaniards had sacked. For three
10 hundred years their fortified <u>citadel</u> remained little more than legend until its rediscovery in 1911 by the American explorer Hiram Bingham. The jungle-clad ruins that he uncovered surpassed even his wildest imaginings: there was
15 a flight of 100 perfectly built terraces, each hundreds of feet long and covered with soil carried laboriously up from the valley floor. Machu Picchu was a huge hanging garden in the mountains, like a New World Babylon. The city
20 was a complex of white granite buildings large enough to shelter many thousands of people and <u>impregnable to</u> attack on all fronts--the Incas had looked for security from their Spanish tormentors, and at Machu Picchu they had fashioned it with
25 the toil of their own hands.

Their city fortress was a masterpiece of construction. The Incas moved great stone blocks over mountainous terrain without the aid of the wheel: no two blocks were alike, yet each
30 irregular shape was cut to precision to dovetail exactly with its neighbors. At Machu Picchu, Bingham uncovered a magnificent royal mausoleum, temple complexes and houses, all tied and keyed into one another by the finest
35 masonry he had witnessed. At the center of his hidden city was a carved stone--sacred to the Incas' sun cult. Each year at the winter solstice in June, the high priest symbolically bound the sun-god Inti to the stone with a chain of pure
40 gold--to ensure that he returned for the southern hemisphere summer.

(Perry, 1985)

41. It can be inferred from the passage that Machu Picchu was built
    1. prior to the Conquistadores' invasion.
    2. after the invasion of the Conquistadores.
    3. by the Conquistadores to house the Inca captives.
    4. prior to the 1600s.

42. According to the passage, Machu Picchu was
    1. located in the southern hemisphere.
    2. destroyed by the Spanish.
    3. easily constructed by the Incas.
    4. the center of Inca trade.

43. As used in the passage, the word <u>citadel</u> means
    1. metropolis.
    2. stronghold.
    3. garden.
    4. prison.

44. Which of the following does the author primarily use to support his ideas?
    1. examples
    2. cause and effect relationship
    3. description
    4. sequence of events

45. The writer may be assumed to be
    1. an archeologist.
    2. a military strategist.
    3. a sociologist.
    4. an Inca descendant.

46. As used in the passage, the term <u>impregnable to</u> most nearly means
    1. vulnerable to.
    2. secure from.
    3. susceptible.
    4. unprotected from.

47. With which of the following would the author agree?
    1. The Spanish spread the legend about Machu Picchu.
    2. Thousands of Incas survived the Spanish attacks.
    3. Conquistadores made the Incas slaves to build the city of Machu Picchu.
    4. The Incas had built Machu Picchu in case of an attack by the Spaniards.

In 1979 sodium carbonate, Na_2CO_3, ranked eleventh among industrial chemicals in amount produced in the United States. Production that year was 7.5×10^6 metric tons, about 25 kg for every inhabitant. Na_2CO_3 is used to make glass, soap, paper, and other chemicals. It is one of the so-called heavy chemicals, perhaps because it is made in such large amounts.

Two hundred years ago, before chemistry was a science, sodium carbonate, then called soda ash since it was obtained from wood ashes, was in short supply, and the French government offered a prize for a synthetic method for its manufacture. A scientist named Leblanc developed such a process in 1790, using common salt, limestone, coal, and sulfuric acid. In the process salt was heated with sulfuric acid and converted to salt cake, NA_2So^4. The salt cake was then heated to about 900° C with a mixture of coal and limestone, producing a mixture of Na_2CO_3, CaS, and various impurities called black ash. The sodium carbonate could be leached from the solid with water and recrystallized. It was a rather messy process, but at least it worked.

The Leblanc process was used to make Na_2CO_3 during much of the nineteenth century. Following its development in 1865, the Solvay process gradually replaced that of Leblanc, and became the source of most of the Na_2CO_3 produced during this century. In 1938 some large deposits of a mineral called trona, Na_2CO_3 $NaHCO^3$ 2 H^2O, were discovered near Green River, Wyoming, and over the past 20 years these deposits have been extensively mined. They now furnish well over half the sodium carbonate needs of this country.

(Slowinski, 1985)

48. The underlined word synthetic means
    1. natural.
    2. man-made.
    3. complex.
    4. simple.

49. During most of the eighteenth century, sodium carbonate was obtained
    1. from wood ashes.
    2. from the Leblanc process.
    3. from the Solvay process.
    4. from deposits of the mineral trona.

50. It can be concluded from the passage that sodium carbonate
    1. is in short supply today.
    2. is used to make many common products.
    3. is the most highly produced chemical in the United States.
    4. is called soda ash today.

51. The primary purpose of this passage is to
    1. reveal the flaws in the Leblanc process of manufacturing synthetic sodium carbonate.
    2. trace the development of the production of sodium carbonate.
    3. compare the natural production of sodium carbonate to the synthetic process.
    4. describe the variety of uses for sodium carbonate in the United States.

52. Which of the following does the author primarily use in this passage?
    1. cause and effect
    2. chronological order
    3. personal opinion
    4. comparison and contrast

53. Between 1791 and 1865
    1. sodium carbonate was ranked eleventh among industrial chemicals.
    2. the Solvay process gradually replaced that of Leblanc.
    3. the Leblanc process was used to make sodium carbonate.
    4. sodium carbonate was obtained from wood ashes.

The most graphic image of the Renaissance is conveyed through its art, particularly architecture, sculpture, and painting. All three art forms in the Renaissance reflect a style that
5   stresses proportion, balance, and harmony. These artistic values in turn are achieved through a new, revolutionary conceptualization of space. Renaissance art also reflects the values of Renaissance humanism, a return to classical
10   models in architecture, to the rendering of the nude human figure, and to a heroic vision of human beings.

Medieval art sought to represent spiritual aspiration, the world was a veil merely hinting at
15   the other world, perfect and eternal. Renaissance art did not stop expressing spiritual aspiration, but its setting and character differ altogether. This world is no longer a shroud but becomes the place where people live, act, and worship. The
20   reference is less to the other world and more to this world, and people are treated as creatures who find their spiritual destiny as they fulfill their human one.

The Middle Ages had produced a distinctive
25   art known as the Gothic. By the fourteenth and fifteenth centuries, Gothic art had evolved into what is known as the International Style, characterized by careful drawing, flowing and delicate lines, harmonious composition, and
30   delightful naturalistic detail.

Renaissance art at its most distinctive represents a conscious revolt against this late Gothic trend. This revolt produced revolutionary discoveries that served as the foundation of
35   Western art up to this century.

(Clucas, 1981)

54. Which of the following is not reflected by Renaissance art?

    1. spirituality
    2. humanism
    3. heroic vision
    4. shrouded world

55. Which period in western art came last?

    1. Medieval
    2. Renaissance
    3. Gothic
    4. International

56. As used in the passage, the best meaning for shroud is

    1. veil.
    2. spiritual life.
    3. place.
    4. delicate line.

57. What is the author's primary idea?

    1. Renaissance art represented a conscious revolt against the Gothic trend.
    2. Gothic art evolved into the International Style.
    3. International Style was characterized by careful drawing and delicate lines.
    4. The world is the place where people live, act, and worship.

58. The reader may infer that the art of the Renaissance expressed

    1. more concern for day to day life and human destiny.
    2. more concern for spiritual aspirations.
    3. vivid perceptions of the world as a veil which separated the earthly from the spiritual.
    4. spiritual truths through careful drawings with flowing, delicate lines.

59. International Style was a

    1. Renaissance Style.
    2. Gothic trend.
    3. revolt against Gothic style.
    4. new art form.

60. The author's primary purpose is to

    1. contrast Renaissance art with Medieval art.
    2. explain the three art forms of the Renaissance.
    3. support the values of Renaissance humanism.
    4. define the spiritual aspirations of Medieval art.

The Reading Test
Practice Test Seven

As he [Charles] grew older he irritated her in more ways than one. He began to contract coarse habits. When he sat at his wine he would cut up the corks of the empty bottles. After meals, he sucked his teeth. He made a gurgling noise whenever he ate soup, and, as he grew fatter, his eyes, which were small in any case, looked as though they were being pushed upwards and outward towards his temples by the increasing puffiness of his cheeks.

Sometimes she [Emma] would tuck the edge of his red knitted jersey out of sight beneath his waistcoat, straighten his cravat, and throw away the faded gloves which he was quite gaily proposing to put on. It was not for him--as he thought--that she did these things, but for herself. Her action was dictated by her egotism, was the expression of a nervous irritability. Sometimes, too, she talked to him of things that she had read, passages from novels or from plays, or would repeat some anecdote of the great world which she had seen in the gossip column of her paper. For at least he was better than nobody, was always there, ready to listen and agree. Many were the secrets which she told her dog. The wood in the fireplace or the pendulum of the clock would have done as well.

But deep in her heart she was waiting for something to happen. Like sailors in distress, she gazed around with despairing eyes upon the loneliness of her life, seeking a white sail on the immensities of the misty horizon. She did not know what chance, what wind would bring it to her, to what shore it would carry her, whether it would turn out to be an open boat or a three-decker laden to the gunwale with pain or happiness. But each morning when she woke she was agog for what the day might bring forth. She listened to the sounds of the world, jumped from her bed, and never ceased to be surprised that nothing happened. Then, when night came on again, sadder than ever, she longed for the morrow.

(Flaubert, 1881)

1. In the last paragraph, "Like sailors in distress, she (Emma) gazed around with despairing eyes upon the loneliness of her life, seeking a white sail on the immensities of the misty horizon," is meant to be

   1. factual.
   2. colloquial.
   3. literal.
   4. figurative.

2. As used in the passage, agog means

   1. depressed.
   2. bored.
   3. excited.
   4. nervous.

3. To Emma, the "white sail" in paragraph 3 is

   1. the boat that will rescue her.
   2. the pain of her unhappiness.
   3. the loneliness of her life.
   4. the hope for excitement and change.

4. The author's purpose in the passage is to

   1. give evidence for the woman's discontent.
   2. describe the woman's preparations for the next day.
   3. explain why the woman talked to the man.
   4. give examples of the man's (Charles) coarse habits.

5. The passage implies that Emma's efforts to change the way Charles dressed were

   1. designed to make him look better.
   2. because she was concerned about him.
   3. because she was ashamed of his appearance.
   4. made to give her something to do.

6. All of the following are sources of Emma's irritation with Charles except

   1. he was always ready to listen to her stories.
   2. he sucked his teeth.
   3. he made gurgling noises when he ate soup.
   4. he cut up corks from empty wine bottles.

7. The last sentence in the second paragraph compares wood in the fireplace or a pendulum of the clock to

   1. Charles.
   2. the sailors.
   3. the newspapers.
   4. the neighbors.

The death in his ninety-first year of Sir
Winston Churchill removes from the
contemporary scene a statesman whose services
to his country are unexampled in modern times,
5 one to whose courage, clear-sightedness and gift
for leadership the world owes many debts of
gratitude. Yet if we must remember him for one
thing above all, it is bound to be for the
inspiration, the will to fight on, that he injected
10 into his country and her allies in the dark days of
1940. He did not achieve this ability by accident.
It was the logical culmination of a way of life and
a way of thought.

   To win wars the qualities required are
15 courage, foresight, an absolute confidence in
ultimate success, combined with an infinite
patience, the power of judging in the heat of the
fray both men and events, tireless energy and
the ability to draw from others over long periods,
20 the best they can give, individually and in
concert.

   All these qualities Churchill possessed in an
exceptional degree. From his youth onwards he
had seen war as the ultimate test of a man's
25 reality. No firebrand--though often labelled one--
he had gravitated to wars like a scholar to books,
offering himself the heightened apprehension of
existence their danger provided as a necessary
part of the complete life. As a subordinate he
30 could be willful and scornful of those in authority,
but nothing within his purview was ever allowed
to stagnate and his loyalty once given was
absolute.

                              (Ferrier, 1965)

8. The author states that Churchill's most
    important contribution was his
    1. willingness to challenge authority.
    2. tireless energy.
    3. ability to judge characters in the heat of
        battle.
    4. ability to inspire others during a world
        war.

9. In the passage, the word purview most nearly
    means
    1. life time.
    2. range of vision.
    3. household.
    4. personality.

10. Which of the following words best describes
    the author's attitude toward Winston Chur-
    chill?
    1. objective
    2. admiring
    3. hostile
    4. detached

11. In the second paragraph the author makes
    his point through the use of
    1. statistics.
    2. sensory appeal.
    3. examples.
    4. cause and effect.

12. The best meaning of the word absolute is
    1. reversible.
    2. reserved.
    3. unconditional.
    4. qualified.

13. Which of the following does the author
    primarily use to support his views of
    Churchill?
    1. factual narration
    2. appeals to emotion
    3. personal opinion
    4. chronology

A steady supply of water is as essential to any city as it is to any farm system. Some cities take their water directly from rivers and during periods of drought must ration its use. A more
5 dependable way to supply water to a city is to collect it in a reservoir for release when needed. (The city and the river can be thought of here as a partial system since we do not consider where the river water comes from or where it
10 goes after being used in the urban area.) In order to regulate the flow of water to the city as it is needed, the reservoir is used as a storage device to smooth out variations in the annual availability of water. Many systems include
15 similar stores or regulators in order that the input to the system will balance the output that follows. (A budget and a bank account serve this purpose in the management of money. To paraphrase Mr. McCawber, happiness is spending one cent less
20 than you earn.") A healthy city depends in part on its having enough water to meet its needs and keeping its needs within the amount of water available to it.

A city reservoir releases a varying flow of
25 water to the city. In turn, it receives varying amounts of water from the rivers that feed it. When the rivers run low, the reservoir contributes more water than it receives. The flow to the city does not alter.

(Wood, 1989)

14. The reason cities utilize reservoirs is
    1. to filter water.
    2. to regulate the output of water.
    3. to hold and collect rain water.
    4. to guarantee the availability of water.

15. When the rivers feeding the reservoirs are low
    1. the reservoir doesn't have to contribute.
    2. the reservoir dries up.
    3. the reservoir contributes more than it receives.
    4. the reservoir contributes less than it receives.

16. In the passage, the following analogy is made:
    1. happiness = money.
    2. reservoir = bank account.
    3. city = farm.
    4. rivers = budgets.

17. As used in passage, the best meaning for reservoir is
    1. input regulator.
    2. storage system.
    3. waterway.
    4. river basin.

18. The author's purpose is to explain the
    1. regulator systems for reservoirs.
    2. use and benefits of reservoirs.
    3. development of healthy cities.
    4. checks and balances of water systems.

It was in Italy and Germany that cannon were manufactured and early firearms developed; and it was from those countries that the French were supplied with guns larger and in every way
5 superior to any possessed by the English. After the Wars of the Roses the English remedied the defect. King Henry VIII was particularly anxious to add to his <u>store</u>, and sometimes, as in 1522, he levied princely blackmail of firearms from the
10 Venetian galleys trading to Flanders; yet as early as 1513 the Venetian Ambassador had reported to the Doge that Henry had "cannon enough to conquer hell." A visitor to the Tower of London in 1515 states that there were then in the Tower
15 about 400 cannon, and that most of them were mounted on wheels. It was in the reign of Henry VIII that cannon were first cast in England. Peter Bawde, a Frenchman, was the artificer; he cast brass cannon in Houndsditch in 1525. Later,
20 about 1535, John O'Ewen was engaged in the work, and by 1543 the industry was flourishing at Uckfield Sussex, then the centre of the iron trade in Britain.

(Greener, 1910)

19. Cannon were first made in England in
    1. 1513.
    2. 1525.
    3. 1535.
    4. 1542.

20. Firearms were first manufactured in
    1. England and France.
    2. Italy and England.
    3. Germany and France.
    4. Italy and Germany.

21. <u>Store</u> underlined means
    1. supply.
    2. future prospects.
    3. shop.
    4. space.

22. We can infer that the reason the cannon in industry flourished in Sussex was
    1. to be convenient for King Henry.
    2. because John O'Ewen lived there.
    3. because Sussex was the center of iron trade.
    4. because cannons were made there.

23. The passage implies that
    1. King Henry VIII increased his supply of arms unethically.
    2. King Henry VIII concealed his depository of arms.
    3. cannons were the most common firearms in 1543.
    4. cannons were first cast in England.

The United States could face a fuel crisis due to constant fluctuations in the cost and availability of foreign petroleum. We now depend on other nations for approximately 38 percent of
5   our liquid fuels. To achieve energy independence, the United States must develop domestic replacements for imported fuels.

Our nation possesses large supplies of oil, natural gas and coal--the traditional fuels used
10 for energy. These resources are <u>finite</u>, and cannot be renewed, but we do possess abundant biomass resources which can be converted to liquid fuels and renewed annually.

Biomass is organic material such as trees,
15 crops, manure, seaweed, and algae. Biomass captures and stores energy through photosynthesis. This energy can be released from any form of biomass through conversion processes to produce a variety of useful fuels--
20 alcohol, syngas, hydrogen, charcoal, methane, and synthetic oils.

Of these biomass fuels, alcohol is considered one of the best near-term keys which can help the United States to achieve more energy
25 independence. Because alcohol can be blended with gasoline to form gasohol, it can displace 10 percent of the 110 billion gallons of gasoline used in American automobiles each year.

(Kolars, 1974)

30
24. According to the passage, <u>finite</u> means
    1. permanent.
    2. enduring.
    3. limited.
    4. rare.

25. Which of the following would be the best title for this selection?
    1. "The Future of Imported Fuels"
    2. "The Availability of Foreign Petroleum"
    3. "Biomass Fuels--A Key to Energy Independence"
    4. "The Future of Petroleum"

26. According to the passage, the United States should
    1. find alternative sources for energy fuel.
    2. use our large supplies of energy fuels.
    3. turn to gasohol for the solution to energy demands.
    4. reduce our fuel exports to a level below 38 percent.

27. The author states that the biomass that would produce gasohol is
    1. renewable.
    2. difficult to obtain.
    3. expensive to obtain.
    4. too ordinary to gain credibility.

28. The passage is written from the point of view of a/an
    1. Federal Trade Commissioner.
    2. a conservationist.
    3. a chemical engineer.
    4. an automobile manufacturer.

29. The tone of the author is
    1. indifferent.
    2. demanding.
    3. pessimistic.
    4. hopeful.

30. The relation of the first paragraph to the remainder of the passage is one of
    1. specific idea to general idea.
    2. cause to effect.
    3. problem to solution.
    4. comparison to contrast.

"What is the shape of Walnut Bends . . .

"My boy, you've got to know the shape of the river perfectly. It is all there is left to steer by on a very dark night. Everything else is blotted out and
5 gone. But mind you, it hasn't the same shape in the night that it has in the daytime."

"How on earth am I ever going to learn it, then?"

"How do you follow a hall at home in the dark? Because you know the shape of it. You can't see it."

10 "Do you mean to say that I've got to know all the million trifling variations of shape in the banks of this interminable river as well as I know the shape of the front hall at home?"

"On my honor, you've got to know them
15 better than any man ever did know the shapes of the halls in his own house."

"I wish I was dead!"

"Now I don't want to discourage you, but.... You see, this has got to be learned; there isn't
20 any getting around it. A clear starlight night throws such heavy shadows that, if you didn't know the shape of a shore perfectly, you would claw away from every bunch of timber, because you would take the black shadow of it for a solid
25 cape; . . . You can't see a snag in one of those shadows, but you know exactly where it is, and the shape of the river tells you when you are coming to it. Then there's your pitch-dark night; the river is a very different shape on a pitch-dark
30 night from what it is on a starlight night. All shores seem to be straight lines, then, and mighty dim ones, too; and you'd run them for straight lines, only you know better. You boldly drive your boat right into what seems to be a solid,
35 straight wall (you knowing very well that in reality there is a curve there). . . Then there's your gray mist. You take a night when there's one of these grisly, drizzly, gray mists, and then there isn't any particular shape to a shore. A gray mist would
40 tangle the head of the oldest men that ever lived."

(Clemens, 1874)

31. This passage is included in the narrative primarily to
    1. warn readers of the dangers of riverboats.
    2. amuse readers who know about steamboat navigation.
    3. describe the dangers of river travel at night.
    4. support river travel.

32. The speaker in the last paragraph is probably
    1. a riverboat passenger.
    2. the riverboat captain.
    3. a young man.
    4. a bystander.

33. In the passage, interminable most nearly means
    1. never ending.
    2. unchangeable.
    3. changeable.
    4. winding.

34. Why does the boy say he wishes he was dead?
    1. He is unable to see the variations in the riverbank at night.
    2. He has been involved in an accident on the river.
    3. He does not believe he can learn what he needs to know about the river at night.
    4. He is afraid on the nights when there are grisly, drizzly, gray mists.

35. The most difficult night to navigate is the one that has
    1. clear starlight.
    2. gray mists.
    3. pitch-dark.
    4. heavy shadows.

36. Which of the following may the reader infer from the passage?
    1. Piloting a riverboat is done through sophisticated instrumentation.
    2. Riverboat pilots are trained at an academy and follow manuals for navigation.
    3. Piloting a riverboat is a boring and uneventful occupation.
    4. Riverboat pilots depend largely on intuition and experience.

37. The language used in the passsage is
    1. poetic.
    2. academic.
    3. technical.
    4. informal.

38. The speaker describes the skills needed in navigation in order to support the idea that
    1. a riverboat pilot must know the shape of the river perfectly to steer at night.
    2. the river is treacherous at all times.
    3. steering a riverboat is impossible to learn.
    4. riverboat pilots must be able to walk in the dark.

Motives and emotions both energize and direct our behavior. The two are closely related and can activate us even without our awareness. Motives are triggered by bodily needs, cues in
5 the environment, and such feelings as loneliness or guilt. When such stimuli combine to create a motive, goal-directed behavior results. Like motives, emotions, which usually refer to such complex feelings as anger, fear, or love, activate
10 behavior, but it is more difficult to predict the behavior and goals affected by emotion than those stimulated by motives.

One of the earliest explanations of motivated behavior focused on instincts--<u>innate</u> tendencies
15 to behave in certain ways. But since not all human behavior is inborn, psychologists began to look for other explanations of motivation. According to drive reduction theory, bodily needs create a state of tension or arousal called a drive;
20 motivated behavior is seen as an attempt to reduce this tension and return the body to a state of homeostasis or balance.

Primary drives are unlearned motives that are common to every animal. They include
25 hunger, thirst, and sex. The primary drives are triggered by physiological stimuli and by both internal and external cues. All of them are subject to learning and experience.

Hunger is regulated by two centers in the
30 brain. The hunger center stimulates the desire to eat while the satiety center signals when to stop. The hunger center is stimulated in response to a drop in the level of glucose or fats in the blood.

(Morris, 1988)

39. The primary purpose of the passage is to define and give examples of
    1. emotions.
    2. motives.
    3. drives.
    4. instincts.

40. As used in the passage, <u>innate</u> means
    1. learned.
    2. behavioral.
    3. inborn.
    4. state of arousal.

41. According to the passage, primary drives
    1. are not affected by external cues.
    2. are universal yet individually unique.
    3. keep the body balanced.
    4. are triggered by motives.

42. Drive reduction theory views motivated behavior as
    1. instinctive.
    2. a "balancing procedure" of the body.
    3. tension in the body.
    4. complex emotions.

43. The passage suggests that
    1. bodily needs create a state of homeostasis.
    2. hunger is unaffected by learning.
    3. behavior is easily predicted.
    4. emotions are more complex than motives.

44. Which of the following would be the consequence of a drop in the blood sugar level?
    1. Satiety signals begin.
    2. Fat levels drop.
    3. Homeostasis is established.
    4. Hunger center stimulates desire to eat.

In the final scenes of the story Mary finds herself at a neighborhood gathering where Mrs. Fullerton's farm is under discussion by a group of young couples putting their heads together to find
5 a way to outwit the local ordinances that have prevented the old place from being appropriated and torn down. Mary feebly argues that they haven't the right--that Mrs. Fullerton was there before any of them were born--but is quickly
10 overruled with a certain gentle indulgence for what appears in this context to be her romantic sentimentality. One young realtor informs her, for instance, that the continued existence of Mrs. Fullerton's house is lowering the resale value of
15 the whole neighborhood. Mary refuses to sign the petition they circulate at the party's conclusion, but leaves the gathering deeply <u>ambivalent</u>, reflecting, "But these are good people; they want homes for their children, they help each other
20 when there is trouble, they plan a community-- saying that word as if they found a modern and well-proportioned magic in it, and no possibility anywhere of a mistake." The story ends with the next line.... "There is nothing you can do at
25 present but keep your hands in your pockets and keep a disaffected heart." It is, like so many modern stories a chronicle of compromise, ending in uncertainty and <u>acquiescence</u> to the confusing imperatives of apparent necessity. To
30 measure the loss against the gain is saddening and at times seems cause for outrage, yet ultimately beside the point.

(Leonard, 1983)

45. The narrator's purpose in telling the story is to
    1. condemn zoning codes.
    2. promote neighborhood involvements.
    3. contrast young marrieds with older single women.
    4. illustrate the complexity of problems which often accompany change.

46. The reader can infer that during the early scenes of the story Mary had been
    1. a real estate agent.
    2. involved in a zoning dispute.
    3. a farmer.
    4. without children.

47. The group's attitude toward Mary is
    1. belligerent.
    2. indifferent.
    3. supportive.
    4. patronizing.

48. As used in the passage, <u>ambivalent</u> means
    1. having mixed feelings.
    2. indifferent.
    3. depressed.
    4. thoughtful.

49. As used in the passage, <u>acquiescence</u> means
    1. a response.
    2. a giving in.
    3. an anger expressed.
    4. a contradiction.

50. At the end of the story, the reader can conclude that Mary
    1. does not like modern stories.
    2. is frustrated.
    3. is about to sell her property.
    4. will express her outrage.

By 1528 it was public knowledge that Anne Boleyn was the King's mistress. She was installed in her own splendid apartments at Greenwich and when Henry banished Catherine

5 from court in 1531 Anne took her place at the King's side. They were <u>halcyon</u> days for Anne. The King was madly in love with her and she could happily ignore the unpopularity shown her by the public.

10 It is not known exactly when King Henry and Anne Boleyn began living together as man and wife, but by January she was pregnant. Clearly a marriage had to be arranged if the heir were to be born in wedlock. The wedding was not the

15 lavish affair Anne must have hoped for, but a simple ceremony held in the utmost secrecy early on January 25--for Henry's marriage to Catherine was still valid....

The child, born between three and four in the

20 afternoon on September 7, was a girl. It had been a difficult labour and a complicated delivery in which Anne must have suffered, but Henry did not try to hide his anger. He could hardly bring himself to look at his new, beautiful daughter. . .

25 Henry became more and more watchful for the slightest misdemeanor which he could hold against her [Anne] . . .

His chance came . . . when Anne dropped her handkerchief for a young jouster in the lists.

30 The incident led to a trumped-up charge of adultery . . Elizabeth . . was barely three years old when her mother was sent to the block.

(Wallace, 1987)

51. The passage implies that Henry's real reason for executing Anne was that
    1. she was interested in another man.
    2. she didn't produce a male heir.
    3. he thought she was old and ugly.
    4. Henry had a lover.

52. According to the passage, it can be inferred that the heir to the throne must be
    1. a descendant.
    2. a son.
    3. a daughter.
    4. a relative.

53. The word <u>halcyon</u> means
    1. glorious.
    2. difficult.
    3. undignified.
    4. routine.

54. Catherine was
    1. Henry's daughter.
    2. Henry's sister.
    3. Henry's lover.
    4. Henry's wife.

55. The passage fails to mention
    1. King Henry's illicit affair.
    2. Henry's animosity toward Elizabeth.
    3. Henry's divorce from Catherine.
    4. Anne's method of execution.

Mozart was among the most versatile of all composers and wrote masterpieces in all the musical forms of his time--symphonies, concertos, chamber music, operas. All his music sings and
5 conveys a feeling of ease, grace, and spontaneity as well as balance, restraint, and proportion. Yet mysterious harmonies contrast with its lyricism, and it fuses elegance with power. Not only do his compositions sound
10 effortless; they were created with miraculous ease and rapidity--for example, he completed his last three symphonies in only six weeks.

Many of Mozart's concertos are among his greatest works. His piano concertos--composed
15 mainly for his own performances--are particularly important; but he also wrote concertos for violin, horn, flute, bassoon, oboe, and clarinet.

Mozart was also a master of opera, with a supreme ability to coordinate music and stage
20 action, a keen sense of theater, an inexhaustible gift of melody, and a genius for creating characters through tone. Most of his operas are comedies, composed to German or Italian librettos. His three masterpieces of Italian comic
25 opera (all composed to librettos by Lorenzo da Ponte) are *The Marriage of Figaro* (1786), *Don Giovanni* (1787), and *Cosi fan tutte* (1790); his finest opera in German is *The Magic Flute* (1791). The comic operas have both humorous
30 and serious characters--not mere stereotypes but individual human beings who think and feel. Emotions in his arias and ensembles continually evolve and change.

"I am never happier," Mozart once wrote,
35 "than when I have something to compose, for that, after all, is my sole delight and passion."

(Kamien, 1990)

56. As used in the passage, versatile means
    1. energetic.
    2. talented.
    3. multi-talented.
    4. well known.

57. The author's attitude toward Mozart is best described as
    1. indifferent.
    2. admiring.
    3. sentimental.
    4. nostalgic.

58. Which of the following could be a fact and *NOT* an opinion?
    1. Mozart was among the most versatile of all composers.
    2. Many of Mozart's concertos are among his greatest works.
    3. Mozart was also a master of opera.
    4. Mozart completed his last three symphonies in only six weeks.

59. According to the passage
    1. Mozart's greatest masterpieces were comic operas.
    2. Mozart's concertos were written for his own violin performances.
    3. Mozart's comic operas have stereotypical characters with static emotions.
    4. Mozart's compositions were created quickly and easily.

60. According to the passage, Mozart's opera characters were often characterized through the utilization of
    1. lyricism.
    2. stereotypes.
    3. tone.
    4. librettos.

The Reading Test
Practice Test Eight

Computers are moving into the workplace at a speed virtually unprecedented by any other piece of business equipment. Not even the telephone, which in its advent revolutionized
5   business communications, had so <u>pervasive</u> an impact on how business is conducted and managed.

Every day, hundreds of companies turn over many of the details of their management
10 functions and controls to these high-tech tools. According to the International Data Corporation, by the end of 1985 American business will be equipped with some ten million personal computers, three out of four of which
15 will be located in small and medium-sized businesses. And this figure does not include the nearly one hundred thousand mainframe computers already in place.

Few successes come without their price, and
20 while these dramatic advancements may improve significantly the quality and cost-effectiveness of a company's services to clients, employees, and stockholders, they also lead to unprecedented opportunities for crime. For example, while the
25 management of a newly computerized business enjoys access to more readily available information, it may also find that it has less direct control over vital business functions and less knowledge of the work supervised. A manager
30 with limited understanding of computer operations may now have to supervise computer programmers, data entry clerks, and others placed in newly created positions of trust.

Perhaps even more potentially damaging is
35 the concentration of massive amounts of vital, often confidential information on small, easily transportable documents.

(Schomp, 1986)

1. As used in the passage, <u>pervasive</u> means
    1. limited.
    2. widespread.
    3. unusual.
    4. complicated.

2. Which of the following does the author primarily use in this passage?
    1. problem/solution
    2. argument
    3. comparison
    4. narrative

3. Which of the following does the author fail to mention?
    1. the attitude of employee toward computers
    2. the cost effectiveness of computer technology
    3. the ethics of computerization
    4. the successes of computer technology

4. The author mentions International Data Corporation to support his point that
    1. computerization of business introduced negative consequences as well as positive results.
    2. managerial responsibilities have lessened through technology.
    3. the impact of computerization on business has come on rapidly and dramatically.
    4. massive amounts of vital, confidential company records are at risk on disks.

5. What is the author's viewpoint toward the computerization of businesses?
    1. critical
    2. objective
    3. admiring
    4. sentimental

6. Which comparison does the author make to illustrate the impact of computers on business?
    1. the mainframe computer
    2. the telephone
    3. small documents
    4. the personal computer

It is probably safe to say that none of the visual elements gives us so much pleasure as color. You will understand this if you have ever been restricted to watching an old black-and-
5 white television and then suddenly have access to a color set. For the same reason, certain entrepreneurs have acquired the rights to classic films like *Casablanca,* and "colorized" them--applied color by painstaking computer methods
10 to what was originally a black-and-white movie. The debate about whether this practice is acceptable, ethically and aesthetically, will continue for many years, but obviously the "colorizers" are hoping to tap a segment of the
15 market that demands full color.

Various studies have demonstrated that color affects a wide range of psychological and physiological responses. Restaurants often are decorated in red which is believed to increase
20 appetite and therefore food consumption. A common treatment for premature babies born with potentially fatal jaundice is to bathe them in blue light, which for reasons not fully understood, eliminates the need to transfuse their blood. Blue
25 surroundings also will significantly lower a person's blood pressure, pulse, and respiration rate. In one experiment subjects were asked to identify, by taste, ordinary mashed potatoes colored bright green. Because of the disorienting
30 color cues, they could not say what they were eating. And in one California detention center violent children are routinely placed in an 8-by-4 foot cell painted bubble-gum pink. The children relax, become calmer, and often fall asleep within
35 ten minutes. This color has been dubbed "passive pink." The mechanism involved in all these color responses is still unclear, but there can be no doubt that color "works" on the human brain and body in powerful ways.

(McCarter, 1988)

7. The primary purpose of this passage is to describe
   1. the "colorizing" of the classic films like Casablanca.
   2. experiments done with changing colors for shock effect.
   3. the way in which the visual element, color, can produce both physical and emotional reactions.
   4. the way color is a function of light.

8. Which of the following statements is an opinion and could NOT be a fact?
   1. The practice of "colorization" is acceptable, ethically, and aesthetically.
   2. Color ~works~ on the human brain.
   3. Children relax, become calmer, in a room painted bubble-gum pink.
   4. The classic film Casablanca was "colorized."

9. As used in the passage, entrepreneurs means
   1. color experts.
   2. business owner-operators.
   3. psychological researchers.
   4. photographers.

10. As used in the passage, the word consumption means
    1. sales.
    2. appeal.
    3. preservation.
    4. intake.

11. The author would probably agree that
    1. entrepreneurs wanted to "colorize" movies to make a profit.
    2. all children's rooms should be painted bubble-gum pink.
    3. ethically no movies should be "colorized."
    4. the coloring of a plate of food has little effect.

12. Which of the following details given in the passage least illustrates the author's point?
    1. Disturbed children relax in bubble-gum pink cells.
    2. Blue environments lower a person's blood pressure.
    3. Black and white movies are "colorized" by tedious computer methods.
    4. Subjects were unable to identify by taste, bright green mashed potatoes.

As man grows older, he is said to become "more like himself." This is meant to imply that the individual increasingly shows a pattern of appearance and behavior that is characteristic of
5　him. He is, of course, always moving forward in time and is in a dynamic transformation from his past to his future. The dynamics of the transformation of the individual from childhood through adulthood are such that mixtures of
10　stability and change, persistence and adaptation, and emergence of new features are seen in the wide range of human characteristics.

Metaphorically, man's development over the life span might be likened to the growth and
15　branching of a tree. Trees, like humans, have characteristic lengths of life and show forms typical of their species. They, like humans, reflect various environmental conditions, trees through the width of their annual trunk rings and humans
20　through the special functions of their nervous system and memory. The growth of human behavior can be likened to the manner in which tree branching occurs. Once tree-branching has occurred, the growth pattern is somewhat
25　determined, and new growth proceeds on previous growth. This is true of human behavior as well. However, unlike the tree that is unable to make selections at choice points in its development, humans can make choices during
30　their growth that can change their "growing" environment. It is those behavior choices that lead individuals to progressively more efficient and productive behaviors. The result is that as individuals change over the life span, new
35　patterns of behavior emerge representing adaptations to past history as well as to present physical and social circumstances.

(Birren, 1964)

13. The passage is primarily concerned with
    1. stability of behavior.
    2. behavioral changes over the human life span.
    3. man's environment.
    4. physical and social circumstances.

14. According to the passage, human behavior
    1. is often misunderstood.
    2. is usually predictable.
    3. is set in childhood and remains set throughout the life span.
    4. is influenced by the environment, yet also influences the environment.

15. As used in the passage, a dynamic transformation means
    1. continual change.
    2. powerful adaptation.
    3. interesting growth.
    4. impressive development.

16. The passage states that
    1. reactions hinder growth.
    2. the human nervous system and memory play important roles in human growth.
    3. life forms depend upon new features.
    4. behavior is set.

17. For what purpose did the author use the analogy, "branching of a tree"?
    1. To compare the structural forms of trees and humans.
    2. To imply that a tree is the same as a man.
    3. To explain the behavioral growth of humans.
    4. To show that trees like humans need pruning.

18. The author indicates that with age, human behavior choices
    1. deteriorate.
    2. regress toward the past.
    3. become more competent.
    4. are uncontrolled.

Adapted from: Birren, J.E. *The Psychology of Aging.* Englewood Cliffs: Prentice-Hall, 1964, pp. 1-2.

James I stopped the Virginia Company but not the flow of Englishmen to America. The social, religious, and economic forces that had made their appearance in the time of Henry VIII were still at
5   work, upsetting the lives of an increasing number of people. Prices were still rising; lands were changing hands; and sheep were grazing where men once drove their plows. To make matters worse, a depression settled over the woolens industry in the
10 1620's and lasted through the next decade. The land seemed weary of her inhabitants; the new king made it seem wearier by levying taxes without the consent of Parliament and by repressive measures against religious dissenters. The result was the
15 Great Migration, in which perhaps as many as fifty thousand people left for the New World. The exodus lasted until 1640, when Englishmen began to see a more hopeful future for their own country. By that year Virginia's population had risen to eight
20 thousand, Maryland had been founded; and so had the Bermudas, Barbados, St. Kitts, and other West Indian islands. About twenty thousand of the emigrants came to that northern part of Virginia now called New England.

(Blum, 1977)

19. The best title for this passage is
    1. The Virginia Company.
    2. Settling of New England.
    3. Great Migration.
    4. Time of Henry VII.

20. Which of the following does the author primarily use in this passage?
    1. comparison-contrast
    2. definition
    3. cause-effect
    4. enumeration

21. The events in the passage most likely occurred in the
    1. early 16th century.
    2. late 16th century.
    3. early 17th century.
    4. early 18th century.

22. Which of the following would NOT be a reason the British left England for America?
    1. religious oppression
    2. financial problems
    3. depression of the woolen industry
    4. unproductive land

23. It can be concluded from the passage that James I's attitude toward his people was
    1. sympathetic.
    2. distressed.
    3. oppressive.
    4. indifferent.

24. As used in the passage, exodus means
    1. existence.
    2. a departure.
    3. a book of the Bible.
    4. exportation.

Psychological aspects of participating in sports provide an opportunity to "let off steam," and to express aggression or hostility either directly or <u>vicariously</u>, as spectators. It has been

5 argued that in past centuries, people had to overcome natural obstacles and dangers found in their primitive environments; today, we have created sports and games which represent mock struggles with artificial dangers.

10 Whether or not one fully accepts this view, there is no doubt that sports, particularly those which are highly combative or physically dangerous, such as football, boxing, bobsledding, or parachute jumping, offer modern men and

15 women a challenge they cannot find elsewhere in their lives.

Beyond the element of physical risk and daring, the urge to compete with others or with oneself, to overcome odds and obstacles and to

20 reach new levels of personal accomplishment is a powerful motivation behind participation in sports.

Social aspects of participating in sports also offer the chance to be a member of a team--a

25 closely-knit human group--with all the reassurance and warmth that may imply. This factor is particularly important today. Many social commentators have described a growth of <u>alienation</u>, a lack of belonging and commitment,

30 on the part of young people today.

Sports, while obviously not the total answer to the problem, do provide a direct and forceful kind of identification and human contact that is the very opposite of alienation. A team under

35 pressure is a very tightly knit group. The athlete identifies closely with his or her rival; they are sharing the same impulses, pressures, and emotions. In other sports or active games which do not stress competition as heavily, the social

40 rewards may be based on a sense of fellowship and companionship, and on sharing experiences with others.

(Kraus, 1985)

25. Which of the following is NOT a psychological motivation behind participation in sports?

1. the urge to compete
2 the urge to overcome odds
3. the urge to be physically fit
4. the urge to reach personal accomplishment

26. It is implied that

1. the author is an athlete.
2. the physical risks of sports are more important than the social aspects.
3. the author is in favor of team sports.
4. the author is not in favor of team sports.

27. As used in the passage, <u>vicariously</u> most nearly means

1. silently.
2. directly.
3. cooperatively.
4. indirectly.

28. The primary purpose of this passage is to show

1. components of community recreational programs.
2. psychological aspects of sports partici- pation.
3. physical aspects of sports participation.
4. social and psychological motivations for sports participation.

29. With which of the following would the author probably NOT agree?

1. Sports participation can give young people a sense of belonging.
2. Sports participation is not the total answer to the problem of identification.
3. Sports participation can be a positive ventilation of aggression.
4. Sports participation is a trivial aspect of modern culture.

30. As used in the passage, <u>alienation</u> refers to

1. association.
2. isolation.
3. obligation.
4. rationalization.

The planet Earth is unique among entities in the infinite series of galaxies, although other worlds may also possess life. The geographer regards the earth as more than a globe
5 suspended in space. In general, he is concerned with the planet's lower atmosphere, surface skin, and thin layer of crustal material, or the land-sea-air interface. Here it is that life occurs, localities differ, various conditions appear simultaneously,
10 different processes have been at work since the earth became relatively stable, and change continues.

All this suggests that geography deals with everything that forms the outer section of the
15 earth. A "geographer," situated on some other planet and interested in the geography of the earth might well accept this <u>holistic</u> approach. On our own planet, however, man has not been limitless in intelligence and capabilities. In an
20 effort to focus his attention on a comprehensible subject he early fell to dividing knowledge into segments, to which he applied <u>diverse</u> terms. The more he understood, the more he divided, until knowledge became so broken into
25 disciplines that, some feel no one man can view the whole.

(Miller, 1991)

31. As underlined in the passage, <u>holistic</u> means
    1. religion.
    2. segmented.
    3. secure.
    4. whole.

32. As underlined in the passage, <u>diverse</u> means
    1. different.
    2. understandable.
    3. crucial.
    4. complex.

33. According to the passage, the more man knew
    1. the more he applied similar terms to knowledge.
    2. the less he divided knowledge.
    3. the more holistic his thinking became.
    4. the more he categorized his knowledge.

34. The passage implies that man
    1. is limitless in intelligence and capabilities.
    2. is limited in intelligence and capabilities.
    3. accepts the holistic approach to geography.
    4. is superior to extraterrestrials.

35. What is the relationship of the second paragraph to the first one?
    1. The second contradicts the first.
    2. The second elaborates on a concept referred to in the first.
    3. The second presents the solution to a problem introduced in the first.
    4. The second shifts the topic entirely.

36. Which of the following does the author use in the last paragraph?
    1. analogy
    2. statistics
    3. contrast
    4. figurative language

As he neared Petersburg, Alexey Alexandrovitch not only adhered entirely to his decision, but was even composing in his head the letter he would write to his wife. Going into the porter's room, Alexey Alexandrovitch glanced at the letters and papers brought from his office, and directed that they should be brought to him in his study.

"The horses can be taken out and I will see no one," he said in answer to the porter, with a certain pleasure, indicative of his agreeable frame of mind, emphasizing the words, "see no one."

In his study Alexey Alexandrovitch walked up and down twice, and stopped at an immense writing-table, on which six candles had already been lighted by the valet who had preceded him. He cracked his knuckles and sat down, sorting out his writing appurtenances. Putting his elbows on the table, he bent his head on one side, thought a minute, and began to write, without pausing for a second. He wrote without using any form of address to her, and wrote in French, making use of the plural *"vous,"* which was not the same note of coldness as the corresponding Russian form. *"At our last conversation, I notified you of my intention to communicate to you my decision in regard to the subject of that conversation. Having carefully considered everything, I am writing now with the object of fulfilling that promise. My decision is as follows. Whatever your conduct may have been, I do not consider myself justified in breaking the ties in which we are bound by a Higher Power. The family cannot be broken up by a whim, a caprice, or even by the sin of one of the partners in the marriage, and our life must go on as it has done in the past. This is essential for me, for you, and for our son. I am fully persuaded that you have repented and do repent of what has called forth the present letter, and that you will cooperate with me in eradicating the cause of our <u>estrangement</u>, and forgetting the past. In the contrary event, you can conjecture what awaits you and our son. All this I hope to discuss more in detail in a personal interview. As the season is drawing to a close, I would beg you to return to Petersburg as quickly as possible, not later than Tuesday. All necessary preparations shall be made for your arrival here. I beg you to note that*

I attach particular significance to compliance with this request.

A. Karenin
"P.S.--I enclose the money which may be needed for your expenses."

(Tolstoy, 1877)

37. On the basis of the signature, the narrator implies that

    1. Alexey Alexandrovitch is the same person as A. Karenin.
    2. A. Karenin is a woman.
    3. the letter is addressed to A. Karenin.
    4. Alexey is not A. Karenin.

38. The narrator implies that if Alexey's wife arrives later than Tuesday, this would mean to Alexey that

    1. she wants to have a reconciliation.
    2. she didn't get the letter.
    3. she doesn't want to have a reconciliation.
    4. she is deathly ill.

39. From the passage, it can be concluded that Alexey believes that husband and wife are

    1. free to do as they like.
    2. always justified in getting a divorce.
    3. never tempted by others.
    4. bound by a higher power.

40. <u>Estrangement</u>, as used in the passage, means

    1. togetherness.
    2. marriage.
    3. courtship.
    4. separation.

41. According to the passage, Alexey gave his wife money because

    1. she might need it for her vacation.
    2. she needed a new dress.
    3. he was paying child support.
    4. she might need it for travel expenses.

42. It is implied in the passage that the problem between Alexey and his wife is

    1. she spent too much money.
    2. she was unfaithful.
    3. he was unfaithful.
    4. he drank too much.

Most animals eat and drink whenever the urge arises. Humans, however, do most of their eating and drinking at certain culturally pre-scribed times and feel hungry as those times

5 approach. These eating times vary from culture to culture. Similarly, a North American's idea of a comfortable way to sleep will vary greatly from that of a Japanese or an African. The need to sleep is determined by biology; the way it is

10 satisfied is cultural.

Through enculturation one learns the socially appropriate way of satisfying one's biologically determined needs. It is important to distinguish between the needs themselves, which are not

15 learned, and the learned ways in which they are satisfied. The biological needs of humans are the same as those of other animals: food, shelter, companionship, self-defense, and sexual gratification. Each culture determines how these

20 needs will be met.

Not all learned behavior is cultural. A dog may learn tricks, but this behavior is reflexive, the result of conditioning by repeated training, not the product of enculturation. On the other hand,

25 nonhuman primates are capable of forms of cultural behavior. A chimpanzee, for example, will take a twig and strip it of all leaves in order to make a tool that will extract termites from a hole. Such toolmaking, learned through imitation, is

30 unquestionably a form of cultural behavior thought until recently to be exclusively human.

(Spencer, 1973)

43. As used in the passage, appropriate means
    1. required.
    2. processed.
    3. prescribed.
    4. unacceptable.

44. The author's primary purpose is to explain that
    1. the overall appropriate way to satisfy biological needs is learned from culture.
    2. humans eat and drink whenever the urge arises.
    3. all learned behavior is cultural.
    4. chimpanzees are capable of forms of cultural behavior.

45. Which of the following is NOT a form of cultural behavior?
    1. the time a Russian eats
    2. the way a chimpanzee makes a tool
    3. the way a dog learns a trick
    4. the way a Japanese sleeps

46. Which of the following is NOT biologically determined?
    1. Humans feel hungry as certain times approach.
    2. Japanese need a certain amount of sleep.
    3. Animals drink whenever the impulse arises.
    4. Humans have sexual urges.

47. Which of the following statements is an opinion and could NOT be a fact?
    1. Biological needs of humans are the same as those of other animals.
    2. Japanese satisfy their cultural needs in a more efficient manner than Americans.
    3. Culture is transmitted from one generation to the next.
    4. Eating times vary from culture to culture.

48. According to the passage, enculturation occurs
    1. through heredity.
    2. through learning.
    3. only in man.
    4. in all species.

The growth of technology and science was so rapid In the industrialized countries during the period 1871-1914 that it influenced or overshadowed all other developments.

5 Industrialization also spread during these years from its early base in Western Europe and the United States to Central and Eastern Europe, Japan, and the British dominions. Steel, oil, and electricity joined or superseded the iron and

10 steam of the preceding age. This was the great era of railroad building. The automobile and the airplane appeared. Communications were revolutionized by the telegraph, the telephone, and wireless telegraphy.

15 Science kept pace with technology. The nature of matter was discovered and it proved to be as shockingly unstable as the old "absolutes" of time, space, and motion. Darwin's evolutionary hypothesis seemed to unlock most of the secrets

20 concerning life on the planet. Medical science had its beginning in this period and the preceding decade. Psychology, sociology, and history made valiant efforts to be scientific. The people in the industrialized countries became fascinated by all

25 this--the masses with the marvels and promises of technology, the intelligentsia with the wonders of science.

The first phase of the Industrial Revolution had belonged to the bourgeoisie. During the

30 second phase, the industrial proletariat, now much more numerous and concentrated in the industrial cities, demanded and got many benefits. Liberalism became much more liberal. By 1914, almost every country in Europe enjoyed

35 universal male suffrage. Liberals abandoned laissez-faire doctrines in favor of government protection for the poor and the weak.

(Harrison, 1975)

49. Which of the following does the author primarily use in this passage?
   1. cause-effect
   2. narration
   3. argument
   4. personal experience

50. As underlined in the passage laissez-faire means
   1. government regulated.
   2. unregulated.
   3. fair.
   4. restricted.

51. The telephone, the telegraph, and wireless telegraphy revolutionized
   1. transportation.
   2. science.
   3. medical science.
   4. communications.

52. Male suffrage is listed as an example of
   1. laissez-faire doctrine.
   2. liberalism.
   3. government protection.
   4. the industrial proletariat.

53. Government protection for the poor and the weak is contrasted with
   1. liberalism.
   2. universal male suffrage.
   3. laissez-faire doctrine.
   4. industrial demands.

54. According to the author, the Industrial Revolution helped to
   1. promote world peace.
   2. influence the formation of labor unions.
   3. open doors for voting rights.
   4. end secret keeping.

In 1884 a woman planted a water hyacinth in her backyard in Florida. Within ten years the plant, which can double its population in two weeks, was a public menace. These plants have clogged boat traffic in many ponds, streams, canals, and rivers in Florida and in other parts of the southeastern United States.

Since 1989 mechanical harvesters and a variety of herbicides have been used to keep the plant in check, with little success. Large numbers of Florida manatees can control the growth and spread of water hyacinths in inland waters more effectively than mechanical or chemical methods. But these gentle and playful <u>herbivores</u> are threatened with extinction, mostly from being slashed by powerboat propellers, becoming entangled in fishing gear, or being hit on the head by oars.

In recent years scientists have introduced other alien species that feed on water hyacinths to help control its spread. They include a weevil imported form Argentina, a water snail from Puerto Rico, and the grass carp, a fish brought in from the Soviet Union. These species can help, but the water snail and grass carp also feed on other desirable aquatic plants.

There is some good news in this story. Preliminary research indicated that water hyacinths can be used in several beneficial ways. They can be introduced in sewage treatment lagoons to absorb toxic chemicals. They can be converted by fermentation to a biogas fuel similar to natural gas and added as a mineral and protein supplement to cattle feed.

(Daniel, 1980)

55. As used in the passage <u>herbivores</u> means
    1. meat eaters.
    2. sea cows.
    3. plant eaters.
    4. alien species.

56. Which point does the writer fail to develop?
    1. the positive way the water hyacinth can serve the community
    2. the way manatees can be protected from extinction
    3. the way the hyacinth has come to be such a threat in Florida waters
    4. the negative way the hyacinth is affecting the water ways

57. The author's tone may be best described as
    1. critical.
    2. exaggerated.
    3. ironic.
    4. objective.

58. The primary topic of this passage is
    1. waterways of Florida.
    2. the water hyacinth.
    3. the playful manatee.
    4. other alien species.

59. Which of the following is NOT a threat to the extinction of the manatee?
    1. injuries from motor boat propellers
    2. entanglement in fishing nets
    3. herbicides used to check the growth of water hyacinths
    4. injuries from boat oars

60. With which statement would the author most likely agree?
    1. The lady should never have planted the hyacinth in the Florida waterway.
    2. The introduction of other alien animal species to feed on the hyacinths was not altogether successful.
    3. The hyacinth can be of no benefit.
    4. The use of herbicides in the waterways of Florida is very dangerous.

The Reading Test
Practice Test Nine

Not all animals have the same basic eye structure as humans do, nor do they necessarily form the same type of images.

Typically, insects have two kinds of eyes.
5 One is a "simple" eyespot, called an ocellus, which is sensitive to light and shade but does not form an image. The other eye is much more complex and is called a compound eye. It is made up of a thousand or more tiny individual
10 "eyes" called ommatidia. These microscopic ommatidia fit together like a honeycomb, or mosaic, with their fused lenses forming the curved exterior of the eye. The lower portion of each ommatidium tapers to a single sensitive
15 reactor cell, at the bottom of which is an axon leading to the center of the eye.

When something (such as a passing bird) moves through the air above the compound eye, various ommatidia are stimulated in turn, each
20 individual response making up only a small part of the total image. Such an arrangement produces what is called mosaic vision; the image is composed of pieces of the complete picture like a mosaic.
25 Insects with compound eyes do not see a sharp picture. Much more important than a clear image is that any motion above and around them is exaggerated, for movement usually means a potential enemy to threaten their survival.
30 Other insects have single eyes, each with one lens and a fixed focus. Spiders often have four pairs of this kind of eye, and each pair has a different fixed focal length. The octopus and squid have eyes quite similar to those of the
35 human. This is a good example of parallel evolution. These eyes are <u>analogous</u> to ours except that in these many armed mollusks, the axons from the retinal cells emerge at the back and there is no network or blind spot over or on
40 the retina, as in the human eye. In that respect, the octopus eye might seem to be superior in function to our own.

1. <u>Analogous</u>, as used in the passage, means
   1. comparable.
   2. identical.
   3. dissimilar.
   4. superior.

2. "Many armed mollusks" (line 37) refers to
   1. squid and octopus.
   2. octopus and spider.
   3. spider and squid.
   4. octopus and insect.

3. Which of the following does the author fail to discuss?
   1. the ocellus
   2. the compound eye
   3. mosaic vision
   4. potential enemies

4. The primary purpose of this passage is to explain
   1. how eye spots affect insect vision.
   2. how insects' eyes are structured.
   3. how ommatidia pick up images.
   4. the function of compound eyes.

5. As described in paragraph 3, mosaic vision
   1. is a visual image composed of many different segments.
   2. produces a sharp image.
   3. is composed of one lens and a fixed focus.
   4. is composed of four sets of eyes.

6. The insect eye structure most directly related to the safety of the insect is the
   1. ocellus.
   2. ommatidia.
   3. simple eyespot.
   4. fixed focus.

In sharp contrast to the Crime Fighter is the sort of police officer one can describe as the Social Agent. Defenders of this type of officer note that police departments are merely part of a

5 larger organization of several government agencies; they believe that officers are responsible for a wide range of duties other than crime fighting. They argue that police could better spend their time trying to do well those things

10 that have to be done rather than attempting to limit police contacts with the public to crime-related events. Proponents of the Social Agent approach argue that establishing new governmental agencies or modifying existing

15 ones to perform the duties relinquished by the Crime Fighter would create an exorbitant drain on municipal resources.

The Social Agent believes that police should become involved in a wide range of activities,

20 without regard for their connection to law enforcement. The Social Agent does not believe enforcement is the essence of policing and may point out the word "police" is commonly used in contexts that have at best only a tenuous relation

25 to law enforcement (e.g. in such phrases as "the state's police power" and "police the parade grounds"). The Social Agent who is well versed in the history of the American police will note, for example, that the Boston police department was

30 developed in the early nineteenth century as much in response to a health and sanitary crisis as for criminal apprehension needs.

Rather than viewing themselves as criminal catchers, Social Agents consider themselves

35 problem solvers.

(Senna, 1990)

7. The primary purpose of the passage is to
    1. explain attitudes toward police.
    2. list police duties.
    3. contrast the Social Agent with the Crime Fighter.
    4. support Crime Fighters.

8. As used in the passage, apprehension means
    1. fearful anticipation.
    2. understanding.
    3. capture.
    4. tension.

9. The author implies that the Social Agent believes
    1. law enforcement is unnecessary.
    2. police duties should not be limited to law enforcement.
    3. crime fighting is unimportant.
    4. criminals should not be arrested.

10. The Social Agent police officer would be known primarily for his or her
    1. crime fighting.
    2. number of arrests.
    3. solving of civic problems.
    4. creative approaches.

11. The author's primary purpose for mentioning the Boston police department is to show that
    1. Boston police were responsible citizens.
    2. U.S. police should know their history.
    3. the first police in Boston were social agents.
    4. health and sanitary crises threaten cities.

12. Consider the purpose of the second paragraph which begins "The Social Agent believes . . ." and choose the word or phrase that could logically be used at the beginning of this sentence.
    1. finally
    2. in the meantime
    3. further
    4. in contrast

During his lifetime Poe entertained thousands of American and European readers with his tales and poems. This, he believed, was the aim of the writer, and no American writer of his day was so well equipped by temperament and training to achieve this aim. His mind was as keen and analytical as it was imaginative. He became, through hard work and self-criticism, a master craftsman in prose as well as in poetry.

Some critics consider Poe a better storyteller than a poet, for the tales allowed him greater freedom to use his imagination. Some of these tales leave the reader with a single impression of fear, horror, wonder, or dread. Some hold <u>him</u> in <u>suspense</u> as a mystery or seemingly impossible crime is exposed and clearly solved. In all of these, the plot is arranged with great skill, and the reader is drawn rapidly to the dramatic climax.

Poe found greater delight in writing poetry; it was "not a purpose but a passion." To make it a "Rhythmical Creation of Beauty" he devised unusual themes and rhythms and used words, and combinations of words, as much for their melodious effect as for their meaning--sometimes more. Both his poems and his tales reveal him to be one of the most painstaking and consistent craftsmen in the history of Western literature.

(Wachner, 1963)

13. In general, the reviewers reaction to Poe's work is
    1. favorable.
    2. mixed.
    3. neutral.
    4. unfavorable.

14. Which of the following could be a fact and NOT an opinion?
    1. Poe entertained thousands of Americans and Europeans with his stories and poems.
    2. He had the best analytical mind of his time.
    3. He was a painstaking and consistent craftsman.
    4. He was a master craftsman in prose and poetry.

15. Poe's primary passion was
    1. prose.
    2. tales.
    3. poetry.
    4. criticism.

16. As used in the passage, <u>suspense</u> means
    1. doubt.
    2. suspicion.
    3. anticipation.
    4. contemplation.

17. It is implied in the passage that Poe's success and recognition as a writer
    1. came after his death.
    2. came because his work was analytical.
    3. came predominantly from his prose.
    4. came through consistent, careful, hard work and self imposed criticism.

18. <u>Him</u> refers to
    1. Poe.
    2. the critic.
    3. the reader.
    4. the storyteller.

Although no one can predict the future in much detail, there are a number of strong trends in the works that should create investment opportunities.

5   Population growth is one of them. By 1990, the population will be approaching 250 million-- roughly 10% higher than in 1981--that means about 20 million more people creating demand for additional goods and services.

10   More important than the total, however, is the mix. The population will be undergoing significant shifts in the years to come.

    The single largest adult age group will be the 25- to 34-year olds. They <u>constitute</u> a prime
15 market for homes and the things that go in them. Sellers of such products should do a brisk business throughout the decade.

    The number of new 18-24 year-olds will shrink, easing the need for the job market to
20 create entry level positions for new workers. The results should be a lower unemployment rate as the decade proceeds. At the same time colleges and other institutions that have depended on young adults as their primary clients will have to
25 widen their appeal or suffer the consequences.

    The growth in practically every other age bracket will mean shifting tastes in the things people buy. Older adults, further along in their working lives, have more money to spend than
30 the youngsters who constituted the major marketing target of the 1960's and 1970's. They represent a potential boon to businesses that serve them.

(Miller, 1981)

19. This passage probably appeared in
    1. a retirement magazine.
    2. an accounting textbook.
    3. a statistics annual.
    4. an investment brochure.

20. Which group constituted the major marketing target of the 1960's and 1970's?
    1. the elderly
    2. the young
    3. the middle-aged
    4. persons age fifty and over

21. The author makes his point primarily through the use of
    1. comparison.
    2. analogy.
    3. opinion.
    4. contrast.

22. The word <u>constitute</u> as used in the business means
    1. direct.
    2. influence.
    3. compose.
    4. govern.

23. It can be inferred that in the future colleges will have to
    1. offer more appealing courses for non-traditional students.
    2. appeal only to the 18-year old population.
    3. admit only 18-to-24 year olds.
    4. close down certain departments to account for low enrollment.

24. The primary purpose of this passage is to explain
    1. the future shifts in population.
    2. how population will grow in the future.
    3. how investment opportunities may be created by population growth and shifts.
    4. that investment opportunities are solely dependent on population growth and mix.

How the body responds to invasion by an antigen for the first time is called, logically, the primary response, while its response to a second or later exposure is a secondary response.

5   When an antigen is introduced into the body for the first time, it takes the system a day or two to begin producing antibodies. This delay is called a latent period (or lag) because all of the early responses are not apparent, and it may

10 look as if the body is doing nothing. Antibody production begins slowly, but by about the fifth day, production reaches a peak, then it plateaus, or levels off, for a while. Over the next 4 to 6 weeks, production slowly ceases.

15   Upon subsequent exposure to the antigen, the secondary response is immediate and more effective. Antibodies may be produced within a few hours; many more antibodies are produced and their defense of the body is more long-

20 lasting.

    Physicians use the principle of the more effective secondary response when they administer active immunizations that give the patient immunity to one particular kind of antigen,

25 but there are also passive forms of immunization. Passive forms employ antibodies already made by another organism; active forms employ antigens that stimulate the organism to form its own antibodies.

30   An active immunity develops from exposure to antigens. This immunity can be naturally or artificially induced. If someone with measles sneezes in your direction, you contract the disease and you develop the immunity naturally.

35 However, such immunity can be artificially induced by immunization, which is the injection of a vaccine containing either measles antigen or weakened (attenuated) or killed virus that are unable to cause a disease. The body launches

40 an immune response against the antigen contained in the measles vaccine and develops memory cells so that future encounters with the same pathogen will be dealt with swiftly.

25. Which of the following would NOT be considered active immunity?
1. contracting measles from an infected person's sneeze.
2. injection of a vaccine containing measles antigens.
3. the use of antibodies already made by another organism.
4. immunization containing a weakened or killed virus.

26. As described in the passage, antigen means
1. antibodies produced for the defense of the body.
2. passive forms of immunization.
3. the immune response of the body.
4. a substance introduced into the body which stimulates production of antibodies.

27. Latent, as used in the passage means
1. acclaimed.
2. dormant.
3. dead.
4. systemic.

28. It, as underlined in paragraph two, refers to
1. peak delay.
2. latent period.
3. early responses.
4. antibody production.

29. The author implies that when an antigen is introduced into the system
1. the secondary response acts quicker than the primary response.
2. the primary response acts immediately.
3. the primary response does not always work.
4. the secondary response does not always work.

30. The author established a tone that is
1. informative.
2. subjective.
3. critical.
4. conversational.

The unsettled West had always occupied a special place in the American imagination. But the vast regions of this last frontier had a particularly strong romantic appeal. Some of the reasons were obvious. The Great Plains, the Rocky Mountains, the basin and plateau region beyond the Rockies, and the Sierra Nevada-Cascade ranges beyond that--all constituted a landscape of such brilliant diversity, such spectacular grandeur, so different from anything white Americans had encountered before, it was little wonder that newcomers looked on it with reverence and awe. Painters of the new "Rocky Mountain School" celebrated the new West in grandiose canvases. They emphasized the ruggedness and dramatic variety of the region.

Even more appealing than the landscape perhaps, was the rugged, free-spirited life style that many Americans associated with the frontier--a life style that stood in sharp contrast to the increasingly stable and ordered world of the East. Particular public interest attached to the figure of the cowboy, who was transformed remarkably quickly into a powerful and enduring figure of myth. Admiring Americans seldom thought about the drearier aspects of the cowboy's life; the tedium, the loneliness, the physical discomforts, the relatively few opportunities for advancement. Instead, in Western novels such as Owen Wister's *The Virginian (1902),* they romanticized his freedom from traditional social constraints, his affinity with nature, his supposed propensity for violence. The cowboy became the last and most powerful symbol of what had long been an important ideal in the American mind--the ideal of the natural man. That symbol survived for more than a century in popular literature, in song, and later in film and on television.

(Current, 1983)

31. The primary purpose of this passage is to describe
    1. the landscape of the American West.
    2. paintings of the "Rocky Mountain School."
    3. the romantic appeal of the Western frontier.
    4. The rugged life-style of the cowboy.

32. As used in the passage, propensity means
    1. dislike.
    2. disgust.
    3. indifference.
    4. inclination.

33. Not included as one of the realities of the cowboy's life was
    1. loneliness.
    2. boredom.
    3. violent nature.
    4. physical discomfort.

34. The overall impression of the Western landscape in the first paragraph is
    1. pleasant.
    2. awesome.
    3. monotonous.
    4. colorful.

35. The author mentions the novel *The Virginian* to show
    1. how the cowboy's life was romanticized.
    2. the realities of a cowboy's life.
    3. that the cowboy's life was dreary and lonely.
    4. how the cowboy became a symbol.

36. The author mentions the "stable and ordered world of the East" in paragraph two to show
    1. how life in the American West was similar.
    2. how appealing life in the East was.
    3. how different frontier life was.
    4. how unappealing the rugged frontier was.

The model followed by the largest Japanese corporation draws on a long cultural tradition that emphasizes the importance of the group over the individual. When people join a major Japanese

5   corporation, they are making a lifetime commitment, which the corporation reciprocates. Unless the employee commits a crime, he or she will not be fired or laid off. All promotions are made from inside the organization; outsiders are

10 not even considered. Most promotions are based on seniority, so people of the same age move more or less together through the organizational hierarchy, with little competition among them. Workers are organized into small teams, and it is

15 the team--not the individual workers--whose performance is evaluated. Over the years, each individual may belong to many such teams, thereby gaining experience throughout the corporation. Decision making is collective: rather

20 than issue new policies, the top officials merely ratify them after they have been discussed and approved at every level of the organization (the Japanese word for this process literally means "bottom-up" decision making).

25   Unlike Western corporations, which usually limit the relationship between organization and employee to matters that are "strictly business," Japanese corporations take considerable responsibility for their workers' welfare. They

30 provide a whole range of services, sometimes including housing, recreation, health care, and continuing education. The workers, in turn, show great loyalty to the company--perhaps by wearing company uniforms, singing the company song,

35 working exceptionally long hours, or taking part in company-organized sporting and other sporting activities. In short, the activities of the corporation and the lives of its members are closely intertwined. This relationship between

40 organization and worker reflects a deep difference between Japanese and Western cultures: to the Japanese, it indicates a bond of commitment that ensures security and solidarity.
                                        (Robertson, 1987)

37. The author's primary purpose is to discuss
    1. Japanese hiring and firing policies.
    2. the unique features of the Japanese corporation which emphasize the significance of the group.
    3. how Western corporations deal with "strictly business" matters within the corporate structure.
    4. the Japanese workers' daily activities within the company.

38. In the second paragraph which of the following does the author primarily use?
    1. chronology
    2. narrative
    3. persuasion
    4. contrast

39. As used in the passage, reciprocates means
    1. retaliates.
    2. returns.
    3. vindicates.
    4. invests.

40. Which of the following is NOT mentioned about Japanese workers' attitudes toward their corporations?
    1. commitment
    2. individualism
    3. loyalty
    4. stability

41. It can be concluded that a Japanese employee in an American corporation might experience
    1. emphasis on group achievement.
    2. a work relationship that is "strictly business."
    3. "bottom up" decision making.
    4. a lifetime commitment from the company.

42. What is meant by the statement that Western corporations limit worker/employer relationships to "strictly business?"
    1. Corporate decision making is collective.
    2. Workers gain experience in many parts of the business.
    3. Promotions are made inside the organization.
    4. Personal lives of workers and work-related activities are not closely linked.

Adolescent children of employed women are better adjusted socially, feel better about themselves, have more of a sense of belonging, and get along better with their families and with
5   their friends at school than other teenagers do. Adolescent daughters of working women make a particularly strong showing. They are "more outgoing, independent, active [and] highly motivated, score higher on a variety of indices of
10   academic achievement, and appear better adjusted on social and personality measures."

On the negative side, latchkey arrangements for adolescents may have less-than-favorable outcomes, depending on how <u>susceptible</u> a
15   teenager is to peer pressure.

A study by the U.S. Department of Education, found a cumulative negative effect on the achievement of high school sophomores and seniors (particularly those in white two-parent
20   families) when their mothers had worked at some time during their growing-up years, and the effect was stronger when mothers had worked full time over the child's lifetime. A possible reason is that students with working mothers tended to spend
25   less time on homework and reading and more time watching television.

But when other researchers reanalyzed the data for a larger sample of sophomores, the negative effects of mother's employment were
30   insignificant. In fact, the sophomores a more mixed group than the seniors, since some disadvantaged students and low achievers drop out before their senior year--did *better* when their mothers worked while the children were in high
35   school. Furthermore, it appeared that high school students' achievement suffered only when their mothers worked full time during the children's preschool years--at a time historically, when most mothers were still staying home and child care
40   options were severely limited.

(Papalra, 1989)

43. The primary purpose of the author is to explain that
   1. children of employed women are better adjusted socially and academically.
   2. latchkey kids may have been unfavorably affected.

3. effects of mothers' employment are insignificant.
4. the effects of mothers' employment on children's achievements are damaging.

44. It can be concluded from the passage that
   1. older children appear at less risk than younger children and may even be at an advantage when mothers work.
   2. all mothers should work so their children will be better adjusted socially.
   3. younger children appear at less risk than older children when mothers work.
   4. researchers need to reanalyze the data to confirm their findings.

45. As used in the passage, <u>susceptible</u> means
   1. inattentive.
   2. sensitive.
   3. intolerant.
   4. responsible.

46. The U.S. Department of Education found which of the following to negatively affect academic achievement?
   1. Students tended to spend less time on social activities.
   2. Students did not get along well with their families.
   3. Students tended to spend more time watching television.
   4. Disadvantaged students and low achievers dropped out.

47. The author would probably agree with which of the following?
   1. Adolescent males of working mothers perform better academically than females of working mothers.
   2. Teenagers of working mothers are more susceptible to peer pressure.
   3. The result of the study done by the U.S. Department of Education were inconclusive.
   4. Mothers should not work during an adolescent's high school years.

What was the best way to educate a future officer? Were great captains born or could they be made? What classroom skills translated into battlefield prowess?

5 West Point had wrestled with these questions for the better part of two centuries. In the years after its founding by Thomas Jefferson in March 1802, the United States Military Academy had remained, in the words of one dismayed
10 contemporary, "a puny, rickety child." No standards obtained. Cadets might be as young as ten and as old as thirty-four. The first superintendent, Jonathan Williams, resigned in disgust in 1803; persuaded to return, he quit again
15 in 1812. The second war with Britain, which began that year, nearly became a national military debacle; Andrew Jackson's postbellum victory at New Orleans notwithstanding, the performance of the American army was marred by incompetent
20 and bickering commanders, and logistical fiascoes.

West Point found its soul with the arrival of the slender, stern, brilliant Sylvanus Thayer. A native of Braintree, Massachusetts, Thayer had graduated with the West Point class of 1808. Returning as
25 superintendent in July 1817, he found the place in an uproar. Most of the two hundred and thirteen cadets had taken an unlimited holiday. The outgoing superintendent, the vain and deceitful Alden Partridge, simply refused to leave.
30 Assembling the corps, he announced to lusty cheers that he was resuming command. Thayer caught the next boat to New York, where he waited patiently until Partridge was arrested for mutiny, and imprisoned.

35 In the next sixteen years, by force of personality and vision, Thayer transformed the Academy into an institution admired and emulated throughout the world!

(Atkinson, 1990)

48. The second war with Britain began in
    1. 1802.
    2. 1803.
    3. 1808.
    4. 1812.

49. Jackson's battle at New Orleans was
    1. misunderstood.
    2. a fiasco.
    3. a turning point.
    4. a farce.

50. The author makes his point through
    1. comparison.
    2. narrative.
    3. chronology.
    4. cause-effect.

51. As underlined debacle means
    1. assault.
    2. disaster.
    3. shortage.
    4. homage.

52. As used in the passage postbellum means
    1. before the war.
    2. during the war.
    3. at the beginning of the war.
    4. after the war.

53. The soul of West Point was
    1. Thayer.
    2. Partridge.
    3. Jackson.
    4. Williams.

54. The phrase "a puny, rickety child" expresses
    1. objectivity.
    2. sympathy.
    3. humor.
    4. satire.

Although interest groups clearly play useful political and social roles, the proliferation of such groups clearly has created serious problems in democratic life. As far back as the Constitutional
5 Convention, James Madison warned of the deleterious effects of "factions" on the political process; in his eyes factions represented potentially dangerous social elements that by nature would oppose the public interest. The only
10 way to counteract the dangers of a faction, Madison believed, would be to ensure that factions counteracted another, so that no majority faction could tyrannize society. This image of counterbalanced factions accords with a
15 commonly held view of the U.S. political process: that no one interest group possesses enough power to enforce its views on a wide range of issues, since each group will be counteracted by other groups.
20 It would be comforting to think that the system of interest groups is balanced such that in the end, the "public interest" (however that is defined) is ultimately served. Unfortunately, there are good reasons for thinking that this is not the
25 case. Perhaps the primary flaw in this theory is that the system is heavily based on the direction of those who have the resource that matters most: money, organizational clout, and political and social legitimacy. The effectiveness of
30 interest groups, in other words, is not decided by the size of their memberships or the intellectual or social worth of their goals.

(Lipsitz, 1986)

55. It can be concluded that interest groups
    1. are unnecessary.
    2. play deleterious roles.
    3. promote the "public interest."
    4. promote their views.

56. To support the idea that U.S. founding fathers were aware of the problems caused by interest groups, the author uses
    1. comparison and contrast.
    2. personal experiences.
    3. sensory appeal.
    4. an example.

57. The passage implies that special interest groups
    1. are more effective with a large membership.
    2. may oppose the "public interest."
    3. are socially unacceptable.
    4. tyrannize society.

58. According to Madison's view
    1. interest groups serve useful political roles.
    2. interest groups should balance each other's political influences.
    3. the U.S. political process is not supported by factions.
    4. interest groups should be illegal.

59. As used in the passage deleterious means
    1. complex.
    2. harmful.
    3. serious.
    4. detracting.

60. Which of the following conclusions about interest groups is supported by the passage?
    1. The effectiveness of interest groups cannot be measured.
    2. Interest groups cannot counteract one another.
    3. Interest groups with small memberships are ineffective.
    4. The effectiveness of interest groups depends upon money, prestige, and power.

The Reading Test
Practice Test Ten

The rhythmic chink of the shovel against the dirt erupted into a sharp, <u>raucous</u> clang of metal against rock. The lantern wavered and the prisoner swore softly at the reverberating sound
5 in the middle of the night.

Hardly daring to move an eyelid, he waited for some sign that he had been overheard. But no alarm was raised by the outside patrol, no barracks doors were bashed in. And so,
10 breathing a little easier, he wiped the grimy sweat from his forehead and began again that slow tedious procedure of removing the dirt from around the offending rock, and then shoveling once more.

15 It was like trying to break up cement--this hard Georgia clay. He'd already broken one shovel handle and it had taken him a whole week to make another.

It was a wonder <u>they</u> had not been caught,
20 especially with all the dirt they had disposed of. But Pershing's regulars, waiting to be relieved, didn't have their hearts in guarding prisoners. Ever since they had been moved from the temporary stockade, the six prisoners had
25 taken turns digging an escape tunnel under the barracks that housed them. A few more days and they would be clear of the fence that encircled the camp, with its layers of barbed wire strung overhead.

30 He was getting dizzy from a lack of air. But that only indicated how far they had dug and how near to freedom he was. Boards in the distance creaked, and the prisoner heard someone crawling in the tunnel toward him.

(Statham, 1982)

1. <u>Raucous</u> as underlined means
   1. harmonious.
   2. muffled.
   3. harsh.
   4. unusual.

2. <u>They</u> underlined refers to
   1. sowers.
   2. Pershing's regulars.
   3. prisoners.
   4. trustees.

3. The author creates a mood which can best be described as
   1. gloomy.
   2. nostalgic.
   3. hysterical.
   4. suspenseful.

4. According to the passage, the prison guards are
   1. anxious to capture the convicts.
   2. indifferent toward guard duty.
   3. building a fence to encircle the camp.
   4. locking the barracks.

5. The man swore softly at the reverberating sound because
   1. he hit his foot with the shovel.
   2. the lantern wavered.
   3. he was caught.
   4. he thought he would call attention to himself.

Topic
MI
Tone
Pattern

175

The most important and significant fur trade of the northern frontier was developed by the Dutch in the valley of the Hudson River. To understand the great significance of this trade,
5   especially its bearing upon Indian affairs and international relations, it is necessary to step back for a broad view of a much larger area. The French, who had established themselves on the St. Lawrence River as early as 1608, began
10   drawing upon the great fur region lying to the north of the Great Lakes. Their trade was based upon friendly relations with the Huron, an important tribe inhabiting the area between Lake Ontario and Georgian Bay, who acquired furs
15   from more remote tribes and brought them by way of the Ottawa River to the French posts on the St. Lawrence. So long as the Huron retained their position and the Ottawa-St. Lawrence route remained secure, this traffic could continue, to
20   the great advantage of both the Huron and their <u>allies</u>, the French.

The Five Nations of the Iroquois Confederacy, dwelling in the area south and east of Lake Ontario, were enemies of the French and
25   their Indian allies, especially the Algonquin tribes. Confronted with a combination of French-Huron-Algonquin power, the Iroquois were anxious to gain support from the Dutch on the Hudson. At first they were handicapped because the
30   Mahican stood between them and the Dutch, but about 1628 the Mohawk defeated the Mahican and gained full access to the Dutch trading post at Fort Orange.

(Leach, 1966)

6. The author's primary purpose is to explain
    1. how the French traded furs with the Hurons.
    2. Indian affairs in the Lake Ontario and Georgian Bay areas.
    3. how the Dutch were established as the most important fur traders of the northern frontier.
    4. the history of Fort Orange.

7. <u>Allies</u> as underlined means
    1. friends.
    2. enemies.
    3. explorers.
    4. fur traders.

8. The French fur trade was dependent on relations with the
    1. Hurons.
    2. Dutch.
    3. Iroquois.
    4. Mahicans.

9. Which of the following languages was NOT spoken in the northern frontier, according to the passage?
    1. Dutch
    2. English
    3. French
    4. Algonquian

10. According to the passage, fur trade was dependent upon
    1. friendly relations with the Indians.
    2. the Ottawa River.
    3. the five nations of the Iroquois.
    4. the allies.

11. The author develops his point through
    1. examples.
    2. analogy.
    3. cause and effect.
    4. personal opinion.

Any <u>hypothesis</u> must depend for its verification on observable evidence. Until recently there has been little evidence about how the brain functions in cognition, precisely how and which
5 of the 12 billion cells within the brain store memory. How much memory is retained? Can it disappear? Is memory generalized or specific? Why are some memories more available for recall than others?
10 One noted explorer in this field is Dr. Wilder Penfield, a neurosurgeon from McGill University in Montreal, who in 1951 began to produce exciting evidence to confirm and modify theoretical concepts which had been formulated
15 in answer to these questions. During the course of brain surgery, in treating patients suffering from focal epilepsy, Penfield conducted a series of experiments during which he touched the temporal cortex of the brain of the patient with a
20 weak electric current transmitted through a galvanic probe. His observations of the responses to these stimulations were accumulated over a period of several years. In each case the patient under local anesthesia was
25 fully conscious during the exploration of the cerebral cortex and was able to talk with Penfield. In the course of these experiments he heard some amazing things....

The evidence seems to indicate that
30 everything which has been in our conscious awareness is recorded in detail and stored in the brain and is capable of being "played back" in the present.... These recorded experiences and feelings associated with them are available for
35 replay today in as vivid a form as when they happened and provide much of the data which determine the nature of today's transactions.

(Harris, 1967)

12. <u>Hypothesis</u>, underlined in the passage, means
   1. fact.
   2. evidence.
   3. memory.
   4. unproved theory.

13. The author mentions "amazing things" to show that Penfield was
   1. shocked at personal comments.
   2. surprised that patients could remember so much.
   3. impressed with the knowledge of his patients.
   4. happy that his patients were not suffering.

14. According to the passage, everything in our conscious awareness
   1. can be recorded.
   2. can be erased.
   3. can be remembered.
   4. can be changed by a galvanic probe.

15. It is implied in the passage that a person's memory affects his or her
   1. ability to recall.
   2. response to anesthesia.
   3. transactions.
   4. tendency to have focal epilepsy.

16. Dr. Penfield is referred to as an "explorer" (line 10) because he
   1. was the first neurosurgeon in Montreal.
   2. was among the first to scientifically study how the brain stores memory.
   3. was the first to study human behavior.
   4. was the first to record brain responses.

17. It can be concluded from the passage that
   1. scientists will soon understand how the brain works.
   2. Penfield's experiments have aided epilepsy victims.
   3. local anesthesia is not needed during brain surgery.
   4. much of human behavior may be interpreted in terms of stored memory.

Chronic dieting wreaks havoc with women's health. A ten-billion dollar diet industry, largely aimed at women, plays on our cultural obsession with thinness to ensure continued allegiance to
5   its myriad programs and products. Let's take a look at women's magazines for one measure of this increasing obsession with thinness. From 1959-78 the number of articles on dieting and losing weight in six popular women's magazines
10   increased from 17.1 per year in the first decade to 29.6 per year in the second. At the same time, eating problems, such as anorexia nervosa and bulimia, are on the rise, among women of all ages, racial groups and socio-economic classes, making
15   for a tyranny of thinness.

This tyranny is couched in erroneous myths. For example, there is a common belief that fat people eat more than thin people. False. Many studies have shown that fat people do not on the
20   average eat more than thin people. Many researchers now believe there is a "setpoint" for body fat, that is, a level of fatness that the body strives to maintain, which may be determined by heredity. To go far above or below this point
25   requires extraordinary measures. A study recently reported in the New England Journal of Medicine revealed that adopted persons closely resembled their birth parents in weight, regardless of their eating habits, and the
30   strongest link was found between mothers and their biological daughters. This does not mean that there is nothing individuals can do, but low-calorie, starvation diets will not improve our health or fitness.

(Norsigian, 1988)

18. With which of the following statements would the author agree?
    1. Fat people eat more than thin people.
    2. Starvation and low-calorie diets have little effect on women's health.
    3. The body tries to maintain a body weight set by heredity.
    4. Adopted people closely resemble adoptive parents in weight.

19. As used in the passage, myriad means
    1. powerful and potent.
    2. varied and numerous.
    3. strange and exotic.
    4. overrated and useless.

20. As used in the passage erroneous means
    1. mistaken.
    2. humorous.
    3. error-free.
    4. common.

21. The author mentions women's magazines to support her primary point that
    1. articles on diet and losing weight are popular.
    2. eating problems such as bulimia and anorexia are increasing.
    3. women are obsessed with dieting.
    4. women of all races and classes have bulimia.

22. The author implies in the passage that
    1. there is nothing persons can do to change their weight.
    2. women continue to use diet products and programs because they are effective.
    3. there is a cultural connection between the increased number of diet articles in women's magazines and the increase of eating disorders.
    4. the diet industry is primarily concerned with women's health.

23. It can be inferred that the author is most concerned with
    1. the diet industry.
    2. eating disorders.
    3. myths about thinness.
    4. women's health.

Steinbeck's preoccupation with life and living is perhaps the main reason for his popularity and influence.

Dozens of his contemporaries write
5 consistently better than he, with greater subtlety and polish, greater depth and force. He can produce pages of beauty and impact, preceded and followed by pages of sheer trash, the emptiness of which is only accentuated by the
10 pseudo-grandeur or pseudo-primitivism of the diction. He can be acutely sensitive and true for a chapter, then embarrassingly sentimental and cheaply trite. He can write dialogue with authenticity and bite, and go on to more dialogue
15 which is reverberant rhetorical noise. He can juxtapose a penetrating analysis of human feeling, especially of sense impression and painfully artificial fabrication. In short, he has at least as many faults as he has felicities in his
20 talent; his books are by no means rigorously weeded.

Still, he has won both critical and popular acclaim, largely, it would appear, because he is, within limits, an affirmative writer. So many
25 novelists in the Thirties and Forties have followed Hemingway's example of necrophilia. Their violent narratives have culminated by forcing the protagonist into a cul-de-sac, death, quick, arbitrary, grim and final extinction, and thus have
30 been a reflection and a propagator of bleak despair with meaningless overtones of defiance.

Steinbeck is different. He does not fit into any of the categories of negativism prevalent in this age's fiction. He is no Pollyanna--far from it. He
35 depicts human existence as conflict, unremitting and often savage battle. But he suggests that life is worth living.

(Kennedy, 1952)

24. Necrophilia underlined in the passage means
    1. respect for life.
    2. fascination with death.
    3. love of excitement.
    4. fear of death.

25. The reviewers reaction to Steinbeck's work is
    1. favorable.
    2. unfavorable.
    3. balanced.
    4. unfounded.

26. According to the passage, Steinbeck's writing is characterized by
    1. the affirmation that life is worth living in spite of hardship.
    2. a preoccupation with death.
    3. a view that life is futile and useless.
    4. the optimistic view that life is filled with beauty and ease.

27. Which of the following statements drawn from the passage could be a fact and NOT an opinion?
    1. Many writers of the Thirties and Forties have followed Hemingway's example of necrophilia.
    2. Dozens of his contemporaries write consistently better than he.
    3. He can produce pages of beauty, preceded and surrounded by pages of sheer trash.
    4. He has as many faults as he has felicities in his talents.

28. As used in the passage felicities means
    1. feelings.
    2. passion.
    3. problems.
    4. delights.

29. The reviewers primary purpose for mentioning Hemingway is to
    1. list another notable writer.
    2. offer an example of contrast to Steinbeck's writing.
    3. condemn necrophilia.
    4. characterize bleak despair.

Just how fragmented the American public school curriculum has become is described in *The Shopping Mall High School,* a report on five
5 years of firsthand study inside public and private secondary schools. The authors report that our high schools offer courses of so many kinds that "the word 'curriculum' does not do justice to this astonishing variety." The offerings include not only academic courses of great diversity, but also
10 courses in sports and hobbies and a "services curriculum" addressing emotional or social problems. All these courses are deemed "educationally valid" and carry course credit. Moreover, among academic offerings are
15 numerous versions of each subject, corresponding to different levels of student interest and ability. Needless to say, the material covered in these "content area" courses is highly varied.
20 Cafeteria-style education, combined with the unwillingness of our schools to place demands on students, has resulted in a steady diminishment of commonly shared information between generations and between young people
25 themselves. Those who graduate from the same school have often studied different subjects. And those who graduate from different schools have often studied different material even when their courses have carried the same titles. The
30 inevitable consequence of the shopping mall high school is a lack of shared knowledge across and within schools. It would be hard to invent a more effective recipe for cultural fragmentation.

(Hirsch, 1987)

30. The author's attitude toward the high school curriculum is
    1. neutral.
    2. optimistic.
    3. critical.
    4. apathetic.

31. A "services curriculum" refers to courses
    1. for the military.
    2. dealing with emotional or social problems.
    3. in the content areas.
    4. which carry credit.

32. Which of the following most directly supports the author's point that our culture is fragmented?
    1. Schools are unwilling to place demands on students.
    2. Students have too many choices to make.
    3. High school graduates do not share a common body of knowledge.
    4. Five year research projects reveal interesting data.

33. Which phrase would the author most likely use to describe the high school curriculum?
    1. educationally valid
    2. teacher-controlled
    3. worthless
    4. diverse

34. The title of the research report, "The Shopping Mall High School" compares
    1. teachers with students.
    2. secondary schools with shopping centers.
    3. shopping with studying.
    4. subjects with customers.

35. As used in the passage fragmentation means
    1. completeness.
    2. destruction.
    3. disruption.
    4. diversification.

The story of William Randolph Hearst is the story of the most inglorious success in American journalism and the gaudiest failure in American politics. His career furnished the greatest
5 possible contrast to that of his leading rival Lord of the Press, Joseph Pulitzer. Pulitzer, starting as a specialist in sensational reporting, brought his newspaper and the whole journalistic world to a new level of liberalism; Hearst, beginning as a
10 vociferous champion of the underprivileged, ended as an enemy of social reform and an instigator of the most reckless sensationalism ever printed. Devoted to the flamboyant, Hearst lived spectacularly in person and irresponsibly in
15 print. If there were not enough sensations around, Hearst manufactured them. He turned current events into daily crises, created a constantly increasing appetite for excitement and, endowed with enormous wealth and
20 unlimited sense of power, became not only a director of a huge network of newspapers but dictator of the printed word.

He was born April 29, 1863, in San Francisco, California, son of a millionaire publisher-senator,
25 George Hearst, and Phoebe Apperson Hearst, a cultured southerner twenty-two years her husband's junior. Born a twin (the other infant died at birth), he grew up an only child devoted to his mother who, in turn, centered everything
30 upon the boy with a passionate and possessive love. Although the grown man was addicted to platitudes, believing that if a platitude was repeated often enough it became a profundity, it was not a commonplace but an Eternal Verity
35 when he frequently repeated, "A boy's best friend is his mother."

(Untemeyer, 1955)

36. The author's primary purpose is to
    1. contrast Hearst with Pulitzer.
    2. compare sensational reporting with liberal journalism.
    3. support good journalism.
    4. narrate a short biographical summary of Hearst's life.

37. The author's primary purpose in mentioning Pulitzer is to
    1. provide support for liberal journalism.
    2. contrast his career with Hearst's.
    3. give an example of a journalistic success story.
    4. explain his views of social reform.

38. The author states Hearst's reporting went from
    1. conservatism to liberalism.
    2. sensationalism to liberalism.
    3. liberalism to conservatism.
    4. social reformation to sensationalism.

39. The author implies that Hearst
    1. always told the truth in print.
    2. felt inferior to others.
    3. fabricated news stories.
    4. tried to "out-do" Pulitzer.

40. According to the passage, Hearst's mother
    1. was not aware of child rearing principles.
    2. spoiled Hearst.
    3. loved Hearst because his twin had died.
    4. enjoyed platitudes.

41. Flamboyant as used in the passage means
    1. conservative.
    2. dark side.
    3. sensational.
    4. humble.

42. Champion as used in the passage means
    1. organizer.
    2. contestant.
    3. winner.
    4. advocate.

The American economy has grown from its revolutionary beginnings almost 200 years ago to become the most productive in the world. The productive capacity created by this growth has
5 allowed the people of the United States to enjoy a continually rising standard of living. In no small measure the economic success of our country can be attributed to a people who in their private lives and in their commerce have acted freely and with a
10 minimum of governmental control. The free enterprise system as it manifests itself in our country has provided a framework of political, economic, and financial stability that has allowed individuals, institutions, and businesses an
15 opportunity to invest their capital profitably. Few countries compare to the United States in providing their citizens with such an abundance of well-developed outlets for their savings and investments. Few other economies offer outlets
20 that possess such varying degrees of risk and reward to meet different individual and institutional needs.

Continued growth and prosperity in the United States depend entirely and wholly on the
25 continuation of our present economic system. Perhaps our economy may continue in the future in a modified social form, but it must retain its inherent basis--the awareness of the moral responsibility of one man to his fellow men. This
30 implies that if our growth as a nation in a competitive world society is to continue, it must depend upon a people who are educated and knowledgeable about investments, who are willing to accept the risks of our economic
35 system as well as the rewards.

(Amling, 1965)

43. In the second paragraph, the author makes his point through the use of
   1. statistics.
   2. personal opinion.
   3. comparison-contrast.
   4. chronology.

44. It can be inferred that the free enterprise system in the U.S.
   1. depends on governmental control.
   2. offers very little risk to the investor.
   3. meets the investment needs of individuals and institutions.
   4. does not provide citizens with ample investment opportunities.

45. Which of the following could be inferred about the author of the article?
   1. The author is a philosopher.
   2. The author is an economist.
   3. The author is a political scientist.
   4. The author is an historian.

46. The author's purpose is to show that the profitable U.S. Investment process
   1. is free of government control.
   2. is without risk to individuals.
   3. is dependent upon our revolutionary beginnings.
   4. depends on the free enterprise system.

47. The tone of the passage is best described as
   1. threatening.
   2. supportive.
   3. ironic.
   4. indifferent.

48. Which of the following statements is a fact and could NOT be an opinion?
   1. The productive capacity created by this economic growth has allowed a continually rising standard of living in the U.S.
   2. Continued prosperity in the U.S. depends entirely and wholly on the continuation of our present economic system.
   3. U.S. growth must depend upon people who are educated about investments.
   4. U.S. citizens must be willing to accept the risks of our economic system.

The ideas of liberal individualism--with their emphasis on the rights of individuals to political freedom, limited government and self-government, private property, and social and economic
5 opportunity--are set forth in the great documents of American political life--the Declaration of Independence, the Constitution, and such speeches as Lincoln's Gettysburg and Second Inaugural addresses. How much have these
10 ideas really shaped American social and political behavior?

In all societies, ideas taken most seriously have sometimes been ignored or <u>flouted</u>. This is not to make excuses for American shortcomings.
15 We can hardly forget that a number of the men who signed the Declaration of Independence, with its bold insistence that all people are created equal, were themselves owners of slaves. Slavery is, of course, a powerful denial of the
20 ideal of individual rights and equality. Yet it survived and even expanded its hold, until it was finally ended by the Civil War (1861-65)....

It is one thing to recognize that the United States has at times fallen far short of the
25 highest ideal professed by its ideology, something else to insist that these shortcomings make the ideology's claims mere sham. If one insists that a set of beliefs always be adhered to before we should take its claims
30 seriously, one ends up dismissing every one of them.... America's ideological commitments, including the emphasis on individual rights have had great impact on the nation's social and political life, even though the dictates of these
35 ideas have sometimes been ignored.

(Ladd, 1991)

49. The primary purpose of this passage is to
    1. oppose liberal individualism.
    2. discuss American shortcomings.
    3. support U.S. ideology.
    4. accuse Americans of hypocrisy.

50. The author assumes that the reader is
    1. questioning America's ideological commitments.
    2. a hypocrite.
    3. indifferent toward ideas which should be taken seriously.
    4. supportive of slavery.

51. The author mentions the great documents of American political life to
    1. give examples of serious American ideas.
    2. show the ideological contradictions of the documents.
    3. challenge American ideology.
    4. reveal their shortcomings.

52. The author states that
    1. American society is unique in its application of ideals.
    2. all societies have at some time ignored their most serious ideologies.
    3. in order to be taken seriously, ideals should be practiced.
    4. American ideologies have had little impact on U.S. society.

53. The passage most likely appeared in
    1. a chapter about U.S. shortcomings.
    2. a preface to a political science textbook.
    3. a summary of the effects of American foreign policy.
    4. a report drawn from records of court proceedings.

54. As used in the passage, <u>flouted</u> means
    1. erased.
    2. scorned.
    3. praised.
    4. upheld.

Asthmatics and those suffering from angina or heart disease can clearly be harmed by passive smoking. And <u>passive smoke</u> has been demonstrated to be a health risk for healthy

5 nonsmokers as well. In addition to the immediate effects of continued exposure--such as eye, nose, and throat irritation along with acute respiratory irritation, headaches, and coughing--passive smoke increases the chances of

10 developing both lung cancer and heart disease. According to the Environmental Protection Agency, passive smoke causes 3,800 lung cancer deaths each year. And other studies have estimated that about 50,000 Americans die each

15 year as a result of passive smoke, 75 percent of them from heart disease. The risks are greatest for individuals who live with someone who smokes; for example, according to a study conducted by Dr. K. J. Helsing of Johns Hopkins

20 University and his colleagues, a nonsmoker living with a smoker has a 20 to 30 percent increase in risk of death from heart disease (the heavier the smoker, the greater the risk). But even those who are exposed to passive smoke for shorter periods

25 may be at increased risk. One study found that rabbits exposed to sidestream smoke for fifteen minutes a day for just twenty days developed lung damage. Another study of humans showed that just twenty minutes of exposure to

30 sidestream smoke can increase the stickiness of the platelets in the blood, thus, making it more likely to clot.

The harmful effects of passive smoking are particularly critical for children. Children--

35 especially young children--who have one or both parents (particularly the mother) who smoke have an increased risk of chronic respiratory symptoms, respiratory problems, decreased lung capacity, and middle ear infections.

(University of California, 1991)

55. The author's primary purpose is to show that
   1. passive smoking is harmful to children.
   2. living with a smoker increases the risk of heart disease.
   3. passive smoke is a health risk for healthy and unhealthy nonsmokers.
   4. asthmatics and heart patients are harmed by passive smoking.

56. The author would probably agree that
   1. smoking should be allowed in public places.
   2. minor health problems are the results of smoking.
   3. scientists can design a harmless cigarette.
   4. parents should not smoke around their children.

57. According to the passage, the person most at-risk to passive smoke is one who
   1. smokes heavily.
   2. lives with a heavy smoker.
   3. is a child.
   4. is asthmatic.

58. As used in the passage, <u>passive smoke</u> means
   1. smoke exhaled by nonsmokers.
   2. smoke inhaled by smokers.
   3. smoke from low-tar cigarettes.
   4. smoke inhaled by nonsmokers.

59. According to the passage, the leading cause of death due to passive smoke is
   1. lung cancer.
   2. asthma.
   3. heart disease.
   4. respiratory infections.

60. In order to develop his main idea, which of the following does the author use?
   1. chronological order
   2. cause and effect
   3. narrative
   4. analogy

Appendix A
Unit Answers

Unit Three: Vocabulary Answer Key

Exercise 1

1. perennial--lasting a long time
   optimist--one who expects a favorable outcome
   travail--trouble; anguish; hard work
2. subtle--slight; not obvious
3. transcripts--official records of grades
4. assimilation--absorption of a distinct minority or cultural group into the majority group whereby the characteristics of the majority are adopted by the minority
5. alienation--isolation; indifference
6. disheveled--untidy; messy
   labored--difficult; hard

Exercise 2

1. multimorts--many deaths
2. transterre--across-earth (cross-country)
   benegamy--good marriage
3. ambispectator--one who looks in both directions
4. gamology--study of marriage
5. contracred--believe the opposite; disagree
6. biometer--instrument to measure life
7. philous--full of love
8. malgraphics--poor or wrong writing
9. eudiction--act of speaking well
10. polyport--carry many
    extramuscular--overly muscled

Exercise 3

1. extraneous--more than needed; not essential
2. eulogy--speech of great praise philanthropist--one who loves mankind
3. predestination--act of determining events before they occur
4. contradict--express the opposite view; to deny
5. malicious--full of evil; wanting to do harm to others

Exercise 4

1. prerequisite--something required beforehand
2. conspicuous--obvious; not hidden; open
3. escalated--intensified; increased; enlarged
4. impervious--not capable of being penetrated or affected

5. disperse--to scatter
   randomly--in no particular pattern

6. tenaciously--holding or clinging firmly

7. exploited--used unfairly or selfishly ruthless--having no mercy or pity

8. garrulous--talkative detriment--harm; damage

9. benign--not harmful malignant--harmful; life threatening

10. exhorting--strongly advise or urge; order

11. speculate--wonder; meditate; reflect; think about

12. endowed--provided with; given omniscience--all or unlimited knowledge omnipotent--all or unlimited power intervene--to come between mortals--human beings; those who will die

13. flora--vegetation; plants

14. fauna--animals indigenous--native to forlorn--sad; hopeless; lonely; abandoned urban--city

15. ambivalent--having conflicting feelings or thoughts

16. remorse--regret; sorrow; guilt; compassion
    rehabilitate--to restore to a former state or to a useful life

17. composed--calm or quiet; not upset
    meticulously--neatly; extremely carefully

18. tentative--uncertain; unconfirmed

19. impassive--showing no emotion inured--hardened

20. anthropologist--one who studies cultures (mankind)
    modify--change

21. affluent--wealthy

Exercise 5

Passage One

1. 2	5. 2	9. 3
2. 1	6. 4	10. 4
3. 3	7. 2	11. 3
4. 4	8. 1	12. 1

Passage Two

13. 3	16. 2	19. 1
14. 2	17. 2	20. 4
15. 4	18. 2	21. 2

Passage Three

22. 3	25. 3
23. 1	26. 1
24. 2	

Unit Four: Literal Comprehension Answer Key

Exercise 1

A. The main idea is stated in the first sentence.

B. Some of the details that should have been listed are:
    ♦ More acres settled and cultivated.
    ♦ Number of farms tripled.
    ♦ Kansas, Nebraska, California, and Texas had large population growths.

Notice how these details support the main idea. Details such as these are similar to ones the reader will be asked to identify on the Regents' Test.

Exercise 2

A. The answer is 2. The passage states that between 1649 and 1660 England was without a king.

B. The answer is 4. This is stated in the last sentence.

Exercise 3

A. There are several clues that indicate that this will be a comparison/contrast passage. The passage begins with ''The differences ...'' indicating that the author is contrasting the two cultures and showing their dissimilarities. The second paragraph begins ''On the other hand ...'' which is an indication the author is going to change the direction of his thoughts and will discuss how the two cultures were alike. The answer to the question should be 4.

B. The answer is 3. It is stated in the first and second sentences.

Exercise 4

A. The answer is 2. In the second paragraph *As a result* indicates a cause and effect pattern of organization. The cause is population growth and the effect of its growth was a demand for farm products.

B. The answer is 3. It states the reasons in sentence three; therefore you can use ''process of elimination.''

Exercise 5

The answer is 2. The last sentence defines the term. But the sentence that precedes this definition serves to expand and illustrate the way an individual might proceed toward becoming excellent.

Exercise 6

The answer is number 3. In this passage the concept of static electricity was explained by a series of examples--lightning, a nylon rug, cat's fur, a balloon, and clothing from a dryer.

Exercise 7

Of course the correct answer is 3. The other referring word *(latter)* refers to prehistoric periods.

Exercise 8

1. 1
2. 4
3. 3
4. 4

Exercise 9

1. 4
2. 3
3. 2

Unit Five: Inference Answer Key

Example 1

Pictures 3 and 4. This is designed to allow the student to draw several inferences; therefore, answers will vary.

A. (individual answers)
B. No
C. The couple would not be holding each other.
D. Boyfriend: likelihood of con artist is not high considering the heart symbols.
E. Boyfriend: evidence is ''hearts,'' closeness of couple.

Example 2

Yes   1.
No   2.
Yes   3.
Yes   4.

Exercise I

Macbeth	Lady Macbeth
reluctant	bad
felt compunction at the	ambitious
thoughts of blood	cared not by what means
	step absolutely necessary

Exercise 2

Inferences about Jo: tomboy, tall
Clues: ''put her hands in her pockets and began to whistle''
        rude, unladylike, long figure

Exercise 3

Inferences: 1. hated by the lords

2. wanted more power

3. coward, turncoat

Exercise 4

1. 1
2. 3

Exercise 5

1. 2
2. 4

Exercise 6

A. Conclusion: *he failed the test*

B. Conclusion: *go out on a date*

C. Conclusion: *man won the lottery*

Exercise 7

Step 2. Key Ideas: heard something; saw another figure; then another on right; another on left; then tall man; all closed in with purpose; looked for means of escape.

Step 3. Answers will vary.

Step 4. The men are going to hurt Clare.

Exercise 8

Scientists say that *certain pollutants may cause a drastic depletion of ozone.* If what scientists say is true, then *the ozone layer will be depleted and high-energy radiation, which is harmful to life, will penetrate the earth's surface.*

Exercise 9

Picture 7 Main Idea: The man is attracted to the woman.

A. Main Idea: Rowena was a beautiful woman who attracted men.

B. The paragraph is different from Picture 7 in that the years are different. Picture 7 takes place in modern times whereas the paragraph from Ivanhoe probably takes place in Medieval times (note the phrase "Knight Templar"). Also, it is clear that Rowena does not like the behavior of the Knight, whereas the woman in the picture does not mind the attention the man is giving her.

C. The paragraph and picture are similar in that both depict a woman who attracts a man.

Exercise 10

A. Characterization: Individual student drawings

B. Main Idea: James II did not trust Douglas, accused him of being a traitor, and then killed him.

Exercise 11

A. 4

B. 2

Exercise 12

1. hungry dogs
2. carving table
3. red meat and butchers
4. jewels

Exercise 13

A. Hamlet: lion
   Words/phrases: as hardy as a lion, bursting from them (implies strength).

B. Joan: cat
   Words/phrases: catlike gray eyes, intelligent, mane

C. Peggoty: apple
   Words/phrases: so hard and red; the birds didn't pick her in preference to apples

D. Kenilworth Castle: sun
   Words/phrases: ''a blaze of fiery red splashed against a golden sea of sky''

Exercise 14

Passage One

1. 4
2. 1
3. 2
4. 2
5. 2
6. 1

Passage Two

1. 4
2. 4
3. 3
4. 2
5. 4

Unit Six: Analysis of a Passage Answer Key

Exercise 1

1. 2
2. how dare I hate him
   you can't be angry with me
   no one gets a disease on purpose
   wasn't I suffering from temporary insanity

Exercise 2

1. Objective--the writer presents both sides of the issue impartially.
2. Pro-abortion--the writer's appeal is in favor of the issue and the woman's right to choose.
3. Anti-abortion--the writer's position is supported by use of negative language, such as "insidious attempt," "killing children," "a violent, degrading event," "mechanical rape," and so forth.

Exercise 3

1. 1
2. 4

Exercise 4

1. 4
2. 4
3. 1

Exercise 5

1. 3
2. 4
3. 4

Exercise 6

1. 2
2. 2
3. 3   The rationale/explanation for #3 in Exercise 6 is that the driver intended to motivate the five uncooperative donkeys to work for rewards. However, by rewarding all donkeys in the incident equally instead of rewarding only the cooperative donkey, he lost his only worker. The outcome was opposite to that which he expected.

Exercise 7

1. 3
2. 2

Exercise 8

1. 2
2. 3
3. 2
4. 3

Exercise 9

1. 4
2. 3
3. 4
4. 4

Exercise 10

1. 4
2. 4
3. 2

Exercise 11

1. 1
2. 4

Practice Passage

1. 2
2. 2
3. 2
4. 3
5. 3
6. 4
7. 4

Appendix B
Practice Test Answer Keys

ANSWER KEY
PRACTICE TEST ONE

DIAGNOSTIC

1.	2 (An)	31.	2 (Vo)
2.	4 (Vo)	32.	2 (Vo)
3.	1 (Vo)	33.	3 (Li)
4.	2 (Li)	34.	1 (In)
5.	1 (An)	35.	3 (An)
6.	3 (An)	36.	4 (In)
7.	3 (An)	37.	2 (Li)
8.	2 (Li)	38.	2 (Vo)
9.	1 (Li)	39.	2 (In)
10.	2 (Li)	40.	3 (An)
11.	4 (In)	41.	3 (In)
12.	2 (Vo)	42.	4 (Li)
13.	3 (In)	43.	2 (In)
14.	1 (In)	44.	3 (Li)
15.	1 (Li)	45.	1 (Li)
16.	3 (Vo)	46.	4 (In)
17.	4 (Li)	47.	1 (In)
18.	1 (An)	48.	3 (In)
19.	2 (An)	49.	1 (An)
20.	1 (In)	50.	1 (Li)
21.	4 (In)	51.	4 (Li)
22.	1 (In)	52.	1 (Li)
23.	2 (In)	53.	3 (Vo)
24.	3 (In)	54.	2 (In)
25.	3 (In)	55.	2 (Vo)
26.	2 (An)	56.	4 (Vo)
27.	4 (An)	57.	4 (In)
28.	1 (In)	58.	4 (In)
29.	2 (Vo)	59.	3 (Li)
30.	1 (In)	60.	2 (Li)

Explanations of Answers: Diagnostic Practice Test One

1. (2An) The writer contrasts communism and democracy. Every other paragraph begins ''Communism'' or ''Democracy.'' Also the last two paragraphs explicitly state ''these differences . . .''

2. (4Vo) In paragraph one the writer discusses communism as being based on ''belief''; therefore, the reader infers that democracy as contrasted is based on ''belief.''

3. (1Vo) Chattel means ''property'' or ''slave.'' One who is a property or slave can be ''forced'' into work.

4. (2Li) ''Man is unable to govern himself'' is stated in the first paragraph; ''Individuals may be arrested without lawful cause'' is stated in the third paragraph; ''Information man receives should be controlled'' is stated in the third paragraph.

5. (1An) The passage is argumentative in that it presents aspects of both philosophies.

6. (3An) The purpose is stated in the last paragraph.

7. (3An) The phrase is figuratively comparing Margaret to an animal. The tigress, like Margaret, is quick-tempered, etc.

8. (2Li) That Margaret was close to Somerset and Suffolk is stated in the last sentence of the second paragraph.

9. (1Li) In paragraph one the passage states about Henry: ''When he recovered from his first madness . . .'' and ''his ineffective, other-worldly nature.''

10. (2Li) This is directly stated in paragraph three: ''but is was her own implacable hostility towards York which converted him to hatred.''

11. (4In) That York feared Somerset is implied in the last sentence since Somerset was sent to the Tower on York's orders.

12. (2Vo) since ''it is doubtful that Henry needed much persuading'' not to have ''his sport'' with the Queen, Henry must have been a modest person. These phrases are found before and after the word prudish.

13. (3In) See the first statement in the first paragraph: ''. . . whether it be English or Malaysian or Thraco-Phrygian.'' It is obvious that English is not given preferential treatment. Therefore, No. 3 can not be concluded from the passage.

14. (1In) See the second paragraph: ''English treated the English control and French controller as synonyms when in fact the English form means 'to dominate or hold power' while the French means simply 'to inspect.' The treaty nearly fell apart as a result.''

15. (1Li) This is directly stated in the first sentence of the second paragraph.

16. (3Vo) The war was prolonged mistakenly because of a misunderstanding in translation.

17. (4Li) See paragraph one: ''One in every three employees of the European Community is engaged in translating papers and speeches . . .''; At the bottom of that paragraph the reader is able to link ''translating papers'' to the word ''linguists''; ''. . . even in multilingual Brussels to find linguists who can translate....''

18. (1An) Persuasion is used from the beginning of the passage: ''There is certainly a good case for adopting an international language.'' Notice the strong words ''certainly'' and ''good.'' Then again, in the beginning of the second paragraph: ''A more compelling reason....'' The word ''compelling'' is used to convince the reader.

19. (2An) Note the phrases ''They weren't at all certain . . .'9, and ''. . . they were sure of nothing....''

20. (1In) The adjectives "old," "lined," "tired" connoted weariness. Also, "the men had seemed no different than any others who had run a long race . . ." is indicative that the men seemed weary.

21. (4In) Even though the men looked tired and uninspired, they held great knowledge in their minds. Their appearances were deceiving.

22. (1In) "Something unforgettable had happened" is especially shown through the following: "with the knowledge they carried ...", and "a brightness, a resolve, a triumph...."

23. (2In) That the knowledge that the men possessed was waiting to be shared is seen through the phrase "for the *customers who* might come by in later years...."

24. (3In) Customers can be linked to future generations by the phrasing which appears before the word *customers: "They* weren't at all certain that the things they carried in their heads might make every future dawn glow with a purer light...."

25. (3In) Montag is concerned about the expressions on the mens' faces: "He was looking for a brightness, a resolve, a triumph over tomorrow that hardly seemed to be there." And again, "Perhaps he had expected their faces to burn and glitter with the knowledge they carried, to glow as lanterns glow, with the light in them. But all the light had come from the campfire, . . ."

26. (2An) The author is contrasting "ordinary" Americans to cowboys. The structure which shows contrast in this paragraph is indicated by the introductory word "Where" at the beginning of the sentences. For example, "Where Americans seemed to be under the thumb of giant institutions and mired down in bureaucracy, the cowboy answered only to himself."

27. (4An) See the first sentence: ". . . the novel took the country by storm."

28. (1In) The passage implies that the cowboy took the law into his own hands in several places. In the first paragraph: ". . . his six-gun, who settled matters of right and wrong with dramatic finality . . ."; in the second paragraph: "the cowboy answered only to himself."; "--all he had to do was catch the rustlers and everything would be settled;" and "Where Americans had increasing difficulty sorting out the right and wrong of things, the cowboy knew precisely which was which."

29. (2Vo) See paragraph two: "Americans had rarely looked backward. They had spoken with enthusiasm of Progress and leaned eagerly into the future." The next sentence begins, "Now . . ." indicating a return to the past.

30. (1In) Refer to "breathed the pure air of freedom."; "answered only to himself"; "always cantered into the sunset of his own heart's desire."

31. (2Vo) Throughout the passage the cowboy's life is depicted as romantic. This life seemed "picturesque": charming, natural--It was the simple life of rustic pleasures.

32. (2Vo) The context clue in this case is common sense. On first thought, **executed** means "killed;" however, in this case, the artist did not "kill pictures," she "produced" them.

33. (3Li) Note the phrase "Often when one least expects it, . . ." found in the first paragraph.

34. (1In) The purpose of the first paragraph is found in the last sentence: "This, in essence, is the phenomenon known as inspiration."

35. (3An) The style of the passage is primarily informative.

36. (4In) The writer does not state that artists must travel. In fact, he states that "One designer may find motivation in travel to other lands, another in films of space flight, yet another in the sight of a familiar weed."

37. (2Li) The referent for this phrase is found in the word "flowers" in the preceding sentence. Since flowers are a natural form (derived from nature), it follows that the author meant this to be the artist's inspiration.

38. (2Vo) The passage states that the star replied without hesitation. "Straightforwardly" means "in a direct manner."

39 (2In) The purpose of the passage is mentioned in the first sentence: ". . . can best be understood by reviewing the various reasons students come to college." And in the first sentence of the second paragraph: "All these reasons...."

40. (3An) The author discusses the examples of the rock star and his success.

41. (3In) A college freshman orientation manual is the best choice since the passage is trying to convince the student to use the entire campus and is reviewing reasons to attend college.

42. (4Li) The inherent values of learning are not mentioned as a reason in this passage; however, the other choices are mentioned in the first paragraph: "You may be seeking to increase your earning power, to gain training, for a good job, or simply to enjoy social activities."

43. (2In) Take note of line 8 in which famous women authors were punished by illness, death, or the loss of love.

44. (3Li) The author states she sought to overcome her writing ambition by marriage and motherhood (line 5).

45. (1Li) The passage states that ". . . Margaret Mitchell and her creation of Scarlett O'Hara" in line 7.

46. (4In) By process of finding clues for the first 3 choices and consequently eliminating them, we can eliminate these by reading one line (12): ". . . had been condemned to death by jurors whose jealous wives insisted upon it." That leaves choice 4 as the answer.

47. (1In) The passage does **not** state that the woman was beautiful, although this may seem a good choice due to the jealousy of the wives. The best choice, however, and the one which has more evidence supporting it, is #1, exceptional. This is indicated in line 17.

48. (3In) The passage states that women authors have been punished for their ambition by illness, death, or the loss of love (line 8).

49. (1An) The passage is factual and contains no emotive words or phrases, no opinions or judgmental statements, and is therefore considered objective.

50. (1Li) In order to understand the function, it is necessary to read paragraphs two and three. Paragraph two discusses oxygenated blood and paragraph three discusses the removal of wastes.

51. (4Li) The following options are mentioned as affecting blood circulation: 1) food intake is mentioned in paragraph four in the phrase "after you eat"; 2) change in body temperature is mentioned in paragraph four; and 3) diabetes is mentioned in paragraph five; therefore, the answer is carbon dioxide which is merely carried by the blood.

52. (1Li) Paragraph four states: ". . . warmer temperatures produce increased flow to the outer layers . . ..

53. (3Vo) In order to understand the meaning of *dissipate,* the reader must recognize the con-

trast being presented. "On the other hand" signals that dissipate is being contrasted to the verb "conserve."

54. (2In) In the first paragraph the vascular system is introduced. The following body paragraphs detail how the system works.

55. (2Vo) The first paragraph explains that a hierarchical form of social organization is best represented by a diagram of a triangle with a few people at the top. The third sentence states that the few people at the top hold the power, thus suggesting a ranking order.

56. (4Vo) Use word structure clues to obtain meaning:
circum = around
vent = to go

57. (4In) The statement that an "informal structure grows up" indicates that the existing structure does not accommodate personal needs. Thus, the bureaucratic structure is bypassed and rules are bent.

58. (4In) The second paragraph states, "Particularly common is the feeling of being manipulated...."

59. (3Li) The second paragraph of the passage states that when top level people have been elected, they "... can be removed by popular vote...."

60. (2Li) In the first sentence hierarchical structure is compared to the shape of a triangle.

ANSWER KEY
PRACTICE TEST TWO

1.	3	31.	4
2.	1	32.	3
3.	3	33.	2
4.	4	34.	2
5.	2	35.	1
6.	3	36.	3
7.	3	37.	2
8.	4	38.	2
9.	1	39.	3
10.	3	40.	4
11.	3	41.	3
12.	3	42.	3
13.	2	43.	2
14.	3	44.	2
15.	2	45.	4
16.	2	46.	1
17.	4	47.	2
18.	1	48.	2
19.	1	49.	3
20.	3	50.	4
21.	2	51	3
22.	3	52.	4
23.	3	53.	2
24.	4	54.	3
25.	2	55.	2
26.	3	56.	1
27.	3	57.	2
28.	1	58.	3
29.	2	59.	1
30.	1	60.	1

ANSWER KEY
PRACTICE TEST THREE

1.	3	31.	2
2.	4	32.	1
3.	2	33.	2
4.	3	34.	2
5.	4	35.	1
6.	2	36.	3
7.	4	37.	2
8.	3	38.	2
9.	4	39.	4
10.	1	40.	2
11.	2	41.	3
12.	3	42.	4
13.	4	43.	2
14.	2	44.	1
15.	4	45.	3
16.	3	46.	3
17.	2	47.	4
18.	4	48.	4
19.	2	49.	2
20.	3	50.	1
21.	4	51.	4
22.	1	52.	3
23.	1	53.	4
24.	3	54.	3
25.	2	55.	2
26.	1	56.	4
27.	3	57.	3
28.	3	58.	4
29.	1	59.	3
30.	1	60.	1

ANSWER KEY
PRACTICE TEST FOUR

1.	1	31.	2
2.	3	32.	3
3.	3	33.	4
4.	1	34.	2
5.	2	35.	2
6.	3	36.	4
7.	3	37.	4
8.	2	38.	1
9.	3	39.	1
10.	3	40.	3
11.	2	41.	4
12.	3	42.	2
13.	2	43.	4
14.	1	44.	2
15.	2	45.	1
16.	2	46.	3
17.	2	47.	4
18.	3	48.	4
19.	3	49.	3
20.	3	50.	2
21.	1	51.	3
22.	1	52.	3
23.	4	53.	3
24.	3	54.	4
25.	1	55.	2
26.	2	56.	2
27.	3	57.	3
28.	1	58.	3
29.	4	59.	1
30.	3	60.	4

ANSWER KEY
PRACTICE TEST FIVE

1.	4	31.	3
2.	1	32.	1
3.	3	33.	3
4.	3	34.	2
5.	4	35.	4
6.	4	36.	3
7.	4	37.	1
8.	2	38.	3
9.	4	39.	4
10.	1	40.	1
11.	4	41.	2
12.	4	42.	4
13.	2	43.	2
14.	4	44.	3
15.	1	45.	1
16.	4	46.	4
17.	1	47.	4
18.	1	48.	1
19.	2	49.	2
20.	4	50.	3
21.	4	51.	1
22.	1	52.	4
23.	3	53.	3
24.	4	54.	3
25.	2	55.	4
26.	3	56.	2
27.	4	57.	3
28.	4	58.	1
29.	4	59.	3
30.	1	60.	3

ANSWER KEY
PRACTICE TEST SIX

1.	3	31.	3
2.	1	32.	2
3.	2	33.	3
4.	3	34.	4
5.	3	35.	2
6.	2	36.	4
7.	1	37.	2
8.	2	38.	3
9.	2	39.	4
10.	3	40.	1
11.	4	41.	2
12.	1	42.	1
13.	1	43.	2
14.	1	44.	3
15.	3	45.	1
16.	3	46.	2
17.	3	47.	4
18.	2	48.	2
19.	4	49.	1
20.	1	50.	2
21.	2	51.	2
22.	3	52.	2
23.	3	53.	3
24.	2	54.	4
25.	4	55.	2
26.	2	56.	1
27.	4	57.	1
28.	3	58.	1
29.	2	59.	2
30.	2	60.	1

ANSWER KEY
PRACTICE TEST SEVEN

1.	4	31.	3
2.	3	32.	2
3.	4	33.	1
4.	1	34.	1
5.	3	35.	2
6.	1	36.	4
7.	1	37.	4
8.	4	38.	1
9.	2	39.	2
10.	2	40.	3
11.	3	41.	2
12.	3	42.	2
13.	3	43.	4
14.	4	44.	4
15.	3	45.	4
16.	2	46.	2
17.	2	47.	4
18.	2	48.	1
19.	2	49.	2
20.	4	50.	2
21.	1	51.	2
22.	3	52.	2
23.	1	53.	1
24.	3	54.	4
25.	3	55.	3
26.	1	56.	3
27.	1	57.	2
28.	2	58.	4
29.	4	59.	4
30.	3	60.	3

ANSWER KEY
PRACTICE TEST EIGHT

1.	2	31.	4
2.	2	32.	1
3	1.	33.	4
4.	3	34.	2
5.	1	35.	2
6.	2	36.	3
7.	3	37.	1
8.	1	38.	3
9.	2	39.	4
10.	4	40.	4
11.	1	41.	4
12.	3	42.	2
13.	2	43.	3
14.	4	44.	1
15.	1	45.	3
16.	2	46.	1
17.	3	47.	2
18.	3	48.	2
19.	3	49.	1
20.	3	50.	2
21.	3	51.	4
22.	4	52.	2
23.	3	53.	3
24.	2	54.	3
25.	3	55.	3
26.	3	56.	2
27.	4	57.	4
28.	4	58.	2
29.	4	59.	3
30.	2	60.	2

ANSWER KEY
PRACTICE TEST NINE

1.	1	31.	3
2.	1	32.	4
3.	4	33.	3
4.	2	34.	2
5.	1	35.	1
6.	2	36.	3
7.	3	37.	2
8.	3	38.	4
9.	2	39.	2
10.	3	40.	2
11.	3	41.	2
12.	3	42.	4
13.	1	43.	1
14.	1	44.	1
15.	3	45.	2
16.	3	46.	3
17.	4	47.	3
18.	3	48.	4
19.	4	49.	3
20.	2	50.	3
21.	3	51.	2
22.	3	52.	4
23.	1	53.	1
24.	3	54.	4
25.	3	55.	4
26.	4	56.	4
27.	2	57.	2
28.	4	58.	2
29.	1	59.	2
30.	1	60.	4

ANSWER KEY
PRACTICE TEST TEN

1.	3	31.	2
2.	3	32.	3
3.	4	33.	4
4.	2	34.	2
5.	4	35.	2
6.	3	36.	4
7.	1	37.	2
8.	1	38.	4
9.	2	39.	3
10.	1	40.	2
11.	3	41.	3
12.	4	42.	4
13.	2	43.	2
14.	3	44.	3
15.	3	45.	2
16.	2	46.	4
17.	4	47.	2
18.	3	48.	1
19.	2	49.	3
20.	1	50.	1
21.	3	51.	1
22.	3	52.	2
23.	4	53.	2
24.	2	54.	2
25.	3	55.	3
26.	1	56.	4
27.	1	57.	2
28.	4	58.	4
29.	2	59.	3
30.	3	60.	2

Appendix C
Answer Sheets With Diagnostic Charts

LAST NAME		FIRST NAME	MI

Practice Tests
Answer Sheet

Diagnostic Test

1 ①②③④ 11 ①②③④ 21 ①②③④ 31 ①②③④ 41 ①②③④ 51 ①②③④ 61 ①②③④ 71 ①②③④

2 ①②③④ 12 ①②③④ 22 ①②③④ 32 ①②③④ 42 ①②③④ 52 ①②③④ 62 ①②③④ 72 ①②③④

3 ①②③④ 13 ①②③④ 23 ①②③④ 33 ①②③④ 43 ①②③④ 53 ①②③④ 63 ①②③④ 73 ①②③④

4 ①②③④ 14 ①②③④ 24 ①②③④ 34 ①②③④ 44 ①②③④ 54 ①②③④ 64 ①②③④ 74 ①②③④

5 ①②③④ 15 ①②③④ 25 ①②③④ 35 ①②③④ 45 ①②③④ 55 ①②③④ 65 ①②③④ 75 ①②③④

6 ①②③④ 16 ①②③④ 26 ①②③④ 36 ①②③④ 46 ①②③④ 56 ①②③④ 66 ①②③④ 76 ①②③④

7 ①②③④ 17 ①②③④ 27 ①②③④ 37 ①②③④ 47 ①②③④ 57 ①②③④ 67 ①②③④ 77 ①②③④

8 ①②③④ 18 ①②③④ 28 ①②③④ 38 ①②③④ 48 ①②③④ 58 ①②③④ 68 ①②③④ 78 ①②③④

9 ①②③④ 19 ①②③④ 29 ①②③④ 39 ①②③④ 49 ①②③④ 59 ①②③④ 69 ①②③④ 79 ①②③④

10 ①②③④ 20 ①②③④ 30 ①②③④ 40 ①②③④ 50 ①②③④ 60 ①②③④ 70 ①②③④ 80 ①②③④

Item Analysis

Vocabulary	Literal Comprehension	Inference	Analysis
2, 3, 12, 16, 29, 31, 32, 38, 53, 55, 56	4, 8, 9, 10, 15, 17, 33, 37, 42, 44, 45, 50, 51, 52, 59, 60	11, 13, 14, 20, 21, 22, 23, 24, 25, 28, 30, 34, 36, 39, 41, 43, 46, 47, 48, 54, 57, 58	1, 5, 6, 7, 18, 19, 26, 27, 35, 40, 49

Practice Tests
Answer Sheet

Practice Test No. __2__

1 ①②③④	11 ①②③④	21 ①②③④	31 ①②③④	41 ①②③④	51 ①②③④	61 ①②③④	71 ①②③④
2 ①②③④	12 ①②③④	22 ①②③④	32 ①②③④	42 ①②③④	52 ①②③④	62 ①②③④	72 ①②③④
3 ①②③④	13 ①②③④	23 ①②③④	33 ①②③④	43 ①②③④	53 ①②③④	63 ①②③④	73 ①②③④
4 ①②③④	14 ①②③④	24 ①②③④	34 ①②③④	44 ①②③④	54 ①②③④	64 ①②③④	74 ①②③④
5 ①②③④	15 ①②③④	25 ①②③④	35 ①②③④	45 ①②③④	55 ①②③④	65 ①②③④	75 ①②③④
6 ①②③④	16 ①②③④	26 ①②③④	36 ①②③④	46 ①②③④	56 ①②③④	66 ①②③④	76 ①②③④
7 ①②③④	17 ①②③④	27 ①②③④	37 ①②③④	47 ①②③④	57 ①②③④	67 ①②③④	77 ①②③④
8 ①②③④	18 ①②③④	28 ①②③④	38 ①②③④	48 ①②③④	58 ①②③④	68 ①②③④	78 ①②③④
9 ①②③④	19 ①②③④	29 ①②③④	39 ①②③④	49 ①②③④	59 ①②③④	69 ①②③④	79 ①②③④
10 ①②③④	20 ①②③④	30 ①②③④	40 ①②③④	50 ①②③④	60 ①②③④	70 ①②③④	80 ①②③④

Item Analysis

Vocabulary	Literal Comprehension	Inference	Analysis
4, 7, 16, 20, 31, 33, 37, 46, 52	3, 8, 9, 15, 19, 23, 28, 32, 35, 48, 49, 58, 59, 60	1, 2, 10, 12, 13, 18, 21, 22, 24, 25, 29, 30, 34, 36, 39, 41, 42, 43, 44, 51, 55, 56	5, 6, 11, 14, 17, 26, 27, 38, 40, 45, 47, 50, 53, 54, 57

210

Practice Tests
Answer Sheet

Practice Test No. ___3___

```
1 ①②③④    11 ①②③④    21 ①②③④    31 ①②③④    41 ①②③④    51 ①②③④    61 ①②③④    71 ①②③④

2 ①②③④    12 ①②③④    22 ①②③④    32 ①②③④    42 ①②③④    52 ①②③④    62 ①②③④    72 ①②③④

3 ①②③④    13 ①②③④    23 ①②③④    33 ①②③④    43 ①②③④    53 ①②③④    63 ①②③④    73 ①②③④

4 ①②③④    14 ①②③④    24 ①②③④    34 ①②③④    44 ①②③④    54 ①②③④    64 ①②③④    74 ①②③④

5 ①②③④    15 ①②③④    25 ①②③④    35 ①②③④    45 ①②③④    55 ①②③④    65 ①②③④    75 ①②③④

6 ①②③④    16 ①②③④    26 ①②③④    36 ①②③④    46 ①②③④    56 ①②③④    66 ①②③④    76 ①②③④

7 ①②③④    17 ①②③④    27 ①②③④    37 ①②③④    47 ①②③④    57 ①②③④    67 ①②③④    77 ①②③④

8 ①②③④    18 ①②③④    28 ①②③④    38 ①②③④    48 ①②③④    58 ①②③④    68 ①②③④    78 ①②③④

9 ①②③④    19 ①②③④    29 ①②③④    39 ①②③④    49 ①②③④    59 ①②③④    69 ①②③④    79 ①②③④

10 ①②③④   20 ①②③④    30 ①②③④    40 ①②③④    50 ①②③④    60 ①②③④    70 ①②③④    80 ①②③④
```

Item Analysis			
Vocabulary	Literal Comprehension	Inference	Analysis
11, 12, 15, 20, 21, 25, 27, 30, 40, 43, 57	1, 2, 3, 7, 8, 10, 13, 16, 18, 22, 23, 29, 33, 35, 37, 39, 44, 45, 49, 55, 56	4, 5, 6, 17, 26, 28, 34, 36, 41, 46, 50, 51, 52, 58, 59, 60	9, 14, 19, 24, 31, 32, 38, 42, 47, 48, 53, 54

Practice Tests
Answer Sheet

Practice Test No. __4__

1 ①②③④	11 ①②③④	21 ①②③④	31 ①②③④	41 ①②③④	51 ①②③④	61 ①②③④	71 ①②③④
2 ①②③④	12 ①②③④	22 ①②③④	32 ①②③④	42 ①②③④	52 ①②③④	62 ①②③④	72 ①②③④
3 ①②③④	13 ①②③④	23 ①②③④	33 ①②③④	43 ①②③④	53 ①②③④	63 ①②③④	73 ①②③④
4 ①②③④	14 ①②③④	24 ①②③④	34 ①②③④	44 ①②③④	54 ①②③④	64 ①②③④	74 ①②③④
5 ①②③④	15 ①②③④	25 ①②③④	35 ①②③④	45 ①②③④	55 ①②③④	65 ①②③④	75 ①②③④
6 ①②③④	16 ①②③④	26 ①②③④	36 ①②③④	46 ①②③④	56 ①②③④	66 ①②③④	76 ①②③④
7 ①②③④	17 ①②③④	27 ①②③④	37 ①②③④	47 ①②③④	57 ①②③④	67 ①②③④	77 ①②③④
8 ①②③④	18 ①②③④	28 ①②③④	38 ①②③④	48 ①②③④	58 ①②③④	68 ①②③④	78 ①②③④
9 ①②③④	19 ①②③④	29 ①②③④	39 ①②③④	49 ①②③④	59 ①②③④	69 ①②③④	79 ①②③④
10 ①②③④	20 ①②③④	30 ①②③④	40 ①②③④	50 ①②③④	60 ①②③④	70 ①②③④	80 ①②③④

Item Analysis

Vocabulary	Literal Comprehension	Inference	Analysis
3, 12, 13, 20, 24, 28, 35, 39, 49, 56	4, 6, 11, 15, 17, 18, 29, 30, 31, 36, 38, 41, 46, 48, 57	2, 7, 9, 10, 16, 21, 23, 33, 40, 42, 43, 45, 52, 53, 58	1, 5, 8, 14, 19, 22, 25, 26, 27, 32, 34, 37, 44, 47, 50, 51, 54, 55, 59, 60

Practice Tests
Answer Sheet

Practice Test No. __5__

1 ①②③④ 11 ①②③④ 21 ①②③④ 31 ①②③④ 41 ①②③④ 51 ①②③④ 61 ①②③④ 71 ①②③④

2 ①②③④ 12 ①②③④ 22 ①②③④ 32 ①②③④ 42 ①②③④ 52 ①②③④ 62 ①②③④ 72 ①②③④

3 ①②③④ 13 ①②③④ 23 ①②③④ 33 ①②③④ 43 ①②③④ 53 ①②③④ 63 ①②③④ 73 ①②③④

4 ①②③④ 14 ①②③④ 24 ①②③④ 34 ①②③④ 44 ①②③④ 54 ①②③④ 64 ①②③④ 74 ①②③④

5 ①②③④ 15 ①②③④ 25 ①②③④ 35 ①②③④ 45 ①②③④ 55 ①②③④ 65 ①②③④ 75 ①②③④

6 ①②③④ 16 ①②③④ 26 ①②③④ 36 ①②③④ 46 ①②③④ 56 ①②③④ 66 ①②③④ 76 ①②③④

7 ①②③④ 17 ①②③④ 27 ①②③④ 37 ①②③④ 47 ①②③④ 57 ①②③④ 67 ①②③④ 77 ①②③④

8 ①②③④ 18 ①②③④ 28 ①②③④ 38 ①②③④ 48 ①②③④ 58 ①②③④ 68 ①②③④ 78 ①②③④

9 ①②③④ 19 ①②③④ 29 ①②③④ 39 ①②③④ 49 ①②③④ 59 ①②③④ 69 ①②③④ 79 ①②③④

10 ①②③④ 20 ①②③④ 30 ①②③④ 40 ①②③④ 50 ①②③④ 60 ①②③④ 70 ①②③④ 80 ①②③④

Item Analysis

Vocabulary	Literal Comprehension	Inference	Analysis
6, 11, 17, 23, 26, 31, 35, 38, 39, 43, 45, 47, 54, 57, 58	3, 4, 12, 13, 16, 19, 21, 30, 34, 37, 50, 52, 53, 56	5, 7, 8, 9, 10, 14, 15, 18, 20, 22, 24, 29, 33, 36, 40, 41, 42, 44, 48, 49, 51, 59	1, 2, 25, 28, 32, 46, 55, 60

Practice Tests
Answer Sheet

Practice Test No. _____6_____

1 ①②③④ 11 ①②③④ 21 ①②③④ 31 ①②③④ 41 ①②③④ 51 ①②③④ 61 ①②③④ 71 ①②③④

2 ①②③④ 12 ①②③④ 22 ①②③④ 32 ①②③④ 42 ①②③④ 52 ①②③④ 62 ①②③④ 72 ①②③④

3 ①②③④ 13 ①②③④ 23 ①②③④ 33 ①②③④ 43 ①②③④ 53 ①②③④ 63 ①②③④ 73 ①②③④

4 ①②③④ 14 ①②③④ 24 ①②③④ 34 ①②③④ 44 ①②③④ 54 ①②③④ 64 ①②③④ 74 ①②③④

5 ①②③④ 15 ①②③④ 25 ①②③④ 35 ①②③④ 45 ①②③④ 55 ①②③④ 65 ①②③④ 75 ①②③④

6 ①②③④ 16 ①②③④ 26 ①②③④ 36 ①②③④ 46 ①②③④ 56 ①②③④ 66 ①②③④ 76 ①②③④

7 ①②③④ 17 ①②③④ 27 ①②③④ 37 ①②③④ 47 ①②③④ 57 ①②③④ 67 ①②③④ 77 ①②③④

8 ①②③④ 18 ①②③④ 28 ①②③④ 38 ①②③④ 48 ①②③④ 58 ①②③④ 68 ①②③④ 78 ①②③④

9 ①②③④ 19 ①②③④ 29 ①②③④ 39 ①②③④ 49 ①②③④ 59 ①②③④ 69 ①②③④ 79 ①②③④

10 ①②③④ 20 ①②③④ 30 ①②③④ 40 ①②③④ 50 ①②③④ 60 ①②③④ 70 ①②③④ 80 ①②③④

Item Analysis

Vocabulary	Literal Comprehension	Inference	Analysis
8, 10, 13, 17, 25, 29, 30, 32, 37, 43, 46, 48, 56	1, 6, 9, 15, 16, 20, 27, 34, 35, 36, 39, 42, 49, 53, 54, 55	2, 3, 4, 5, 7, 12, 14, 18, 22, 23, 28, 38, 41, 45, 47, 50, 57, 58, 59	11, 19, 21, 24, 26, 31, 33, 40, 44, 51, 52, 60

Practice Tests
Answer Sheet

Practice Test No. ____7____

1 ①②③④ 11 ①②③④ 21 ①②③④ 31 ①②③④ 41 ①②③④ 51 ①②③④ 61 ①②③④ 71 ①②③④

2 ①②③④ 12 ①②③④ 22 ①②③④ 32 ①②③④ 42 ①②③④ 52 ①②③④ 62 ①②③④ 72 ①②③④

3 ①②③④ 13 ①②③④ 23 ①②③④ 33 ①②③④ 43 ①②③④ 53 ①②③④ 63 ①②③④ 73 ①②③④

4 ①②③④ 14 ①②③④ 24 ①②③④ 34 ①②③④ 44 ①②③④ 54 ①②③④ 64 ①②③④ 74 ①②③④

5 ①②③④ 15 ①②③④ 25 ①②③④ 35 ①②③④ 45 ①②③④ 55 ①②③④ 65 ①②③④ 75 ①②③④

6 ①②③④ 16 ①②③④ 26 ①②③④ 36 ①②③④ 46 ①②③④ 56 ①②③④ 66 ①②③④ 76 ①②③④

7 ①②③④ 17 ①②③④ 27 ①②③④ 37 ①②③④ 47 ①②③④ 57 ①②③④ 67 ①②③④ 77 ①②③④

8 ①②③④ 18 ①②③④ 28 ①②③④ 38 ①②③④ 48 ①②③④ 58 ①②③④ 68 ①②③④ 78 ①②③④

9 ①②③④ 19 ①②③④ 29 ①②③④ 39 ①②③④ 49 ①②③④ 59 ①②③④ 69 ①②③④ 79 ①②③④

10 ①②③④ 20 ①②③④ 30 ①②③④ 40 ①②③④ 50 ①②③④ 60 ①②③④ 70 ①②③④ 80 ①②③④

Item Analysis

Vocabulary	Literal Comprehension	Inference	Analysis
2, 9, 12, 17, 21, 24, 33, 40, 48, 49, 53, 56	6, 8, 15, 19, 20, 26, 27, 35, 42, 44, 54, 55, 59, 60	3, 5, 7, 14, 16, 18, 22, 23, 25, 32, 34, 36, 38, 39, 41, 43, 46, 47, 50, 51, 52	1, 4, 10, 11, 13, 28, 29, 30, 31, 37, 45, 57, 58

Practice Tests
Answer Sheet

Practice Test No. ___8___

1 ①②③④ 11 ①②③④ 21 ①②③④ 31 ①②③④ 41 ①②③④ 51 ①②③④ 61 ①②③④ 71 ①②③④

2 ①②③④ 12 ①②③④ 22 ①②③④ 32 ①②③④ 42 ①②③④ 52 ①②③④ 62 ①②③④ 72 ①②③④

3 ①②③④ 13 ①②③④ 23 ①②③④ 33 ①②③④ 43 ①②③④ 53 ①②③④ 63 ①②③④ 73 ①②③④

4 ①②③④ 14 ①②③④ 24 ①②③④ 34 ①②③④ 44 ①②③④ 54 ①②③④ 64 ①②③④ 74 ①②③④

5 ①②③④ 15 ①②③④ 25 ①②③④ 35 ①②③④ 45 ①②③④ 55 ①②③④ 65 ①②③④ 75 ①②③④

6 ①②③④ 16 ①②③④ 26 ①②③④ 36 ①②③④ 46 ①②③④ 56 ①②③④ 66 ①②③④ 76 ①②③④

7 ①②③④ 17 ①②③④ 27 ①②③④ 37 ①②③④ 47 ①②③④ 57 ①②③④ 67 ①②③④ 77 ①②③④

8 ①②③④ 18 ①②③④ 28 ①②③④ 38 ①②③④ 48 ①②③④ 58 ①②③④ 68 ①②③④ 78 ①②③④

9 ①②③④ 19 ①②③④ 29 ①②③④ 39 ①②③④ 49 ①②③④ 59 ①②③④ 69 ①②③④ 79 ①②③④

10 ①②③④ 20 ①②③④ 30 ①②③④ 40 ①②③④ 50 ①②③④ 60 ①②③④ 70 ①②③④ 80 ①②③④

Item Analysis

Vocabulary	Literal Comprehension	Inference	Analysis
1, 9, 10, 15, 24, 27, 30, 31, 32, 40, 43, 50, 55	3, 16, 22, 33, 41, 45, 48, 51, 52, 53, 54, 56, 59	7, 11, 12, 13, 14, 18, 19, 21, 23, 25, 26, 28, 29, 34, 37, 38, 39, 42, 44, 46, 58, 60	2, 4, 5, 6, 8, 17, 20, 35, 36, 47, 49, 57

Practice Tests
Answer Sheet

Practice Test No. ____9____

1 ①②③④ 11 ①②③④ 21 ①②③④ 31 ①②③④ 41 ①②③④ 51 ①②③④ 61 ①②③④ 71 ①②③④

2 ①②③④ 12 ①②③④ 22 ①②③④ 32 ①②③④ 42 ①②③④ 52 ①②③④ 62 ①②③④ 72 ①②③④

3 ①②③④ 13 ①②③④ 23 ①②③④ 33 ①②③④ 43 ①②③④ 53 ①②③④ 63 ①②③④ 73 ①②③④

4 ①②③④ 14 ①②③④ 24 ①②③④ 34 ①②③④ 44 ①②③④ 54 ①②③④ 64 ①②③④ 74 ①②③④

5 ①②③④ 15 ①②③④ 25 ①②③④ 35 ①②③④ 45 ①②③④ 55 ①②③④ 65 ①②③④ 75 ①②③④

6 ①②③④ 16 ①②③④ 26 ①②③④ 36 ①②③④ 46 ①②③④ 56 ①②③④ 66 ①②③④ 76 ①②③④

7 ①②③④ 17 ①②③④ 27 ①②③④ 37 ①②③④ 47 ①②③④ 57 ①②③④ 67 ①②③④ 77 ①②③④

8 ①②③④ 18 ①②③④ 28 ①②③④ 38 ①②③④ 48 ①②③④ 58 ①②③④ 68 ①②③④ 78 ①②③④

9 ①②③④ 19 ①②③④ 29 ①②③④ 39 ①②③④ 49 ①②③④ 59 ①②③④ 69 ①②③④ 79 ①②③④

10 ①②③④ 20 ①②③④ 30 ①②③④ 40 ①②③④ 50 ①②③④ 60 ①②③④ 70 ①②③④ 80 ①②③④

Item Analysis

Vocabulary	Literal Comprehension	Inference	Analysis
1, 8, 16, 22, 26, 27, 32, 39, 45, 51, 52, 59	2, 3, 5, 6, 15, 18, 20, 25, 28, 33, 40, 46, 48, 53	4, 9, 10, 13, 17, 19, 23, 24, 29, 31, 34, 37, 41, 42, 43, 44, 47, 49, 55, 57, 58, 60	7, 11, 12, 14, 21, 30, 35, 36, 38, 50, 54, 56

Practice Tests
Answer Sheet

Practice Test No. ___10___

1 ①②③④	11 ①②③④	21 ①②③④	31 ①②③④	41 ①②③④	51 ①②③④	61 ①②③④	71 ①②③④
2 ①②③④	12 ①②③④	22 ①②③④	32 ①②③④	42 ①②③④	52 ①②③④	62 ①②③④	72 ①②③④
3 ①②③④	13 ①②③④	23 ①②③④	33 ①②③④	43 ①②③④	53 ①②③④	63 ①②③④	73 ①②③④
4 ①②③④	14 ①②③④	24 ①②③④	34 ①②③④	44 ①②③④	54 ①②③④	64 ①②③④	74 ①②③④
5 ①②③④	15 ①②③④	25 ①②③④	35 ①②③④	45 ①②③④	55 ①②③④	65 ①②③④	75 ①②③④
6 ①②③④	16 ①②③④	26 ①②③④	36 ①②③④	46 ①②③④	56 ①②③④	66 ①②③④	76 ①②③④
7 ①②③④	17 ①②③④	27 ①②③④	37 ①②③④	47 ①②③④	57 ①②③④	67 ①②③④	77 ①②③④
8 ①②③④	18 ①②③④	28 ①②③④	38 ①②③④	48 ①②③④	58 ①②③④	68 ①②③④	78 ①②③④
9 ①②③④	19 ①②③④	29 ①②③④	39 ①②③④	49 ①②③④	59 ①②③④	69 ①②③④	79 ①②③④
10 ①②③④	20 ①②③④	30 ①②③④	40 ①②③④	50 ①②③④	60 ①②③④	70 ①②③④	80 ①②③④

Item Analysis

Vocabulary	Literal Comprehension	Inference	Analysis
1, 7, 12, 19, 20, 24, 28, 35, 41, 42, 54, 58	2, 4, 8, 14, 16, 18, 26, 31, 32, 38, 52, 57, 59	5, 9, 10, 13, 15, 17, 21, 22, 23, 33, 36, 39, 40, 44, 45, 46, 49, 56	3, 6, 11, 25, 27, 29, 30, 34, 36, 37, 43, 47, 48, 50, 51, 53, 55

Acknowledgments: Units*

Adler, J. and McCormick. (April 1992). ''Abortion's Long Siege.'' *Newsweek.*

Alcott, Louisa May. *Little Women,* 1868.

Berne, Eric. *What Do You Say After You Say Hello?* New York: Grove Press, Inc., 1972.

Beaber, Rex Julian. (1983). ''Stress--And Other Scapegoats.'' *Newsweek.* Vol. 101.

Blough, Glenn, J. Schwartz, and A. Huggett. *Elementary School Science and How To Teach It.* New York: Holt, Rinehart and Winston, 1958.

Excerpt from THE NATIONAL EXPERIENCE, A HISTORY OF THE UNITED STATES by James Blum, copyright © 1977 by Harcourt Brace Jovanovich, Inc., reprinted by permission of the publisher.

Brontë, Charlotte. *Jane Eyre,* 1847.

Bulletin of Georgia Southern University, General Catalog, 1994-1995, p. 87.

Reprinted from WESTERN CIVILIZATIONS, Their History and Their Culture, 8th Edition, Volume 1, by Edward McNall Burns, by permission of W. W. Norton & Company, Inc. Copyright © 1973 by W. W. Norton & Company, Inc.

Burns, James M. *John Kennedy: A Political Profile.* San Diego: Harcourt Brace and Company, 1960.

Conroy, Pat. *The Lords of Discipline.* Boston: Houghton Mifflin Company, 1980.

From THE AUTOBIOGRAPHY OF WILL ROGERS, edited by Donald Day. Copyright i) renewed 1977 by Donald Day and Beth Day. Reprinted by permission of Houghton Mifflin Company.

Dickens, Charles. *David Copperfield,* 1850.

Fox, Frank and E. Pope. *American Heritage.* Dubuque: Kendall Hunt, 1990.

Hardy, Thomas. *Tess of the D'urbervilles,* 1891.

Johnson, James. *Psychology Today.* New York: John Wiley & Sons. 1972.

Kagan, Donald, S. Ozment, and F. Turner. *The Western Heritage Since 1648.* New York: Macmillan Publishing Co., Inc. 1983.

Kagan, Jerome and Cynthia Lang. *Psychology and Education.* New York: Harcourt Brace Jovanovich, Inc., 1978.

Kaplan, D.A April 1992. ''Is Roe Good Law?'' *Newsweek.*

''The Need for Handgun Control'' by Senator Edward Kennedy. Reprinted with permission from *Current History.* Copyright © 1976 by Current History, Inc.

Lamb, Charles and Mary. *Tales From Shakespeare,* 1807.

Levey, Judith and Agnes Greenhall. *The Concise Columbia Encyclopedia.* New York: Columbia University Press, 1983.

McConkey, Dale. (1974). ''The 'Jack-Ass Effect' in Management Compensation.'' *Business Horizons.*

Melville, Herman. *Moby Dick,* 1851.

Norton, Mary Beth, David Katzman, Paul Escott, Howard Chudacoff, Thomas Patterson, and William Tuttle, Jr. *A People And A Nation,* Vol. II: since 1865, Third Edition. Copyright © 1990 by Houghton Mifflin Company. Used with permission.

Excerpt from ASTRONOMY: FROM THE EARTH TO THE UNIVERSE by Jay Pasachoff, copyright © 1983 by Saunders College Publishing, reprinted by permission of the publisher.

Rait, R. S. *History of Scotland,* London: Williams and Norgate, 1914.

Registrar's Office, Unpublished Document. Mike Deal, Registrar, Rita McPhearson, Assistant Registrar. Georgia Southern University, 1991.

Scott, Sir Walter. *Ivanhoe,* 1820.

Sterling, J.C. *The Women's Movement: Revolution and Evolution.* New York: Newsweek Education Program, 1992.

Stewart, George. ''The Smart Ones Got Through.'' *American Heritage.* 1955.

The Committee on the Regents' Reading Test, Unpublished Committee Proceedings. University System, State of Georgia.

Ward, David A. *Alcoholism: Introduction to Theory and Treatment.* Dubuque: Kendall/Hunt, 1980.

Weiten, Wayne. *Psychology Themes and Variations.* Belmont: Wadsworth, Inc., 1989.

*Some passages were adapted to facilitate comprehension.

Acknowledgments: Practice Test Passages *

Test One

Bevlin, Marjorie E. *Design Through Discovery*. New York: Holt, Rinehart and Winston, 1977, p. 15.

Bradbury, Ray. *Fahrenheit 451*. New York: Ballantine Books, 1987, pp. 154-155; 164.

Bryson, Bill. *The Mother Tongue, English and How It Got That Way*. New York: Wm. C. Morrow and Co., Inc., 1990, p. 188.

Fox, Frank and Claynen Pope. *American Heritage*. Dubuque: Kendall Hunt, 1990, p. 467.

Fraser, Antonia. *The Lives of the Kings and Queens of England*. New York: Alfred A. Knopf, 1975, pp. 89-90.

Gardner, John N. and Jerome A. Jewler. *College Is Only the Beginning*. Second Edition. Belmont: Wadsworth Publishing Co., 1989, p. 202.

Hawthorne, Nathanial. *The Scarlet Letter*, 1850.

Larson, David E. (ed.) *Mayo Clinic Family Health Book*. New York: Wm. C. Morrow and Co., 1990, p. 834.

Rose, Caroline B. Sociology, T*he Study of Man in Society*. Social Science Seminar Series. Columbus: Charles E. Merrill Books, Inc., 1965, pp. 4849.

Truman, Harry S. "Presidential Inaugural Address," 1948.

Test Two

Brinton, Crane and Christopher Wolff. *A History of Civilization*, Volume 1. Second Edition. Englewood Cliffs: Prentice Hall, Inc., 1963, p. 450.

Bronfenbrenner, Martin, Werner Sichel and Wayland Gardner. *Macroeconomics*. Second Edition. Boston: Houghton Mifflin Company, 1987, p. 24.

Dickens, Charles. *Great Expectations*, 1861.

Goldberg, Herb. *The Hazards of Being Male*. New York: signet Books, 1977, pp. 46-47.

Greaves, Lorraine and Margaret L. W. Buist. "The Tobacco Industry: Weeding Women Out." In *Women's Health* by Nancy Worcester and Marianne H. Whatley (eds.). Dubuque: Kendall Hunt Publishing Company, 1988, pp. 81-82.

Greenburg, Edward S. *The American Political System*. Fifth Edition. Boston: Scott Foresman and Company, 1989, p. 228.

Norton, Mary Beth, David Katzman, Paul Escott, Howard Chudacoff, Thomas Patterson, and William Tuttle, Jr. *A People and a Nation*, Vol. II: since 1865, Third Edition. Copyright © by Houghton Mifflin Company. Used with permission.

Peterson, Morris S. and Keith J. Rigby. *Interpreting Earth History*. Dubuque: Wm. C. Brown Company, 1982, p. 74.

Reader's Digest Complete Do-It-Yourself Manual. New York: Reader's Digest Association, Inc., 1973, p. 282.

Sarfo, Kwasi. *Life in the Third World*. Dubuque: Kendall Hunt Publishing Company, 1988, p. 15.

Test Three

Dixon, Robert R. *Dynamic Astronomy*. Fifth Edition. Englewood Cliffs: Prentice Hall, 1989, p. 106.

Friedman, Jonathan Block. *Creation In Space Volume 1: Architectonics*. Dubuque: Kendall Hunt Publishing Company, 1989, p. xiii.

Gibbons, Don E. and John F. Connelly. *Selected Readings in Psychology*. St. Louis: The CV Mosby Company, 1970, p. 1 18.

Gronbeck, Ehninger and Monroe. *Principles of Speech Communications*. Tenth Brief Edition. Glenview: Scott Foresman and Company, 1989, p. 76.

*Some passages were adapted to facilitate comprehension.

Lamb, Charles and Mary. *Tales From Shakespeare, 1807.*

Lewis, Sinclair. *Babbitt* New York: Harcourt, Brace, Jovanovich, Inc., 1922, p. 6.

Lincoln, Abraham. ''The Gettysburg Address,'' 1863.

Severin, Timothy. *Vanishing Primitive Man.* New York: American Heritage Publishing Company, 1973, p. 31.

Strickland, Agnes. *Queens of Scotland,* 1851.

Whatley, Marianne. ''Women, Exercise, and Physical Potential.'' In *Women's Health* by Nancy Worcester and Marianne Whatley (eds.). Dubuque: Kendall Hunt Publishing Company, 1988, p. 251.

Test Four

Brontë, Charlotte. *Jane Eyre,* 1847.

Cooper, James F. Homeward Bound; The Chase. A Tale of the Sea, Vol. 1., 1838.

Fox, Frank and Clayne Pope. *American Heritage.* Dubuque: Kendall Hunt Publishing Company, 1990, p. 52-53.

Graham, Thomas M. Biology, The Essential Principles. Second Edition. Dubuque: Kendall Hunt Publishing Company, 1987, p. 405.

Johnson, Peter H. Parker, America's Fine Shotgun. New York: Bonanza Books, 1961. p. 93.

Kamien, Roger. *Music, An Appreciation.* New York: McGraw Hill, Inc., 1980, p. 258.

Kiely, John. (1991) ''A Million Years in the Making.'' *American Way, Vol. 24,* No. 3, p. 20.

Norton, Mary Beth, David Katzman, Paul Escott, Howard Chudacoff, Thomas Paterson, and William Tuttle, Jr. A People And A Nation, Vol. 11: Since 1865, Third Edition. Copyright (3 1990 by Houghton MiMin Company. Used with permission.

Sternhell, Carol. ''We'll Always Be Fat But Fat Can Be Fit.'' *Ms.* Magazine, May 1985.

Truman, Harry S. ''Truman's Address to Congress,'' March 12, 1947.

Test Five

Barnouw, Victor. An Introduction to Anthropology, Physical Anthropology and Archaeology. Volume 1. Revised Edition. Homewood: The Dorsey Press, 1976, p. 221.

Blitzer, Charles (ad.). *The Age of Kings.* New York: Time-Life Books, 1967, p. 85.

Boston Children's Medical Center and R. I. Feinbloom. *Child Health Encyclopedia.* New York: Delta Publishing Co., 1978, pp. 48-49.

Bowra, C. M. *Classical Greece.* New York: Time Inc., 1965, p. 7.

Reprinted from WESTERN CIVILIZATIONS, Their History and Their Culture, 8th Edition, Volume 1, by Edward McNall Burns, by permission of W. W. Norton & Company, Inc. Copyright if 1973 by W. W. Norton & Company, Inc.

Francis, Grant R. *Scotland's Royal Line, The Tragic House of Stuart.* London: J. Murray, 1928, pp. 12-13.

Lehane, Brendan. *Dublin.* Amsterdam: Time-Life International, 1978, p. 8.

Long, William. *English Literature, Its History and Its Significance For the Life of The English Speaking World.* Boston: Ginn and Company, 1945, p. 156.

Runyan, Milton A. and Violma F. Bergane (eds.). *Around the USA in 1,000 Pictures.* Garden City: Nelson Doubleday, Inc., 1955, p. xvii.

Wren, Daniel. *The Evolution of Management Thought.* Second Edition. New York: John Wiley & Sons, 1979, p. 49.

Test Six

Clucas, Philip. *Wonders of the World.* New York: Colours Library International, Ltd., 1981, p. 49.

Flaubert, Gustave. *Madame Bovary,* 1881.

Givens, Charles J. *Wealth Without Risk.* New York: Simon and Schuster, 1988, pp. 21-22; 26.

Kennedy, John F. ''Inaugural Address,'' 1960.

Lamb, David. ''A Season in the Minors.'' *National Geographic,* Vol. 179, No. 4, April 1991, pp. 50-51.

McQuade, Walter and Ann Alkman. *Stress.* New York: Bantam Books, 1975, pp. 26-27.

Excerpt from ASTRONOMY: FROM THE EARTH TO THE UNIVERSE by Jay Pasachoff, copyright © 1983 by Saunders College Publishing, reprinted by permission of the publisher.

Perry, Marvin, et al. *Western Civilization* Boston: Houghton Mifflin Company, 1981, pp. 279-280.
Rathje, William L. ''Once and Future Landfills.'' *National Geographic,* Vol. 179, No. 5, May 1991, p. 123.
Slowinski, Emil J., Wayne C. Wolsey, and William S. Masterson. *Chemical Principles in the Laboratory.* Philadelphia: Saunders College Publishing, 1985, p. 131.

Test Seven

Clemens, Samuel. *Life on the Mississippi,* 1874.
Ferrier, Neil (ed.). *Churchill--Man of the Century.* New York: Doubleday and Company, 1965, p. 5.
Flaubert, Gustave. *Madame Bovary,* 1881.
Greener, W. W. The Gun and Its Development. New York: Bonanza Books, 1910, p. 30.
Kamien, Roger. *Music, an Appreciation.* Bray Edition. New York: McGraw-Hill Publishing Company, 1990, p. 139.
Kolars, John F. and John D. Nystuen. *Geography. The Study of Location, Culture, and Environment.* New York: McGraw-Hill Company, 1974, pp. 248-249.
Leonard, David and Peter McGuire. *Readings in Technical Writing.* New York: Macmillan Publishing Company, 1983, p. 45.
Morris, Charles G. *Psychology, An Introduction.* Sixth Edilion. Englewood Cliffs: Prentice Hall Inc., 1988, p. 45.
Wallace, Ann and Gabrielle Taylor. *Royal Mothers.* London: Piatkus, 1987, pp. 73-76.
Wood, Robert C. ''Rethinking the Suburbs.'' In *Suburbia Re-examined* by Barbara M. Kelly (ed.). Westport: Greenwood Press, Inc., 1989, p. 219.

Test Eight

Birren, J.E. *The Psychology of Aging.* Englewood Cliffs: Prentice-Hall, 1964, pp. 1-2
Excerpt from THE NATIONAL EXPERIENCE, A HISTORY OF THE UNITED STATES by James Blum, copyright © 1977 by Harcourt Brace Jovanovich, Inc., reprinted by permission of the publisher.
Daniel, Rose Mary. *Fatal Flowers.* New York: Avon Books, 1980, p. 10.
Harrison, John B. and Richard E. Sullivan. ''The Growth of Technology.'' In *A Short History of Western Civilization: Vol. 2 Since 1600.* Fourth Edition. New York: Alfred A. Knopf, Inc., 1975, p. 599.
Haviland, William A. *Anthropology.* Third Edition. New York: Holt, Rinehart and Winston, 1982, p. 272.
Kraus, Richard G. *Recreational Leadership Today.* Glenview: Scott Foresman and Co., 1985, p. 101.
McCarter, L. Gilbert. *Living With Art.* Second Edition. New York: Alfred A. Knopf, Inc., 1988, pp. 114-115.
Miller, G. Tyler, Jr. *Environmental Science.* Third Edition. Belmont: Wadsworlh Publlshing Co., 1991, p. 362.
Schomp, Virginia (ed.). *How to Protect Your Business.* Einsford: The Benjamin Co., Inc., 1986, p. 170.
Spencer, J. E. and W. L. Thomas. *Introducing Cultural Geography.* Ncw York: John Wilcy & Sons, Inc., 1973, p. 1.
Tolstoy, Leo. *Anna Karenina,* 1877.

Test Nine

Atkinson, Rick. ''The Long Gray Line.'' In *Today's Best Nonfiction* by Morgan, Barbara (cd.). Pleasantiville: The Reader's Digest Association, Inc., 1990, p. 33.
Current, Richard N. et al. *American History.* New York: Alfred A. Knopf, 1983, pp. 499-500.
Lipsitz, Lewis. *American Democracy.* New York: St. Martin's Press, 1986, pp. 266-267.
Miller, Theodore J. (ed.). *Make Your Money Crow.* New York: Dell Publishing Company, Inc., 1981, pp. 231-232.
Papalia, Duane E. and Sally Wendkos Olds. *Human Development.* Fourth Edition. New York: McGraw-Hill Book Co., 1989, p. 321.
Robertson, Ian. *Sociology.* Third Edition. New York: Worth Publishers, Inc., 1987, p. 186.
Roohk, Bonita and Arnold Karpoff. *Introducing Biology.* Dubuque: Kendall Hunt Publishing Co., 1990, p. 348; 442.

Senna, Joseph and Larry J. Siegel. *Introduction to Criminal Justice.* Fifth Edition. New York: West Publishing Company, 1990, p. 252.

Wachner, Clarence W., Frank E. Ross, and Eva Marie Van Houton. The Early Years of American Literature. New York: The MacMillan Company, 1963, pp. 141; 254.

Test Ten

Amling, Fredenck. *Investments, An Introduction to Analysis and Management.* Englewood Cliffs: Prentice Hall, Inc., 1965, p. 1.

Harris, Thomas A. *I'm OK--You're OK.* New York: Avon Books, 1967, pp. 25-26; 32-33.

Hirsch, E. D. *Cultural Literacy, What Every American Needs to Know.* Boston: Houghton Mifllin Company, 1987, pp. 20-21.

Kennedy, John S. "John Steinbeck: Life Affirmed and Dissolved." In *Fifty Years of the American Novel* by Harold C. Gardiner (ed.). New York: Charles Scribner & Sons, 1952, pp. 219-220.

Ladd, Everett Carll. *The American Polity, The People and Their Government.* Fourth Edition. New York: W. W. Norton & Company, 1991, pp. 54-55.

Leach, Douglas Edward. *Histories of the American Frontier,* The Northern Colonial Frontier, 1607-1763. New York: Holt, Rinehart, and Winston, 1966, p. 97.

Norsigian, Judy. "Dieting is Dangerous to Your Health." In *Women's Health* by Nancy Worcester and Marianne Whatley (eds.). Dubuque: Kendall Hunt Publishing Company, 1988, pp. 235-236.

Statham, Frances. *Phoenix Rising.* New York: Ballantine Books, 1982, p. 9.

University of California, Berkeley: Editors of the Wellness Letter. *The Comprehensive Family Resource for Safeguarding Health and Preventing Illness.* Boston: Houghton Mifflin Company, 1991, pp. 488-489.

Untemeyer, Louis. *Makers of the Modern World.* New York: Simon & Schuster, 1955, p. 311.